CW00338079

God

Is Always

Right

PHYLLIS JEMMOTT

© Copyright 2021 Phyllis Jemmott

All rights reserved.
No part of this publication may be reproduced, stored in a retrieval
system, or transmitted, in any form or by any means, electronic,
mechanical, photocopying, recording or otherwise, without the prior
written permission of the publisher.
British Library Cataloguing in Publication Data.
A catalogue record for this book is available from the British Library

ISBN 978 0 86071 821 5

A Commissioned Publication Printed by

MOORLEYS
Print, Design & Publishing
info@moorleys.co.uk • www.moorleys.co.uk

The views, thoughts, and opinions expressed in this book belong solely to the author,
and do not necessarily reflect the views of the publisher or any of its associates.

DEDICATION

I dedicate this book to my late daughter Yvonne Paisley,
Endeavoring to keep her fresh in my mind for the legacy she
has left to be continued, gone but not forgotten;

CONTENTS

INTRODUCTION

Welcome, to these introductive and useful guidelines of this remarkable book. The reason for choosing and writing on this subject is to draw the attention of everyone both young and older people from all nationalities, people of faith and un-faith, to the realities of getting to know God through the person Jesus Christ, and hopefully, you might acknowledge the fact that there is a God who is always right. I feel extremely humbled and at the same time delightful to introduce this informative book to you.

I hope after you have carefully read the contents you may become inquisitive and ask 'why this book? You'll find this book presents a brief and fast-moving summary of messages found in God's word, though the summaries could not give a full account of the whole theme, The Naked Truth and God is Always Right'

The book is designed with relevant topics relevant to intuitive readers who might wish to improve their knowledge of the naked truth about humans, God's character, and personality. I pray you will experience the loving hand of God that he shared in the lives of his disciples, friends, enemies, prophets, healing the sick, and raising the dead, and generally loving humanity in the face of adversities. God deals with human nations, is unquestionable, he has proven many times and times again that God is always right.

Human conscience can be aroused by the words of God and bring man to experience repentance to salvation. Through the pages of this book, you will experience God's voice through his prophets, speaking, pleading, calling out to man to come to him, it does not matter if you feel you'll never be right, nevertheless, the most important fact remains that God is always right and he is willing to help you to get it right.

This book is written with you in mind, I hope you will enjoy the contents as I do, and take away something to consider, finding God. I've made a positive decision to retract my Christian belief and share it with my readers. While journeying on this particular road, named the Christian journey, many obstacles presented themselves to block my view and anticipation, some were to dampen my faith, as a distraction, and some were to stir disappointments, bereavement, mental traumas and so much more. These life experiences were incredibly and significantly harsh and left negative effects on the human emotion, but by God's help and with a strong determination to keep focusing, I decided no matter what, God is always authentically right, he will not allow me to go under. Whilst trying to grapple with inward thoughts, feelings and revisiting my conscience and emotions, these notions entered my mind and brought awareness of getting things right with God, because, the naked truth is God is always right. I would like everyone reading this book to come to grips with the reality that there is a God who is the creator of every human being, and no matter, the rich and poor black and white one day we all have to stand before God to give an account how we have spent the time that was allotted to each of us, whether doing good or doing otherwise.

What brought me to such a place, I realize accepting Christ as my Savior, I've got a voice to tell, share and foremost my life must speak volumes regarding my belief. There was always a gentle voice echoing inside, saying, 'Don't be afraid, I am your shield, trust me when the going gets tough and the tough gets going, I've got you' Wow, that was good enough to take hold of every word from my Savior, nothing should slip, and nothing must be lost, it's precious and overwhelming, and all together, Wonderful!

Recovering from the edge and going forward was important, maintaining positive desire and at the same time leaving valuable experiences as traces in my tract that I was here, perusing my dreams and hoping others may read, and find something worthwhile to share with their generations. I seriously developed an effective reaction that stirs my conscience to seek more of God's intervention, and realizing there can be only one way to gain confidence is by communication with God through the medium of prayer. He graciously heard my cry, and his presence was evident, he poured oil into the cracks of my broken wounds. The oil was refreshing and effective; it acted as relief soothing and softens the pain as it becomes more bearable.

Finally being awakened up to reality as out of deep sleep and restarted my quest, pulling on the resources initially, God knew how much more I could bear. Recollecting many years ago as a driving instructor brought back many useful memories regarding the people I come in contact with, the conversations, the exchange of thoughts, as I revisited the source of my inner patience and strength.

Passing on instructions, it must be relevant, direct and easy to understand, for instance, when it is safe to turn right or left, or going straight ahead, these decisions must be decided while still focusing on the path ahead, and very rarely, a driver scarcely experiences smoothness on the road that brings comfort and relaxation; however, there are always vital concerns of the various changes of directions and challenges for all road users. The importance of alertness cannot be ignored at all times during maneuvering, especially in poor weather, and at the same time, paying close attention to reactions of other road users, factors such as observing road signs, widespread frost, diversion, slowing down, while approaching crossroads. Some road junctions, going forward must be with caution, bearing in mind icy patches in disguise that cause danger to life or even death, all these factors are important, and each must be taken into consideration.

Thankfully, road maps are provided; it contains useful guidelines for road users, your journey in life can be similar, it is important to consistently overhaul your spiritual development, and making the right choice and frequently evaluating before making decisions regarding your daily lifestyle, thus, your spiritual vehicle must be genuinely clean including positive thought of whatever is lovely pure and of good report, serviceable worthy to withstand bumps, broken parts, and delay the answer to prayers.

In the spiritual realm, God provides his word, as a map for guidance, teaching, directions, and instructions to assist all who believe in him, and his son Jesus Christ, so that none may be lost it is also important to check regarding our spiritual performances, using the word of God as a master tool. It is an effective way for Christian status; it gives clear and concise readings, and guidelines to followed and obey. The people who desire to have an encounter with God must acknowledge that God is always right in everything, therefore we must read, follow, and obey the signpost he has prepared getting to know him.

However, much has been said, let this become a positive story not so much about you, or me, but about the compassion and mercies of God, how he can reach out to broken people, who have to undergo, brokenness, in families, between friendship. There are positive aspects, God will not leave you as he found you, certainly, not, he will bind up the broken pieces and put them back together again. It's an amazing principle about God, he does not patch our brokenness, he graciously granted us new life and a new outlook.

It is important to make a conscious decision to love God amid un-holy practices, though it might create uneasiness, comfortableness. God has done this for me and I'm sure he will do the same for whoever comes to him, therefore, I received complete healing for the bones which seem broken, even though times of brokenness, was not beyond repair. These are suggestive principles as examples, for daily reading, useful for bible study among the congregation. It will assist and awaken your conscience to take the opportunity of reviewing and evaluating your status in Christ and make the necessary decision to change into the right perspective. There is nothing out of character taking actions to evaluate one's desire. The book highlights examples of bible characters, expressions and experiences in various ways finding God's, on a human point of view, you will share experiences with those whom you come into contact with.

Throughout this book, you will understand more about God's love for the whole human race, and how he has demonstrated this love in the lives of his disciples, friends, enemies, his prophets, the sick and generally this universe. God makes his own decisions in matters of human invention, at large; and God has extraordinary knowledge of worldwide systems.

CHAPTER ONE

WHO IS GOD?

GOD IS ALWAYS RIGHT

God is the creator of heaven and earth. God was from the beginning of things and space; God is and always will be, is always right, and without him, there will be absolutely nothing can be compared to his greatness. God works with his Son Christ Jesus, he was at the beginning with God. God is the only being in the universe that possesses independence from his creation, and the only limits to God's freedom are in his nature and attributes. God is the light of the world, and in him, there is no darkness.

Even the most experienced scientist baffled at God's knowledge, doctors, lawyers seek to understand now can it be, how God is so accurate, supreme, unlimited, and unstoppable. The knowledge and wisdom of God surprise the wise and put their devices to naught. God can be trusted in all areas of life or even death; he is faithful in all things in the past present and future. God is God by himself.

God is unlimited in his existence, because his existence relates to his nature, rather than his will, therefore God exist forever. He exists because of his nature, rather than his violation, and will continue to exist forever. God's name emphasizes himself in existence as clearly God has always existed and always will, neither anyone nor any outside force will affect God's relationship with us; he will deal with us according to his nature because he is free from outside influences. For instance, when

God revealed his name to Moses at the burning bush, he identifies himself, The 'I AM' (Exodus 33:15)

God works with the persons of the Trinity, as the three persons in one, as Father, Son, and Holy Spirit. No one has ever seen God at any time, for this cause he sent his son Jesus Christ to reveal him to men who ought to know about him. God can never be in any wrongdoings as men do, and men cannot figure out God, or expect to find fault or wrongdoings with him. God is always right, and various people searched and research diligently for alternatives about God, and obsoletely nothing has ever been found, or any failure in God, because he is faultless and strong. God is not like men, and very seldom would men blame God, one would hardly found anything, rather that God is always right. In the books of the Old Testament, it has proven empathically that God is always right, and throughout the beginning of the human living on earth in the Garden of Eden with Adam and Eve. In Genesis God was Jehovah, in Exodus God showed his power in leading the people from darkness into light, in Leviticus God urged people regarding dietary habits, to eat wholesome food, and dismisses false gods.

God is accurate, supreme, unlimited, and unstoppable, God suppresses the wise and puts their devices to ought, God can be trusted in all areas of life and death. He is faithful in things in past and present, and future. Since we have made our own choices, God alone originates and accomplished our salvation because of His grace; we did nothing to earn it. To be chosen by God does not remove the necessity for people to have their own choices, of the force they follow. When the people step out of line by disobeying God, he will disciple with his justice, nevertheless yet, he remains his right and good causes of righteousness by entreating them to repent and return to him.

God makes his discussion in matters of human inventory, knowledge, worldwide systems, and scientist baffled at his knowledge, doctors amazed at his ability to heal the sick, even incurables, and lawyers cannot understand his knowledge of solving everyday crises, they all seeking to understand, *how can it be?* The fact that God knows all persons, events and decisions beforehand, and he even ordained them beforehand, yet, does not mean that God forces the actions of his creatures or leaves them with no choice.

Instead, God foreknowledge the means and initiative he chose before they had anything to deserve it. Therefore, God credibility should not be tested by humans, whether he is God, or not, God is always right full stop, this has proven in moments of doubt, fear, anxieties and all areas in human history. God can bring about light and deliverance in the darkest moments, and humans are happy of being delivered out of difficult circumstances, scriptures also show examples of people who have been delivered from impossible situations, even when the journey of life has a miserable impact.

God has intimate knowledge of these future events and believers can be assured that God personally knew who would believe in him and those who would disown him. God's chosen people were known by him as their father, who knows his children; God knew them from eternity past. God is not just trapped in time, what he knows is from eternity past into eternity the future. God has a deliberating and expressing concern for everyone, if by reason you decide to accept the truth, then, you will develop stronger desires to enable you to experience stability, growth and commitment to live a Christian life. Therefore, each of us is chosen, but not against our will, all parts of our lives and character are in the process of becoming conformed, both inwardly, and outwardly, to God's standards.

Although after committing our lives to Christ, we may sometimes feel a pullback and returning to the old habits, and old desires. The apostle Peter encourages us to be like our heavenly father, who is holy in everything we do, and for such reason be holy, means to be devoted and dedicated to God, being set aside for his special use, and also set apart from sin and its influences. With this mind, we must make a difference by setting ourselves apart from defiling our bodies, minds and attitude from the deceitfulness of the world system, and by not blending in with the crowd, and yet not being different just for the sake of being different. God qualifies our lives and make an incredible difference, thus your focus and priorities must be his, all this is in direct contrast to our old lives, so much so, and God gives us the Holy Spirit to help us obey him and power to overcome.

The coming of Christ the one whom God anointed with his spirit to be the universal king, had been foretold centuries before Jesus's birth. However, at the birth, Jesus was not yet the Anointed one or Christ. In foretelling his birth, the angel instructed Joseph, you must call his name Jesus. The personal name of Jesus followed by the title 'Christ may call your attention to the person himself and that he is the one who became the Anointed One of God. This occurred when he reached thirty years of age, was baptized in water and was anointed with God's spirit visibly observed at Pentecost. God made him both Lord and Christ, this Jesus, evidently observed in the form of a dove descending upon him.

ACCESS TO GOD THROUGH JESUS
THE WAY-TRUTH-LIFE

One of Jesus disciples enquired concerning *the way*, he said 'Lord, we know not the way you go, and how can we know the way'. This disciple confession of his ignorance was commendable enough; if good men are in the dark, and only know it partially, yet they are willing to know their defects, Christ gave a full answer to this complaint. Jesus tenderly explains that he is the way to the father and no man can come to the father without first going through Him, Jesus.

The nature of Jesus explanation when he said that, 'I am *the way* to God' he is *the truth, the life*. Here, three aspects are brought together, for instance, we cannot get to the tree of life in the way of innocence, but Christ is another way to it.

JESUS IS THE TRUTH

As truth is opposed by falsehood and or unrighteousness, the truths is trustworthy, stable, faithful true or establish facts. Like the father Jehovah Jesus Christ is 'full of undeserved kindness and truth. While on earth Jesus has always spoken the truth as he has received it from the father. He committed no sin or deception found in his mouth. Jesus represents things as they were and besides the truth, Jesus was himself, 'and truth came through him. When men enquire for truth, we need no more learning than the truth that is in Jesus, as truth is opposed to fallacy and deceit. As you consider all these jointly, Christ is the way to the father. He is truth and the life, the beginning, the middle and the end. He is the true and living way; there are truth and life in the way, as well as at the end of it. Christ is the true way to life, another way may seem right, but the end of them is the way of death. God's Word represents times as they are, revealing his attributes, purposes and commands, as well as the true state of affairs among mankind. God's Word of truth shows what is required of one to be sanctified or made holy, set apart to use in God's service. 'Sanctify them by means to the truth; your word is truth'.

WALKING IN THE TRUTH

Therefore, Christianity is the way of the truth and those who assist others in furthering the interest of Christianity become fellow workers in the truth (3 John 8) The entire body of Christian teachings which later becomes part of the written Word of God, is the truth, or the truth of the good news. Jesus is *the life*: for we are alive to God only in and through Jesus Christ. Those who desire to gain God's approval should walk in his truth and serve him in truth. This would include abiding by God's requirement and serving him in faithfulness and sincerity.

THE NATURE OF JESUS IS HOLY

Jesus Christ, God's Son had to be free from the sinful nature passed on to all other human beings by Adam, Because Jesus was born of a woman, he was a human being, but as the Son of God, Jesus was born without any trace of human sin. Jesus was born without the sin that entered the world through Adam. Just as Adam was created sinless, Jesus is both fully human and fully divine. In contrast to Adam who disobeyed God, Jesus obeyed God his father, and thus, was able to face sin's consequences in our place and made us acceptable to God. Adam was a pattern, he is the counterpart of Christ, just as Adam was a representative of creation, so humility is Christ representative of a new spiritual humility. Because living as a

11

man, you know that he understands your experiences and your struggles. He was like us and had experienced a full range of temptation throughout his life as a human being, so you can take comfort knowing that Jesus faced temptation, he can sympathize with you and shows that you do not have to sin when facing the seductive lure of the enemy. (Romans 5:14)

JESUS RIGHTEOUS SERVANT

God declares Christ as his righteous servant, he will justify many, tells of the many enormous families of believers who have become righteous, rather, it's not by their works, but by the Christ great work on the cross. Thus, they are justified because they claimed Christ, the righteous servant, as their Savior and Lord. Their life of sin is stripped away, and they are clothed with Christ goodness. One would never believe that God would choose to save the world through a humble, suffering servant rather, than a glorious king? This idea might seem contrary to the world of human pride and worldly ways but always work in the ways that we don't expect. Therefore, there was nothing beautiful or majestic in the physical appearance of this servant, and some would consider him an ordinary man and even though Jesus might not attract a large crowd on his physical appearance would bring salvation and healing to the world.

HE IS GUILTLESS

Jesus has never committed any sin and no deceit was found in him, Jesus suffering was part of God's plans and was intended to save the world and all who follow Jesus must be prepared to suffer For instance in the Old Testament this was the procedure of the guilty, although the guilt was always brought liability,

12

with no exceptions, however, neither can guilty be overlooked, whatever the law demands, the punishment had to be administered or, some compensation made. For the guilty person to make peace with God it was required to present an offering at the sanctuary.

Whether it was intentional sin that brought guilt, a sacrifice, in any case, was required for atonement. For the guilty acts of man, there is a way to be declared not guilty; it is by trusting Jesus Christ to take away your sins, trusting Jesus Christ means putting your confidence in him to forgive, and make you right with God, thus, God's solution is available to everyone regardless of your background or past behavior. (1Peter 2:22)

JESUS IS SINLESS

Because Christ was sinless therefore you can make an exchange for his righteousness. Your sin was poured out into Christ at his crucifixion, and His righteousness is poured into you at conversion, this is what Christianity means by Christ atonement for sin. In the world, battering works only when two people exchange goods of relatively equal value, but God offers to trade his righteousness for your sin, something of immeasurable worth for something completely worthless. The purity of the mediator knew no sin, the sacrifice that he offered, was made sin offering, so you might be made the righteousness of God in him. (2 Co. 5:21)

JESUS IS SPOTLESS

No spot or wrinkles, or traces of sin were found in Christ, for example as slaves were redeemed when someone paid to buy his or her freedom, God redeemed you from the tyranny of sin, not with money, but with the precious blood of His own Son, even though you cannot escape from sin by your own, only the life of God Son can set you free. Christ sacrificed for the sin of man was not an afterthought, it was not something God decided to do when the world spun out of control, no, certainly not, this plan was set in motion by the all-knowing eternal God long before the world was created (1Peter 1:19)

JESUS WAS INNOCENT

Jesus was innocent of the crime that was put on him. Countless people were accused of crimes they had never committed and were put to death. The role of the priest was to teach people about God also to act as an intercessor for them, helping to administer the sacrifice to cover their sin, but the priest was so selfish and corrupt and not having any concern on behalf of the people whom they should be serving.

In the time of Jesus trial, when Judas return the money to the priest, acclaiming that he had sinned, rather than helping Judas to find forgiveness, the priest said, 'That is your responsibility' thus, rejected his role as priest, the chief priest was corrupt, and felt no guilt that Jesus was innocent, and return the money to Judas to betray an innocent man, the priest could not accept it, because it was very wrong to accept blood money payment for murder, it seems they had lost all sense of justice, because of hating Jesus.

JESUS WAS HUMBLE

Jesus humbled Himself to the death on the cross was in the form of capital punishment that Romans used for notorious criminals. It carries excruciating pain and humbling. In those days prisoners were nailed or tied to a cross and left to die, and death might not come for several days and usually comes by suffocating when the weight of the weakened body made breathing more and more difficult. When you understand that Christ suffered pain and faced temptation, it should help you to face your trials with confidence. Jesus understands our struggles because he faced them as human beings.

Therefore, trusting God will strengthen you to survive suffering and overcome temptation. To many onlookers, Jesus died as one who was cursed, how amazing that this perfect man should die this shameful death so that you would not have to face eternal punishment. 'Wherefore, God has exalted Jesus, because he humbled himself, and exalted his whole person, the human nature as well as the divine. His exaltation is consisting of honor and power and has a name above every name, that every knee must bow to him, the whole creation must be in subjection to him, things in heaven, and things on earth, and things under the earth, the inhabitants of heaven and earth, and the living and the dead. In the name of Jesus, all should pay solemn homage, every tongue shall confess that Jesus Christ is Lord. Therefore, the kingdom of Christ reaches to heaven and earth and the entire creature, to the dead as well as the living, to the glory of God the Father.

JESUS IS MERCIFUL

The term mercy is most frequently use with God's dealing with his covenant people. God's pity towards these is compared with that of a woman towards the children of her womb, and with a father's mercy towards his Son. Since the nation of Israel frequently strayed from righteousness and came into sore straights, they often became especially in need of merciful help. If they showed the right attitude and turned to God, though he was angry with them, yet, he would express compassion, favor, and goodwill. Ever since Jesus came to live on earth people who are sick and in distress are always crying out to him for mercy, thus, the mercy of the Lord is manifested in the general idea of feelings, sympathy with those in misery.

CHAPTER TWO

HUMAN CONSCIENCE

It is incredible how the conscience of man sometimes acts as an inner judge of moral issues; therefore, mankind conscience is inherent in man, having been made a part of him by God. The conscience is an inward realization or sense of right or wrong that excuses or accuses one, hence, man's conscience can become a judge, or sometimes caused conviction that speaks without saying a word. The human conscience that exists within can be convicted and awaken to act in a right or in a bad way. A man's conscience will drive him or her into either guilt resulting in repentance, or, to his death because of refusal to repent, or it might take no act of kindness to make him feel better, or guiltier, who knows if he will turn and repent and to turn to God. (Joel 2:12)

At the beginning of man existence, he was given a pure conscience, but from the time in the Garden of Eden when Adam and Eve both decided to disobey God; from that time man's conscience was no longer speaking to him or sending warnings of wrongdoings. After the couple disobeyed God their eyes were open and they because afraid and ashamed.

Adam and Eve both knew they were naked, they felt guilty and embarrassed and took hold of the conscience of their nakedness. The guilt within their conscience was very strong and causes them to hide from God. Thus, God has placed a warning signal in every human if ever man decides to take the wrong course of action that signal will go off automatically.

Comparing the sin of Adam and Eve in the Garden of Eden, they were exposed by their guilty conscience and thought it was a good thing to hide and cover their nakedness. They were creative and use what was available at the time; fig leaves were close at hand, they organized the leaves and made aprons to cover their nakedness.

Although Adam and Eve covered their outward body, yet, inwardly their conscience stood uncovered, and fig leaves could not cover their guilty conscience, but thankfully God found them and deliver them from their guiltiness of sin and shame. The price of disobeying God comes with bitter consequences, for instance, shame is a dreadful consequence, you cannot hide from shame, it's an inside job, you carry the shame of guilt around until it is exposed and uncovered.

It might be a possibility regarding man's conscience can be trained by thoughts, acts, conviction, and rules that are implanted in studies and experiences, based on these proposals and making a comparison with the course of action being taken, or contemplated, then the human conscience will send out warnings of rule and the course of the conflict. If for some reason a person's conscience is seared and having a sense of feelings, violation or warning, then the conscience can be morally a safe device that imparts pleasure, inflicts pain for one's conduct, whether it's positive or negative.

The naked truth is that all humans who were born into this world are responsible for their destiny, therefore they must rise above each challenge they encounter and, endeavoring to endure all hardship, realizing that the time of trial was not sent to kill or to destroy, but to purify and improve character. There is evidence of this; God has provided healing of the body, soul and spirit, renewing of the mind, and refreshment. You must seek and share in the gifts of God's salvation to enable you to hope in God, even in times of brokenness, because God is always right.

Therefore, your conscience must be enlightened, and trained in the right standard, and truth, otherwise it can be deceived, and be an unsafe guide. The conscience can also be wrongly influenced by the local environment, costumes, worship and habits, and can also be a judge in matters of right or wrong, incorrect standards or value. Thus, Jesus warns his disciples saying, 'Those who have the power to do it, they will put you out of their synagogues, because their conscience is snared against the truth, they shall kill you, thinking that they were doing a service and be put to death for preaching the gospel, except John.

The word of God declares, 'do not be careful about the body, our great care is to provide for our souls' neither should you be perplexing ourselves with an inordinate care, by stretching our wits, and set your thought on the tender hooks, in making this provision, and although the necessities of the body must be considered, yet the lust of it must not be gratified, therefore natural desires must be answered and wanton appetites must be checked and denied. (Romans 8:14)

It is impossible to serve or please God without having a renewed mind and a cleansed conscience. Otherwise, you will not have a clear idea of doing and living right to please God, You will be miss-guided by the in-between actions of selfishness when it pleases. Instead, you must confess and repent of your sins, and God will apply the blood of Jesus Christ. He will sprinkle and cleansed the heart from an evil conscience, from guilt and whatever evil the conscience is subjected to employing sin. (Heb. 10:22)

19

A GOOD CONSCIENCE

It is possible to possess a good conscience; it will enable you to live in peace with God and with others. It gives freedom to face trials, conflicts or anything with confidence and treasuring your faith in Christ.

A person who has a good conscience can make good judgments and right decisions when the inner tugs wanting to do otherwise, yet, your and conscience can remain clear for what is right. Each time a person deliberately ignore his conscience, he is hardening his heart, and then, over a while cannot tell right from wrong, to avoid this action, the person must walk with God; by faith, and God will speak through the conscience, and allowing you to understand the difference between good and evil, right and wrong. This can be a soothing feeling when your conscience is at peace within, you will be able to think positively, speaking with assurance, sing praises to God, meditation will be sweet, and also loving to others with a clear conscience.

Christians who have experienced the knowledge of God can maintain clear conscience towards others who might be experiencing weakness. At the same time, by not imposing their freedom or insisting on their rights, or doing as they please, they can gain an understanding of the duty of praying for others. As well as, strengthening the inner man and realizing that your prayers are the door that God enters in your situation; therefore, you must feel free to have conversations about every situation through connection with God, and his forgiveness and your determination to live right can give you a clear.

Thus you should do all that lies in your power to maintain a cleanse conscience at all times, especially when approaching God. The satisfaction is rewarding, as you draw near to him in a right manner, and drawing nearer in conformity, and communion with him, and still endeavoring to get nearer and nearer until you come to dwell in his presence, with a true heart, knowing that God is the searcher of hearts. God requires truth in the inward parts, with full assurance of faith, laying aside sinful distrust and come boldly to the throne of grace.

Those who fear God must constantly strive for an honest conscience from wrong attitude and behavior. Therefore, man must continually and constantly steer his course of life according to God's word, and the teachings of Christ, because the final analysis, God is always right. Ultimately a man by his conscience will make a judgment, and since men are unable to make the final judge of themselves or a judge of others, therefore, it is only God's judgment that must determine yours. When you listen to your conscience and acting on what is right, you will develop a stronger desire and clear guidance to experience stability, growth and commitment to living the Christian life.

The fact that God has accepted you in Christ, therefore, we ought to accept ourselves, otherwise, it would not be possible to accept others. First, acceptance involves your will; when someone or a situation is accepted it is viewed as a right, therefore, since God loves and accept us in Christ, he says, we are the righteousness of God through Jesus Christ. Unfortunately, some may not act on this glorious opportunity, the opportunity might have been neglected or lost, but while time is still available you may consider accepting the opportunity that comes your way. God loved the world and provided salvation through Jesus Christ his beloved Son; that whosoever believes in him shall be saved.

One of the worst steps you can take to eliminate conviction and guilty feelings, without eliminating the cause, is like taking a pain killer, this does not treat the cause of the pain, after a while when the pain killer wore out, the pain will reoccur, because the root cause is still lying dormant. To enable a cure for any pain and its root caused it must be located where the pain is before any diagnosis may be considered.

However, you should be thankful for the conscience that awakes guilty feelings, and the awareness of sin that causes unhealthy feelings, when this happens, the right thing to do is seek God's forgiveness and then correct the wrongdoings. Even though there are times when your conscience sends out a busy signal of what to get done, and why, and you may choose to ignore it, and harbor forgiveness in your heart, until the day of your passing. Forgiveness is known as the worst ailment that causes serious illnesses, examples, heart disease, cancer, and sometimes death. Therefore you should never harbor such a poisonous attitude, rather you should get rid of those deadly diseases that endanger life.

The apostle Peter spoke of his experience and indicates that those who receive salvation by their good conscience and claiming right conscience should put away the filth of the flesh, and considering this benefit of their salvation, could never be granted through their efforts, it has to be requested, from God, as the pledge of a clear conscience. Peter was insisting on believers to keep a clear conscience so those who speak maliciously against their good behavior in Christ may also become ashamed of their slander, for it is better to suffer doing God's will rather than suffering doing evil.

Therefore you should be an example of doing right, and also hold a good conscience in the face of opposition. In times of the law, none of the gift and sacrifices that were offered could make a person perfect in regard to his conscience, yet considering being free from guilt. It is through the application of Christ's ransoming sacrifice, and having faith, their conscience is cleansed, but those who worshipped other gods would be unable to deliver their conscience from the dread of the wrath of God. In the Old Testament times, there was no free access to God, since the way to the holies was not yet manifest, but now in the New Testament, God has open a wider door through his Son Jesus Christ, which gives all access to the throne of grace.

AN EVIL CONSCIENCE

You do not need to need to look far to find people with an evil conscience, there are many such people in society, but it might be useful to start with yourselves, and amine your conscience, you may not want to own up to this controlling person inside of you called 'conscience', and unless you can control yourself, you must also pray for others, and be clear how you treat one another without compromising the truth with regards to your conscience.

For example Saul a man with an ill-informed conscience and thought he was doing God's service, it was not until he was confronted by the risen Christ and brought face to face with the truth of the gospel. Saul's general rage was against the Christian religion, and thought he had the upper hand over the lives of the Christians, and breathed death to the Christian. His action was breathing out threatening and slaughter against the disciples of the Lord, and his wicked behavior was natural to him, and his very breath was like venomous creatures, and pestilential. Whenever Saul speaks he was under his character of hate and persecution, which breaks the spirit of man.

For a while, Saul's acted in his old self, until the Lord met with him and changed his character, into the person he was meant to be. There will always be a positive change in the life of the person whom God meets. Saul was changed from a persecutor of Christians to a preacher of Christ, and many lives were touch through his testimony. Even years after, and now people are still touched in amazement of who Saul was and whom he became. Nothing is wasted when God works in the lives of bad people, he transforms lives from bad to good, and from good to better. Paul, life was challenged by meeting Christ and nothing was wasted, Paul name was changed, his background, his training, his citizenship, his mind, or even his weakness affected the changes.

There is much to learn from the life of Paul, how through the good news, and forgiveness, eternal life as gifts from God's grace receive through faith in Christ, and this is made available to all people. God does not waste your time he will use your past and present so you will serve him with your future.

However, Saul's former behavior showed a lack of God's knowledge and word, for instance, when the Jews were seriously misled into fighting against God's word and the consciences of many Jews were seared, they had difficulty understanding God's message that was intended for both Jews and Gentile alike. Some Jews had a wrong conception of God's plan for the Gentiles, and believe the Gentiles should become

Jews before they could become Christian, but God planned to save the whole world of sinners, and he fulfilled this through Jesus Christ.

Saul had such a remarkable encounter with God, and was willing to share his experience of his conversation, because in time past, even though his hearers thought, 'Is it this same man? Yet, it must have been something very extraordinary that brought so great changes in this man, and not only to profess but to preach the doctrine, which he had before so vehemently opposed. When Paul met Jesus his life was miraculously changed, and then directed all his energies towards building up the Christian church. (Gal. 1:13-16)

Paul aimed at nothing but to please God and doing his duty, he had a character of an honest man, and set God before him and lived in his sight, Paul makes his conscience what he says, and does, though many a time he thought of some mistakes he had made before his conversion, as a universally conscientious man, Paul continues to declare, 'I have lived so until this day.

Whatever changes passes over Paul, yet, he was still the same strictly conscientious, and reckoned, 'If the blood of goats and bulls and the ashes of a heifer sprinkled on those who were ceremonially unclean, could sanctify and they were outwardly clean, how much more, will the blood of Christ, who brought the eternal spirit and offered himself unblemished to God, cleansed your conscience from acts that lead to death, to serve the living God!

Thus, Christians can take examples, when Paul was accused by the Jews for preaching Jesus; he knew he was innocent of doing no wrong, He declared 'Men and brethren, I have lived in all good conscience unto this day' city' he spoke as a man whose conscience was alive and who was governed by the naked truth.

Therefore, when a man's conscience is renewed in the word of God he can correctly and specifically access matters that are relevant to him, and the lives of others. Although nothing can be hidden from God's sight because everything is uncovered, even secrets lay bare before him whom we must all give account, even when we are unaware of his presence, God is present, and if anyone tried to hide from God, it will be futile, because his eyes run through the earth, beholding the good and the evil, although God knows us intimately, yet, he remains God.

Considering the word of God when planted in our heart by the Holy Spirit, enables you to make proper evaluations of yourselves. Thus, an untrained conscience may be weak in discovering the truth and possible hiding the findings and become weaker and easily injured, easily offended by actions, words or deeds of others. Another while the disciples of Jesus were in an intimidating situation, they brought God into their situation, said, 'Lord, behold their threatening's.'

In such times the disciples stood with confidence knowing that Jesus listens to every threat from the enemy and give strength to stand strong. Sometimes people might have strong feelings against others, using threatening and verbal abuse causing fear, but you should not be afraid of their threatening behavior, because God listens to every conversation whether good or evil. Many biblical characters have left untold testimonies of how they overcame deal diverse encounters while still trusting God. Imagine a Godly person as Job. He endures severe accusations by his friends, yet, his conscience was clear, he was able to deal consciously in a Godly manner, and uphold his faith in God. Job believed and reassured himself, 'though he slays him, yet he will trust him. Job claims a sinless life and forgiveness, and only then when confession is made to God for the forgiveness of sins can a person be free from a clear conscience.

AN EVIL/DEFILED CONSCIENCE

There is a difference between a person who has a clear conscience and the one with an evil and defiled conscience. A person's conscience can be so scorned and abused that he feels untouched when sending out warnings against safety and guidance. There is a difference between some people who are alert and observes around them, while others see nothing but evil, thus, our soul can become filters through while you perceive goodness or evil, people with such conscience cannot sense right or wrong, or will not appreciate the freedom that God grants against rebellion, they will disown or accepting help, and eventually become slaves to a bad conscience.

On the contrary, those who believe in Christ are noted as pure, and in control of their lives, they have learned to see goodness and purity, in this evil world, but corrupt and unbelieving people finds evil in everything because their minds and hearts color in even the good they see and hear.

Whatever you choose to fill their mind, will affect the way they think and act, therefore, it is profitable to turn your thoughts to God, we will discover more good, even while you living in an evil world. Paul instructed believers concerning maintaining a good conscience, and of others, he spoke of those who are weak and those who are strong, although you might be weak in some areas and strong in others, nevertheless, he said, 'Your faith will become weak in some area if you keep on interacting with sinful people, such will affect your thinking process and cause you to fall in their patterns.

Thus, you should endeavor and avoid such traps in certain areas and activities, people or places, to protect your spiritual values' you may need to consider taking a self-inventory of your strength and weakness and be fearful of being defiled by the world system, and if you have strong faith, the apostle urged, 'Receive the one who is weak in faith but you should not dispute over doubtful things, such as what to eat and who has the right not to eat certain meat; For example, some people may choose to be vegetarian, while others make distinctions of meats, or, and what day of the week they should observe. Concerning meat some believed they can eat everything, that person might be satisfied that every creature is good, and nothing to be refused, and nothing is unclean of itself, on the other hand, another person might be weak and dissatisfied in this point and may decide to eat no flesh and all only herbs, and other may be contented to eat only the fruits of the earth, we should give allowance to people to decide and not become a dictator regarding the choices that others make.

Nevertheless, as Christians, you should consider the infirmities of the weaker person, since you have your weaknesses. How amiable and comfortable a society would be if the church of Christ study to please one another and try pleasing your neighbor, perhaps not in everything, but for his good especially for the good of his soul, to edification, not only for his profit, but for the profit of others, and to edify the body of Christ, because even Christ did not please himself; according to self-denial of your Lord Jesus, yet, he provides the best argument against the selfishness of Christians believers. (Romans 15:1)

The apostle Paul gave references regarding a person with a bad conscience, he said, the persons who practice evil, that person's conscience is marked as with a branding iron that indicates snared as flesh that is covered over with scar tissue and avoiding the nerve ending and has no sense of feelings. It is usually when men's conduct is sometimes controlled by fear of exposure and punishment rather than conscience. Another example; regarding Saul, was later, named Paul the apostle.

The Christian life is governed by love for God, and love to your neighbor, this act of love was put on public display, and it is a most notable relationship to all Christians, in reality, you are indebted to one another as brothers and sisters in Christ, but this indebtedness does not equal forced conformity, instead, the scripture gives instructions and encouragement of divers' forms of culture and practice in living out the Christian faith. When our diversity is embraced within an attitude of unity, then, God is glorified, though, there is one debt the Christian will continue to owe; it is the debt to love one another.

Persons can satisfy earthly or civil claims, but the claims of love can never be fulfilled without knowing the author of love. For instance, a person may try paying this debt of love, yet, he gets deeper into debt because the practice of love makes the principle of love deeper and more active, and though, there may be a tendency of temptation to settle and accommodate yourselves to the world system, yet, resting in the victories of the past, and forgetting that a new generation exists who may not experience the greatest gift as love.

Thus, other Christians need our witness, teaching, and setting examples, therefore, mature Christian leaders and teachers should teach others about the freedom that Christ gave in matters that are and expressly stated in Scriptures, and especially, of the reality of the power of the blood of Jesus and the glory, and of Pentecost, surely this experience must be passed on to new believers that the world to be saved.

IGNORING THE CONSCIENCE

Although it might not be easy to act immediately on what your conscience might be pointing to do or say because of what is happening around you, if for example, you might be experiencing trials, sickness, disappointment, or some delays that shows up uninvited, nevertheless you should still be in the right frame of mind to deal with such, for there is nothing impossible with God. Amongst all these many people, some individuals chose to ignore the wooing of their conscience, whether to do well or to do the wrong, but, every time a person gives in to the wrong voice of their conscience, there is an effect resulting in serious consequences. Here, is a typical example of a man who was nominated to the office in a high position of prominence and all authority to do well, yet he ignorantly ignored his conscience and confirmed the death of our Lord Jesus Christ.

Pilate was a Roman governor and a leader of Judah during Jesus earthly ministry and was expected to administer justice in Jesus trial. When Jesus stood before the governor as the prisoner, before a judge, Pilate had a conference with the persecutors regarding Jesus, they were called first to share their views regarding Jesus as the prisoner, in our time we would say, they were in a cook up meeting to discuss the fate of Jesus, what one says, all must also agree on the same decision. The result of the conference found Jesus guilty of three things, his diligent and close applications to business, his condescending to the humor of the people, which might suggest, if the people were so nice to come and see him, now let them go home as they came.

Pilate listened to the accusations and did not agree, he went to see the people and was amazed at the accusation against Jesus of adherence to the role of justice in demanding Jesus to be such a criminal. Pilate asked, 'What accusation have you brought against this man? The prosecutors demand judgment against Jesus upon a general surmise that he was a criminal; this was very spiteful and malicious towards Jesus, they say he was an evildoer who went about doing well, but the judge remands them to their court, he said, 'Take him and judge him according to your law, yet when the angry mob heard these words from Pilate they thought he complimented them and acknowledging their power and allowing them to do as they wish.

Pilate was willing to grant the Jews a pleasure, but unwilling to do the service they required, he said, 'Since you have found him guilty by your law; condemn him if you dare, by your law!

Here, the people disown no authority as judges, they say, it was not lawful for us to put any man to death, and some think that they had no power and even if they had power it was taken from them by the Romans, now, they realize their rudeness and wanted to acknowledge Pilate's actions towards them, and Pilate conference with the chief priest he called Jesus into the judgment hall with him, thus, Pilate conscience was hot inside him, and again examined the accusation that was laid on Jesus to perverted the nation, and forbidding giving tribute to Caesar.

Pilate questioned Jesus on the ground of these accusations, he asked, 'Are you king of the Jews? Pilate may have asked Jesus this question with scorn and contempt, 'What, are you a king?

Again, 'are you king of the Jews, by whom you are hated and persecuted?

Christ had never complained of the Jews being his haters and persecutor, and Pilate was seeking a statement to add more on Jesus. There are people in this world during a conversation who seek to add more or less to what comes out of your mouth and maliciously turn it and use for their advantage against you, and Jesus knowing the all-knowing thoughts of man, Jesus answered the question with another intimidation to Pilate to consider, 'Says thou this thing of thyself or did others tell you about it? And when Pilate perceived the answer that Jesus answered him, he was cautious regarding Roman's interest in government, so, he did his best to please them in all his decision.

Jesus was on top of Pilate case, he says to him, 'if others tell about me, you must consider whether they represent me as an enemy to Caesar and not such themselves. When Pilate understood he found the true reason about the matter, the chief priest was outrageous against Jesus because he did not set up a temporal kingdom to opposition to the Roman power.

Pilate happened to resent Jesus answer and taken it very ill because it was a direct answer to Jesus question. Christ had asked Pilate whether he spoke of himself, he said no, and ask, 'Am I, Jew? For a man like Pilate to ask Jesus, 'Am I, Jew?
Because Jesus had asked Pilate whether someone told him, Pilate answered 'Yes, and those were your people, like the priest' 'and I have nothing to do but to proceed against their information.

Pilate's conscience was wakening, he asked Jesus again, 'Are you king of the Jews, 'What have you done? Surely, there cannot be smoke without fire, 'What is it? Christ gave a next reply and a full answer when he was asked, 'Are you king of the Jews?

Jesus explains in what sense he was a king, in an account of the nature and constitution of Christ kingdom and it is not of this world. The nature of his kingdom is not worldly. It is a kingdom within men, set up in their hearts and conscience, and its guards and support are not of this world. It is a spiritual weapon, its tendency is not of the world, and its subjects although they are in the world, they are not of this world. Jesus gave a more direct answer to Pilate query, but Pilate plain question again to Jesus, 'Are you a king then' 'You speak as one who has a kingdom, 'Are you a king then?

Pilate was losing it by asking Jesus repeatedly the same questions, Our Lord made a good confession before Pontius Pilate, Jesus declared, 'Thou say that I am a king, it is as you have said.'

Christ explains himself and showed how he is a king, as he came to bear witness of the truth. He rules in the minds of men by the power of the truth, and the subjects are those that are of the truth, Pilate put a good question to Jesus, but he did not stay for an answer, Pilate asked, 'What is truth?'

Nevertheless, Pilate showed fear, likely a superstitious fear, upon hearing that he was dealing with one claim to be God's Son, though not the condescending type; he displayed the politico's lack of integrity. He was concerned primarily as to his position as to what his superiors would say if they heard of further disturbances in his providence. He was fearful of appearing to be overly lenient towards those accused of sedition. Pilate recognized Jesus innocence and the envy that motivated his accusers, yet he gave into the crowd and turned an innocent victim over for them to slaughter rather than risking damage to his political career.

Pilate sound as a leaner as one who began to think well of Christ, Pilate thought, 'You speak of truth, 'Can you tell me what truth is, and give me a definite answer, Pilate's question sound like men with no religion who takes no pleasure in bantering all religion, Pilate ridicules both sides, and therefore, Jesus made him no answer.

The results of both conferences with the prosecutors and the prisoner, Pilate as the judge appeared to be Jesus friend, declared Jesus innocent, and said, 'I found no fault in him?' Pilate was bound by his conscience to release Jesus, but the people appeared to be Jesus enemies, they cried out all again, 'Not this man, but Barabbas' although Pilate proposed the thing to them calmly, yet the people resolved in heat, and they gave their resolution and clamor and noise.

There was cause to suspect a deficiency of reason and justice on that side which calls the assistance of popular tumult. The people were foolish to choose Barabbas a robber and breaker of the law of God and yet he shall be spared, as an enemy of the public safety and personal property. Those who prefer to remain in their sins before Christ, though sin is a robber, yet foolishly chosen rather than Christ who would truly enrich them.

This was a rather unfair trial which they imposed on Jesus, the persecution carried out with great confusion among the judge, and the people and the judge accused the prisoner though he declares him innocent, and was disappointed in his project of releasing Jesus on the people's choice, yet took Jesus and scourged him, though he was only to pacify the Jews. The Romans scourging was very severe and was not limited, as among the Jews, to forty stripes, yet it was pain and shame Christ submitted to for your sake, that the scriptures might the fulfilled which spoke of your peace be upon him, that by his stripes you are healed.

Jesus fate was now turned over to the soldiers to be ridiculed and made sport of as a fool, the soldiers put a crown of thrones on his head, they put on him a purple robe, and they complement Jesus shouting 'Hail, king of the Jews' and then smooth him with their hands. Yet, Pilate was still ignoring his conscience and brought Jesus out to the people wearing a crown of thorns and his head and face covered in blood, said, 'Behold the man 'worthy of your compassion as to silent their jealousies, behold a man not worthy your suspicion. The persecution was the more exasperated, the chief priest and officers joined in with the people crying, 'Crucify, him, Crucify him!' The common people perhaps acquiesced in Pilate's declaration of his innocence. Pilate said, 'Take him and crucify him yourself' although he knew they could not, they durst not and he did not have enough courage to act according to his conscience.

The persecutors gave the people their demand, 'we have a law, and by our law, he ought to die, he made himself the Son of God. They had indeed an excellent law, but in vain they boasted and abused the law in bad purposes, and they perverted the law and made it instruments of their malice.

Pilate was at this point yielding to the voice of the people and the chief priest, he finally gave in that it should be as they required. Barabbas was released and cast into prison, and Pilate could not deal more barbarously with Jesus than to deliver him to the people's will'

Pilate intended to release Jesus because he was convinced Jesus was innocent, and he knew that the prosecution was malicious against him yet, Pilate had not the courage to acquit Jesus, he ought to have done so by his power, but he hopes to satisfy both his conscience and the people. It is not surprising regarding these unusual practices among common people who seek to please men rather than pleasing God. Pilate proved rather of having more concerned about political expediency rather than doing what was right. Pilate asked the crowd another time, 'What shall I do then with Jesus who is called Christ? They again, shouted, 'Crucify him!'

In all the confusion, God sends a dream to Pilate's wife. The dream was evidently of divine origin, even as the earthquake and usual darkness and rending of the curtain. Her dream should have warned Pilate that this was no ordinary defendant, yet, as Jesus said, 'the one delivering him to Pilate bore the greater guilt of sin, even though Pilate's guilt did not equal theirs yet this act was extremely reprehensible, yet, he dictates for the promoters of the crime was reflected in the sign he had placed over the impaled Jesus identifying him as King of the Jews.

It was not that this woman heard of anything before, concerning Christ, most probably she was one of the devout and honorable women with a sound sense of religion. She explained how she suffered many things in a dream, and seems as it was a frightening dream, as she recalled, she experienced troubling thoughts so she sends her husband this very wise notice, 'Have nothing to do with this just man'.

This was an honorable testimony of our Lord Jesus witnessing for him, that he was a just man when Jesus friends were afraid to speak up for him. God made even those who were strangers and enemies to speak in his favor, for instance, when Peter denied Jesus, and yet, Judas confessed him, and the chief priest pronounced him guilty of death, here, Pilate declared, 'he found no fault in him, and the people were now in pandemic wondering what will be the outcome, so they cried out the more, 'Let him be crucified. Even though the people had no evidence of what Jesus did wrong, yet, Pilate's objection regarding the people's decisions, cause him to endeavor to transfer the decision from himself to the high priest, because he sees it of no purpose.

See how strong the stream of lust and rage sometimes is, that neither authority nor reason will prevail to check against it, while the people were still in raged and began threatening Pilate what they would do if he did not gratify their wishes to crucify Jesus. The priests also had an agenda and were apprehensive that endeavors to seize Christ that would have caused uproar especially on the feast day, and this would put Pilot into a great strait betwixt peace of his mind, and the peace of the city. Some argued if a man is faultless he ought not to be crucified, upon any presence whatsoever to gratify any man or company in the world. Thus, Pilate thought of trimming the matter, to pacify both the people and his conscience by doing and drowning it, and therefore, he had a plan in his head, to wash his guilty conscience, he called for a basin of water to wash his hands from the guilt of a decision his conscience had ignored.

Thus, for men to protest innocence against a thing, and yet to practice it, is only to proclaim that they sin against their conscience. In the midst of all this, the Jews threaten to report Pilate to Caesar, so he became more afraid and thought his job was in jeopardy, and considering one of his main duties was to do what was necessary to maintain peace, he was baffled by making a decision and allowing the people's desire to crucify Jesus. At this crucial moment of Pilate, a leader of the people was now standing between popularity and his conscience, and took comfort by washing his hands with water, before the multitude, that was not enough to ease his guilt-ridden conscience. This action only gives merely a false sense of peace, before God, and to acquit him before the people, he thought he had cleared himself and saying, 'I am innocent of the blood of this just person and he took the awful decision against his conscience and allowing Jesus to be crucified.

EXAMPLE: King Nebuchadnezzar ignored his conscience, and though it could break off his sins, and showed mercy to the poor captives. God gave him space to repent, instead, his pride and haughtiness, abuse God's patience. As he walked in the palace of the kingdom of Babylon, in pomp and pride, he thought everything looks great, he said to himself, 'This Babylon I have built' he proudly claimed ownership of what was not belonging to him in the first place, all had belonged to God who so kindly permits him to look after it until he is removed by mercy or by force. Sadly, the king had no knowledge that Babylon was built' many years before he was born, yet, he foolishly boasted that he had built it. Just as how Augustus Caesar boasted concerning Rome, he said, 'I have found it as bricks, but I left it marble' Caesar boasted that he built it for the house of the kingdom, the metropolis of the empire.

This king demonstrated an unreasonable behavior of pomp and pride and displayed self-abasement feeling in himself more than a mortal man, and therefore, God had justly to make him less than a man and put him on the level with the beast, (lessons) Those who set up themselves as a rival with their maker, is the behavior of Satan. The king thought of himself too big for his boots, and much more powerful above his Creator, so he had to be cut down to a size of a mere man.

God was not pleased or was impressed by the king's pride; God sees the proud afar off. The Nebuchadnezzar continued in his prideful attitude and thought to himself untouchable by neither God nor man, God's eyes behold the humble and the proud, and give time for men to repent. God will not allow a mere man to pass their boundaries; he was punished by powerful words from heaven which he immediately was deprived of his honor as a king. The words from heaven, 'The kingdom has departed from you. The king was deprived of his honor as a man, and his lost his reason, and by such reason he lost his dominion and was driven from men to the behavior of an animal the same hour, everything followed so sharply and suddenly the king felt starling mad, his understanding and his memory were gone, and all the faculties of a rational soul were broken.

His nakedness was revealed, as a four feet animal like a brute that ran wild into the fields and woods and was made to eat grass like oxen; can you imagine a king got himself being away from other humans? Yet, that was the reward of a person getting too big for himself. There are lessons to be learned from this remarkable king, who was placed in a prominent position, but once his heart was departed away from God, you know he was on a downward path that leads to no good.

God asked all people, whether kings or ordinary people, to be true in their commitment because only by trusting him sincerely you will avoid otherwise, find yourselves alienated from him. However, when people rebel by doing evil because they did not set their heart on seeking the Lord will be at a lost. Any person who chose to live a prayer-less life will soon realize it was a terrible mistake some would continue in the sinful path rather than turning their heart fully to the only true God.

People will ignore the inner wooing of their conscience and refuse to change their attitudes and wrong behaviors. Similarly, the extent when a person deviates from righteousness may be major or minor, the degree of regrets will logically be commensurate with the degree of deviation. Those who have long been without God in the world shall now seek God. People who have no desire to serve God will come to ask forgiveness in times of adversity; 'where is God my maker?' and might begin to inquire after him. Even so, the great God would take pleasure in welcoming them and there will be joy in heaven over all sinners who repent.

CHAPTER THREE

GOD'S DISPLEASURE

There are certain traits in a man that God declared his displeasure and has strong feelings of the sin of man, and because the man was born in sin and shaped in iniquity, it seems the man is helpless in dealing with his sin. It was man's sin that broke the fellowship between man and God, man was helpless trying to live from these inherited sins that reach in their hearts, although God has always shown man mercy and forgiveness, nevertheless, it seems that man always reverts to their usual ways of sinning, and so God provides a remedy for our sinful nature, by sending his only begotten son Jesus to pay the penalty for sin and to redeem man back to a right relationship with God.

As humans, all living humans all inherited sin from Adam the first human committed by disobeying God in the Garden of Eden, then humans are under the curse of sin and cannot live free from sin unless man applied to the blood of Jesus to cleanse them from sin. The book of Proverbs specifies and gives notable displeasure of things that God dislike although God does not count our sins one by one, yet, he declares, 'All have sinned and come short of God's glory.

The debt of man sin paid and fulfilled at Calvary and settled when Jesus cried out; 'It is finished' man's redemption is fully paid' yet, man has always maintained a tendency to turn back and spoil the relationship with God who has a remarkable love for man, he loved man so much that he will never give up on opening the door of salvation so that man can come again and cry, 'Abba father who is in heaven, Hallowed be thy name.'

Humans have always had needs for God, and cannot live without God. That is one of the reasons why God leaves an open door of opportunity that all man can come to him. God declares he will wash away the sins of man, who come to him;

God made it clear the things that please and the things that displease him, although all sin and unrighteous behavior are not pleasing to him, yet he specifies six sins that he hates. Sin is missing the mark of God's righteous standards. Yet, God so loves the whole of the human race, he shows kindness, sympathetic compassion and justice; he tells us in his word how to live from this deadly monster called sin. God is interested in what happens to his creatures, he made a way to bring us back to him, and if we put aside our sinful ways and adhere to him, it will be well with us, therefore, as sinners, we need to ask God for his forgiveness.

It is important to avoid these things that are displeasing to God after you have received his forgiveness, to keep in harmony with God. Catalogues of a special manner of sin are odious to God are generally found in man. God dislikes every sin, but there are some sins which he does especially and what God dislikes so we most dislike in ourselves also. The word *hate*, the definition of dislike and it should not be taken in an absolute sense, however, because it means rejection from fellowship, so these are the kind of sins in people whom God rejects. Six things are listed that God dislikes and seven are an abomination to him.

UNBELIEF

Unbelief is a serious indictment against man, how can man not believing in God the creator and continue to reject God who has done so much for us as humans. Unbelieving is non-submission to the righteousness of God; you have a choice of believing, or not believing. Whatever choice you made carries serious consequences, which will catch up either through life or at the end of life. Everyone believes in something whether good or evil, but especially believing and putting our trust in God early part of one's life will pave a good path for the rest of one's life.

The main cause of unbelief is ignorance and unrighteousness; for instance, the ignorance and unrighteousness of the people of Israel, they did not consider what was the need of their righteousness, and to appear before God, if they had, they would never expect justification by their works. Thus the sinner cannot justify themselves before God's justice in themselves. For example, a man with *a proud* conceit of his righteousness, and goes about establishing the righteousness of his working, and by his works, he cannot please God, for the truth is, every man must belief and repent of unbelief because Godly sorrow will work true repentance.

The nature of unbelieving men has not submitted themselves to the righteousness of God. Therefore, true faith there is a new requirement for submission, and everything we do in life has a requirement towards taking the right actions and making the right decisions because every action carries consequences. The sin of unbelief is gruesome to mankind; it prevents man from knowing and receiving the true and living God. An unbelieving heart will always lose out on the blessings of salvation and the wonderful gift that God offers.

However, the end of the law is Christ, and the design of the law is to lead people to Christ, and the use of the law was to direct people of the righteousness to Christ. Rather than living by faith in God, the Jews established customs and traditions in adding to God's law and trying to make themselves acceptable in God's sight. Human efforts no matter how sincere can never substitute for the righteousness of God. Whereas the only way to earn salvation is to be perfect and that is impossible, we can only hold out our empty hands and receive salvation as a gift from God our father.

The Psalmist declared, 'I will declare my iniquity, and not cover it, I will be sorry for my sin, and not make light-matter of it' David concluded his prayer and said, Forsake me not, 'Oh Lord!, though my friends forsake me, and though I deserve to be forsaken by thee, be not far from me as my unbelieving heart is ready to fear who thou art. (Psalms 38:18)

The written or spoken word of God is the means of persuading men and bringing conviction of the wrongness of their ways, 'Be it known to all mankind that God is not far from God, he is everywhere present, and he is an infinite Spirit that is not far from us. God is near to us both to receive the homage we render to him, and to give the mercies we ask of him, whether we are, though near or far, whether you are in a cottage, church, or temple, in a crowd, or a corner, in a city, or a desert, in the depth of the sea or far off from the sea, this is certain God is not far off from every one of us. Do you believe it?

Thus, you must believe God and acknowledge his word and find answers in the Word of God to help you believe in the Son to who is the only way to the father. The word of the Lord, quick, very lively, active, in seizing the conscience of the sinner

44

in cutting him to the heart, and in comforting him in binding up the wounds of the soul. The word of the Lord is powerful, it convinces powerfully, and it is powerful to batter Satan's kingdom, and to set up the kingdom of Christ upon the ruins.

The word of God is sharper than any two-edged sword; it has the power to enter where no sword can, and make a more critical dissection, by piercing and dividing asunder of the soul and the Spirit, the sword which is the word of God divides between the joints and the marrow, and this sword can make men willing to undergo the sharpest operations for the mortifying of the heart.

The word of God teaches us to put the best construction on words and actions that people will hear, and take notice of what is commanded even from bad people. It may be quite evident of open blasphemy, and vocal misuse of God's name, or worship of other gods, as by use of images, is involved, but even in that it might consider as a private matter, or something between oneself and another person, therefore, any wrongs committed must be recognized as a sin against God and treating God with disrespect, that is committed in ignorance. (1Tim 1:13-16)

The spoken word is full of power, making it active, operative, energizing, and effective, it will turn the inside of a sinner out, and let him see all that is in his heart. It was the word of the Lord that enabled Paul to clearly and unashamedly testified, and confessed, 'Though, I formally blaspheme and persecuted the Christians, and outrageously and aggressively insulted God, 'nevertheless, I obtained mercy because I acted out of ignorance and in unbelief' There are many people who feel extremely guilt-ridden by past behavior and a bad attitude; they ashamedly believe God could never forgive them.

When considering Paul's past life, he had scoffed at the teachings of Jesus, as blasphemy, and hunted and murdered God's people; yet, God has forgiven Paul and use him mightily for his kingdom, but no matter how your past has been. God is still able to forgive and use you as his own. When the apostle Paul visited the city of Athens he took notice of the magnificent buildings and many gods. Athens was the center of Greek culture, philosophy and education, but educated men of the city were in everything except in the word of God. These educated persons were interested to hear something new from Paul, therefore a meeting was called and they invited Paul to hear from him of anything new, but when the people gathered around, Paul stood on a hill so the audience could look down at the city and notice the many idols, these gods were worthless and good for nothing. (Hebrews 4:12)

Paul began addressing the people, he openly proclaimed, 'Since you are offspring of God, you ought not to think that the divine nature of God is like gold or silver or stone, or something that is shaped by art and man's devising will suffice, 'truly these times of ignorance God overlooked, but now commands all men everywhere to repent.

He empathetically expressed the true God; he was well prepared to speak to groups, and he did not doubt unbelief in his heart that Jesus is the Son of God. Paul mentioned regarding the gods they worshipped, even though he had no intention of drawing the people to atheism, yet, his intention was to the service of the true God, and he had rather reduce their hearts to the knowledge of the one God.

The apostle Paul also warned the people who were present at his preaching to flee from the wrath to come, by accepting the message of repentance, and those professing repentance were highly concerned to live like a penitent and bring forth fruit for repentance; else they could not escape the wrath to come, because only changes of our ways are evident in changes of your mind. Quite rightly, the people especially the Jews had the zeal of God; yet, their opposition to the gospel was from a principle of respect to the law, because they had a blind misguided zeal. Paul showed the unbelievers how they had lost the knowledge of the true God that made them, in contrast to the worshipping of the false gods, because of their unbelief. yet, they were not enlightened according to correct and vital knowledge, because of their unbelief.

UNBELIEVING PEOPLE IN THE DAYS OF JOHN THE BAPTIST

Unbelief is not a new concept it existed from the beginning. So many people have lost faith in Christ and others because they do not and will not believe. In the days of John, the Baptist was preaching the gospel, the people made many excuses, rather than listening and adhere to the preaching, changing their ways and accept the gospel, they were preventive, so, John asked, 'what is your presence?'

The religious leaders relied more on their family lines than on their faith for their relationship with God, for them religion was inherited from one generation to another, but by far, one having a personal relationship with God is not handed down from parents to their children. It is required that everyone take the initiative to make their commitment with God; because it is futile depending on someone's faith for salvation, by having your faith in Jesus Christ. For this, cause God has mercifully sent his prophets and preachers calling men everywhere to repentance, through publishing the Good News through the Christian congregation, and this was made possible from the time of the Cornelius conversion, God has been telling mankind everywhere to believe and repent.

God's law is perfect, and perfectly free from all corruption, perfectly filled with all goodness, and perfectly fills with all. It is designed that nothing should be added to it, nor taken from it. It is a useful tool giving comfort to the soul, and bringing us back to ourselves to our duty, and back to God which is framed in the infinite wisdom that is altogether true. (Romans 10:2)

Even in the course of your own life, you may choose whom you believe and what not to believe and the most important person to trust and believe in is God. This is because God's laws are guidelines and lights for our path, rather than chains on our hands and feet. They point at dangers and warn us, then point towards success and guidance, for instance, the testimony of the Lord is sure, it is a sure fountain of living comforts, and a sure fountain of the lasting hope, and make even the simple wise, and eternity, and those who are simple shall be made wise by the word of God.

There should be no unbeliever in the status of the Lord, they are right, exactly agreeing with the eternal rules and principles of good and evil, and because they are right, they rejoice the heart, the status of the Lord is trustworthy, exactly agreeing with the eternal rules and principles of good and evil. The law as we see is in the hands of Christ, it gives cause for joy, and when it is written in our hearts, it lays a foundation for lasting joy, by restoring our right minds.

The commandments of the Lord is pure, enlightening the eyes; it brings us to the sight and sense of our sin and misery, and directs us in the way of duty. The fear of the Lord will cleanse our way, and it will endure forever, even the ceremonial that has long since gone away, but the law concerning the fear of God is ever the same, and time will not alter the moral of good and evil. The work of the prophets was largely one to convincing Israel of their sins, whether it was idolatry, injustice and oppression of their fellowman, immorality, or failing to trust God, but people rather trusting in men and the military might of nations.

In the time of Samuel when the people saw God's expression of his displeasure, they earnestly begged Samuel's prayers, they asked, 'Pray for thy servant that we may not die because we have added to our other sins the evil of asking for a king'. The people were apprehensive of their danger from the wrath of God and could not expect that he would hear their prayers, so they entreat Samuel to pray for them.

The people saw their need and asked Samuel's intervention, which they had rejected, now in their distress, they desire Samuel's praying for them. It's a common behavior among people, they tend to take others for granted, and will use their kindness in times of their distress, and when it is over they will drop you like hot potatoes, but we must continue praying for people everywhere, in season and out of season.

Samuel promised the people he will not only pray for them but also teach them, though they were not willing to be under his government as a judge, he would not deny them his instructions as to their teacher. (1 Sam 12:19)

God is still calling you to be active in your obedience. John compared people who refuse to live for God to unproductive trees that will be cut down. To be productive for God you must obey his teachings, and resist temptation, actively helping others, and sharing your faith.

The message of John and Jesus produce truth to strip away from the people and their religious leaders the cloak of self-righteousness, and observance of man-made traditions, hypocrisy, exposing their sinful state. Some people who listen to John's message were convicted and chose to be baptized by John, so they could escape eternal punishment, but not believing and turning to God for salvation. John had harsh words for such people, John says, 'God's value of reformation must be above rituals, it is a person's faith motivated by a desire for a new and changed life.'

The gospel of Jesus Christ must not be seen as a vaccination or assurance's policy against possible disease, it's a deep belief from the heart and confession by the mouth. John the Baptist was a voice crying in the desert, and he cried, 'Prepare the way of the Lord and make his path straight' and sinners shall be converted to God' The crooked ways and the crocked spirit shall be made straight' God by his grace can make straight which sin has made crocked' John the Baptist declared, 'the guilty corrupted race of mankind has become a generation of vipers, and not only poison, but poisonous, hatful to God, and hating one another.

It was mainly Jews who seem to hateful they have Abraham as their father, to plead for them without asking God for their forgiveness, therefore, carnal hearts are apt to say within it is well we can find God some other ways apart from repentance, and putting their convincing commanding power of the word of God. Therefore, we must be careful in saying this, neither should we rock ourselves to sleep, nor flatter yourself into a fool's paradise, but you must be aware that God takes notice in what you say as they did, think not to say you are a seed of Abraham, and not sinners like the Gentiles.

John reiterates that all people must adhere and repent otherwise they will perish, and many of his disciples were shocked when John said, 'you being Abraham descendants was not enough for God unless you repent. (Luke 3:7)

INDIVIDUAL SINS

All individuals are responsible for their wrongdoings, and will be called to give account, for example, *haughtiness* and *contempt* of others, a *proud look*; Pride is the first because it is the bottom of many sins, haughtiness and contempt of others. When men show off their countenance it will witness against them that they are overvaluing themselves and undervaluing others, this can be seen in pride that can interfere with your ability to reason.

Pride is such a negative force in man; it interferes with their ability to reason, and it is the presage of ruin, and ruin will, at last, be the punishment of pride. God has the power to change a soul who has a long time spirit of pride to become humble, and also those who have a perverse spirit to become meek and obedient. The sin of pride can affect our values, for instance, Jesus disciples were caught up in constant struggles for personal success, and we are interested to know who was the greatest in the kingdom? When Jesus told them about humility, they were embarrassed to answer Jesus question. It was always painful to compare our motives with Christ's, however it is not wrong for believers to be industrious or ambitious, but when ambition pushes obedience and service to one side, it becomes sin.

Therefore, pride or insecurity can cause us to overvalue position and prestige, and in God's kingdom, such motives are destructive, and the only safe ambition must be directed to Christ's kingdom and advancement, thus, pride and God's presence is incompatible; as there is an incompatibility between blind arrogance and the presence of God in our hearts. For instance, the proud person depends on himself rather than God, but when God's presence is welcome there is no room for pride because he makes us aware of our true selves.

Pride is the inner voice that whispers and says. '*My way* is best, resisting God's leadership and believing that you can live without his help and whenever you find yourself wanting to do it your way, and looking down on other people, you are being pulled down by pride, you might consider ridding yourself of pride then God can use you in his service. There is a penalty that is attached to an individual or collative sins and all humans guilty of sin and must come to acknowledgement, and ask God for his forgiveness.

The apostle Paul describes the heart of man is desperately wicked, and their throat is as an open tomb. It is like a deadly poison that is compared to the asps, that is as small and deadly as a poisonous snake that is under the lips, whose mouth is full of cursing and bitterness.

LYING TONGUE

The tongue is the organ of the body playing a prominent role in tasting. The taste buds distributed on the tongue surface defect only acid, sweet, salt and bitter. More importantly, the tongue is also essential to speech because the articulation of words requires active maneuvering on the part which it does with dexterity and remarkable speed.

Nothing can be more an abomination to God than a *lying tongue*, and nothing more sacred than the truth, more necessary to the conversation when speaking the truth.

The tongue is a system, a world of iniquity that sets on fire the whole course of life, and is even set on fire by Satan. The book of James states that the *tongue* cannot be tamed, and mankind can control every lesser creature, but no one can control his or her tongue. James wrote about the human tongue; he said, 'It is but a small part of the body, yet it makes a great boast, on average a person opens his mouth approximately 700 times a day to speak. This small member is a powerful member that can control the rest of your body.

Men usually teach their tongue to speak lies, and those who take the liberty to tell lies in discourse are relatively to be guilty of the greater wickedness of bearing false witness. Whenever they are tempted by it, though they seem to detest it, they shall not escape the righteous judgment of God, who is jealous, and he will not suffer his name to be profaned, and those who are affected by it; afflicts them by reproaches because he hates the sin of lying.

The mischief of this member of our body is obvious; the use of the tongue afflicts, and has the ability cause serious damage to oneself and others, and a flattering lie secretly works ruin, and easily suspected and men betray themselves of being credulous of the compliments that are passed on them. A wise man will be more afraid of a flattering tongue than kisses, and by a slanderer tongue that proclaims war, but rather the mouth of the righteous is a fountain of life, but violence overwhelms the mouth of the wicked.

The mouth can be used either as a weapon, or a tool, hurting relationships, or building them up. In truth, it is often easier to destroy than to build up, and most people have received more destructive comments than those that build up. Therefore, every person you meet on the way is either a demolition site, or a constructive opportunity, but your words will make a difference, whether to build or to tearing own. There cannot be a greater affront to God, and a greater injury to our neighbor than knowingly giving false testimony. The people who make mischief between relations and neighbors, and using all wicked means, even so, but the God of love and peace hates those who sow discord among brethren. We must look at the word of God both as a light and a law. Therefore, God hates a false witness who breathes lies even under oath, and who sows discord among the brethren, rather, pleasant words are a honeycomb that is sweet to the soul and healing to the bones. (Proverbs 6:16-19)

It might be beneficial and wise to adopt David's attitude regarding the rule of his tongue by asking God's to keep from speaking evil and his tongue from speaking lies. Knowing the power of the tongue, it might be advisable to ask God to guard what we say so that your words may bring honor to him. It is the best policy if you have nothing worthwhile to say, by taking the opportunity to listen and learn, by doing so you might learn something in common from others, and making sure you pause to listen when you do speak, o you will have something important to say, though a good tongue is healing to sin-sick souls by convincing them and reconciling parties at variances, this is the healing of the tongue, which is as a tree of life, and the leaves have a sanative virtue. He who knows how to have discussion will make the place where he lives a paradise, but an evil tongue is wounding.

God is willing to help you control your tongue, there is nothing impossible with him, he is interesting even with a little member of your body such as your tongue and he who guards his lips guards his life, and who speaks rashly will come to ruin. You might consider mastering self-control in what you say because words can cut and destroy, if you need help regarding self-control, it is right, to begin with, your tongue, it is best to stop and think before you react or speak.

HANDS THAT SHED INNOCENT BLOOD

God expresses his displeasure of hands that shed innocent blood, your hands are very important members of your body, some people are born with both hands, and some with one, but whatever the case your hands are a useful and necessary member of your body. It is the nature of man to use your hands for the manner of activities, such as clapping for joy in worshipping God, signing an agreement, writing, washing clothes, bathing, feeding holding, carrying, greeting, lifting, it is a good idea to use our hands positively and not shedding the blood of the innocent. A person might use their *hands* to shed innocent blood; because they have in them the devil's image and does his service, and bad people used their hands to kill and destroy each
other, God dislikes such selfish behavior and desire clean hands to be lifted in prayer and praises to him, on behalf of yourselves and anthers.

GOD DISLIKES A BAD HEART

The heart of mankind was originally good, God says so when he made man in the beginning. The heart in man is a very important organ in the body that is known as the center of all emotions, and out of man's heart are the issues of life. The heart of man where all plans are developed, and good or evil, battles for truth and lies are developed, the heart of man is described as being desperately wicked, and full of wicked devices and vile imaginations, and is also capable of manufactures wicked thoughts and plans.

Yet the heart can become anxious and that weigh you down, but a kind word from the heart will cheer up the lonely. A heart that is regenerated and believes in Christ and loves God; considers, pure and prayerful, perfect, contrite, steadfast, sincere and enlightened, any others that comes from the heart is considered displeasing to God the creator, that person's heart will need regeneration to be back in fellowship with God. Yet the heart of man is in God's hands. God, he has the power and authority to change men's mind into newness from what they intended.

FEET THAT RUN SWIFTLY TO DO EVIL

Your feet or foot are frequently used to denote a person's inclination of the course it takes, whether good or bad. God directs the feet of his faithful servants in the right path, figuratively showing them the right way that prevents them from stumbling in a spiritual fall or be ensnared in evil and sometimes even safeguarding them against capture by the enemy. God has a special regard for the feet of those proclaiming the good news of the Kingdom, he calls the comely, and you should have its feet shod with the equipment of the good news of peace so that he can safely carry the good gospel of Jesus Christ to the world.

Your feet are a gift from God and should make the best use of them. Normally people used their feet for walking from place to place, standing, dancing, and running. It is recorded in the bible of some excellent runners in the bible, in that time past there was transport, such as motor vehicles, or travel by air, or sending a telegram to take a message from place to place; people were employed as runners to take urgent messages to any place no matter how far a journey. For example, the Christian is in a race compared to athletes' runners; there are guidelines for taking part in such race, it's not a walking race, but for trained runners who desire to be winners in competitions, Christians are encouraged to be active in the spiritual race, and run to win.

When people use their feet to go about shedding innocent blood, God says, he dislikes it, and when you consider the height incidence of violent crime, murder, and abortion that affects our society destruction and misery are in their ways, and whatever man touches he corrupts, in their sinful pursuit, this is a great affront to God.

CRUELTY/BLOOD-THIRSTINESS

Therefore, blood-thirstiness is the works of the devil from the beginning as a liar and a murderer, for out of the heart proceeds evil thoughts, murders that result from anger. Thus, a person who has a quick temper is like a fire out of control, it can burn us and everyone else in its path. The spirit of anger drives and pushes us in making hasty decisions and cause bitterness and guilt. When you feel yourself getting angry it is suggested to take a little step back and look for the causes, then pray that God will grant you help to control your quick temper and use your energy challenging into effective actions through humility.

HAUGHTINESS

Haughtiness is described as disdainful pride: such as arrogance, superciliousness, and haughtiness is the opposite of humility, the word has also carried the meaning of feeling high, exalted and swelling; therefore, a person who displays a spirit of haughtiness feels esteem and superior, and lifted above his fellowmen. As a result such a person usually claims honor and attention beyond what is due and treats others with disrespect and insolence. For example, when the Israelites went deep in their revolt against God and were rotting away in their transgression, yet they resisted paying the price by looking to God and repenting of their sinful ways.

Instead of asking God for help; they bypass God's previous instructions to them and realizing it is their sins that caused them not to approach God because being unclean we cannot approach God. Haughtiness is bad quality or characteristic that is deeper than a mental conclusion. Jesus Christ name haughtiness the same it along with murder, thievery, blasphemy and other wrongdoings and said, these things come from the heart, and even persons who have been humble in service of God can become haughty because of gaining wealth or power, or because of beauty, success, wisdom, or acclaim of others.

Your best effort is still infected, our only hope is faith in Jesus Christ who can cleanse and bring us into God's presence. The prophet Isaiah recorded, the Lord's voice crying in the city, and the voice of the prophet interpreting the judgment of Jerusalem, *Turn* you from your evil ways, unto God, 'return to your allegiance, 'O children of Israel have revolt'.

The prophet reminded said, 'they have been backsliding children, therefore, let them return and their backsliding shall be healed. God loved his people with compassion, and he will always send a word to his prophet to remind man of their wrongdoings, yet, people refused to pay the price of looking to God and repenting of their sinful ways, they thought they could get away from seeking God for his forgiveness, and bringing them back into the right relationship with him.

There is no way around it, sin must be confessed and turned from, when you are experiencing problems, it is good to seek help, but you must never bypass God or his previous direction he has for us, the apostle reminding how a man takes some false steps before they are aware of it. In some cases a person of discernment and spiritual qualifies can readjust a person in spiritual mildness, with no notice taken, so the Christian or no-Christians should never think that he or she is independent and doesn't need help from others; neither should anyone excuse the task of helping others. Where there is a will there will be away, we must try and find the way without making excuses.

A story was told of a frog trying to get up some steps by jumping over each step, instead of climbing the steps one at a time, the frog made several attempts trying to jump over several steps at the same time in a hurry, eventually, he jumps over too many steps at a time aiming to reach to the top, only finding himself tumbling to the bottom. He realizes his mistake, and had to start climbing up the stairs one at a time all over again, lesson learnt, patience is a virtue, it is wise taking one step at a time, you'll learn patience, understanding and confidence and effective lessons that are useful to pass on to others.

A story was told of the turnaround of a criminal; about fifteen years ago at the Church of God national convention, a humble pastor was surrounded by his family; he was receiving his ordination certificate from the national oversee. The heart of this story is; at one time this man had been greatly feared in his city because of his ruthless behavior, which even included murder. One day an evangelism team was witnessing on the street, seeing the criminal they looked with gazing eyes and went to the other side, except for one saintly lady who cared, and shared the Gospel of Jesus with him, he gladly made a commitment to Christ that day, shortly thereafter he became a minister of the Gospel, it's amazing about God, he does not patch up our lives, he gives us, a clean slate to start over, all new.

God is mercifully and consideration of the fleshy weakness of his servants; they need not stay in a constant state of remorse, due to their error resulting from inherent imperfection. God understands that humans are fragile, but God's care is eternal, thus, we can be assured that God cares for his people who obey him. Though you might often focus on God as a Judge and Lawgiver who ignores his compassion for you when God examines your life he remembers your human condition. Nevertheless, your weakness should never be used as a justification for sin. God's mercies consider everything, and he will deal with his people compassionately, and so you may trust and rely on him.

Since some have not yet accepted grace to repent, yet, it is mercy to them to have space to repent, therefore, you owe it to Christ the great intercessor, why barren trees are not cut down immediately. You are encouraged to pray to God the merciful retriever of barren trees, 'Lord let them alone, bear with them a little longer, and wait to be gracious. You must stand in the gap, to turn away wrath, but retrieve of mercy, or but for a time, 'Let it alone for this year also' Although, God has borne long, you must hope he will bear a little longer, yet, you should not expect he will always. To retrieve, it must be obtained by prayers of others for you, but not pardon, you must have our faith, and repentance and prayers.

DEAD WORKS OF SINS

The term dead works do not means merely sinful works of wrongdoing, but works of the fallen flesh that leads one to death, and although all works in them might be spiritually dead, vain and fruitless. This would include works of self-justification, efforts by men to establish their righteousness apart from Christ and his ransom sacrifice. The formal observance of the Law by the Jewish religious leaders and others constituted dead works because it lacked the vital ingredient of faith. Anything dead is useless and must be buried, or burn, otherwise, it needs a resurrection, not everything is worth being brought back to life. Therefore works that are dead is finished with and has no more use in the Christian faith or any value in society.

The foundational doctrine served as a base for Christian maturity, it begins with repentance from dead works and faith towards God. The formal observance of the Law by the Jewish religious leaders and others constituted dead works because it lacked the vital ingredient of faith. Christians must live in their endeavor growing to maturity, teaching new believers the basics, and not always laying again the foundation of repentance, and the young believer must grow and building up to perfection, though some believers might seem weak, and others who have gained strength should provide encouragements and suitability for the weak.

Those who are trying to get it right by keeping the law, and having their ideas, attending church regularly, working in the church, paying to offer, and being nice and good, and may even play by all the rules. Paul instructs that certain elementary teaching is essential for all believers to understand. For instance, the basics, that includes the importance of faith, the foolishness of trying to be saved by good deeds, and the meaning of baptism, spiritual gifts, and the facts of resurrection and eternal life and growing to maturity in our understanding, we need beyond the elementary teachings to a more complete understanding of the faith.

This approach will never succeed; he explains that God's plans are never for those who try to earn his favor by being good, and those who think they can never be good enough, must depend on Christ to earn God's favors. He explains an individual can only be saved by putting their faith in what Christ has done, and when you recognized this and put it in practice you will never be put to shame or, be disappointed. An instance of the Gentiles was alienated from righteousness; however, God was delighted to dispense grace in the way of sovereignty and absolute dominion on their behalf. They attained righteousness by faith; and by embracing and believing in Christ, on the other hand, the Jews, sought righteousness, but not in the right way, rather they followed after the law of righteousness, that cause many to be stuck in their old Jewish principles and ceremonial, they embraced of the shadows, and not the substance.

These people fell short of accepting God, and this attitude will cause seeking people to stumble at Christ Jesus who is 'the

'Chief Agent" to give repentance to Israel and forgiveness of sins and instead of seeking repentance, they still practice the observance of the law, as if it was still in force, so it becomes dead works after Christ Jesus had fulfilled it.

Therefore, God exalted Jesus to be his right as prince, leader, and deliverer, to grant repentance and forgiveness of sin to Israel, and release from sin. Similarly, all works that men have done might otherwise be of no value and become as dead works if the motivation is not in love, the love for God, love for neighbor, and truth, and harmonizing with God's will communicates to us through his Word. (Matt 7:21)

CHAPTER FOUR

GOD'S PLEASURE

The sin of man that pleases God is written in his word, and in every chapter of the bible contained his word that is profitable for guidance and instructions, for man to follow and live. Some words are written and highlighted in bold and sometimes in red, so that man will not miss the mark. Just like a child who does the right that pleases his parent and causes pleasurable countenances, in the same way, God feels pleasurable of his creatures' obedience. By doing the right thing to others will not always be easy, but when we can make the sacrifice by doing what pleases God, we will be rewarded by him. At times you might work hard at what you are asked to do, and patiently waiting to receive a word of gratitude from our employer, parents, pastors, to say well done, but it never happens, are they afraid to render to others what is right and fair?

God takes pleasure when you care and appreciate others, and does delay it until the person cannot touch and smell flowers of appreciation. Can you imagine when at the end of our lives when we stand in God's presence and he opens his records and presents us with a well-done crown? The prophet Micah tells what the Lord requires of you, he said you need not trouble yourself to make your proposal; the terms are already settled and laid down. What God has spoken to man everywhere in general, all should it to us, in particular. What the Lord requires paying for the pardon of sins, because no sin cannot be bought or paid for by your effort, it is already purchased by Jesus when he died on the cross to pay the penalty for mankind. God is pleased when you do no wrong to anyone, but doing right to all, in bodies and good name.

You should love mercy and, not only be just to all, but to all you have to deal with, and be kind to all that needs you neither must you show mercy, but you must also love mercy.
God is pleased when you walk humbly with your God, this includes all the duties of the first table, as the two former includes and all the duties of the second table. In the whole course of your conversation, you must confirm yourselves to the will of God, by keeping up your communion with God and study to prove yourselves to him and every thought within must be brought down into obedience to God. That is what requires, and without this, the most earthly are vain obligation, and there is more than burnt offerings.

An example, of Enoch walking with God and how he pleases God, Enoch was one of the two great clouds of witnesses who were outstanding examples of faith in ancient times. The great cloud of witnesses is composed of the people described in Hebrews11. The faithfulness of these heroes of faith is a constant encouragement to us, yet, we do not struggle alone and we are not the first to struggle with the problems we face. Others have run the race and won, witness's stirs and won also, examples like Enoch who was exceptionally rare, believers are encouraged to keep walking with the true and living God, as he did.

The life of Enoch is an example, although Enoch was the son of Cain the man who was guilty of his brother's death, and ran away as a fugitive. Enoch was born in that period. It was said Enoch was born in the land of *Fugitiveness*; this is because his father Cain was a fugitive on the earth. Nevertheless, Enoch's life should be blamed for the sin of his father. God saw Enoch loved him and made something wonderful out of him for his glory.

Enoch did not allow the negatives of his family or friends or his place of birth to deterred his faith in God, he loved God and seek to walk with him, amid persecution, in the end, it pays a dividend. The prophet of God Micah foretold God's coming with his holy myriads to execute judgment against the ungodly. Although severe persecution was brought against Enoch because of the prophesying, nevertheless, God did not permit those who oppose killing Enoch. Instead, God took him that is, cut short his life at an age far below most of his contemporaries. Enoch was transferred he did not experience the pangs of death, he died at the age of 365; and it seems as if God disposed of his body for he was nowhere to be found, like the body of Moses.

God is pleased when you humble yourselves in his eyes, and though God does not owe mankind anything, yet, in underserved kindness he is ready to show mercy and favor to those humbling themselves before him, those are the ones who are not boasting in themselves, but looking to him, he opposes the haughty, and gives undeserved kindness to the humble.

God is also pleased when you care for the widow, fatherless, caring and sharing your time with and afflicted and showing compassion, and loving your neighbor as ourselves.

OBEDIENCE PLEASE GOD

Obedience has many aspects, such as submitting to authority, the doing of what is commanded; complying with what is required, or abstaining from what is forbidden.

Thus, in some translations the word obedience is expressed by '*shama*,' meaning, basically to hear and listen, and at times it can refer to simple hearing, and becoming aware of something through the auditory senses. Example Adam and Eve in the garden, God called, 'Where are you? 'They did not understand the reason for his command so they chose to act in another way that looks better to them. All of God's command is for our good though we may not understand the reason behind them; the difference is people who trust God will obey him whether they understand or not. (Gen. 3:10)

Obedience to God is essential for life; God has the first claim to the obedience of all his creatures. They are right to own to him implicit obedience as their maker. God is the source from whom life derives and on whom life depends. Because God is all-wise and Almighty God, what he says merits the utmost respect and attention. There is no substitute for obedience, no gaining for God's favor without it. As Samuel told Saul, does the Lord delight in burnt offerings and sacrifice, to obey, to listen is better than a sacrifice, to pay attention than the fat of lambs.

Failing to obey is to reject the word of God, and demonstrate that one does not believe, trust or have faith in that word and its Source. Hence if one does not obey he would be like a person practicing divination or using idols. Therefore, verbal expressions of assent mean nothing if the required action does not follow; the lack of response proves a lack of belief or respect for the source of instructions. (Matt 21:28)

Those satisfying themselves with only hearing and giving mental acceptance to God's truth, but not doing what it called for, are deceiving themselves with false reasoning and would receive no blessing, James 1:21-25, Get rid of what is wrong in

67

your lives and humbly accept the salvation message you have received that, is the word planted in you, it is only what can save you. Therefore Jesus makes it clear that even those doing such things similar to the command, but evidently in a wrong way, or a wrong motive, would never gain entrance into the kingdom but would be completely rejected.
(Matt 7:16-23).

OBEDIENCE TO SUPERIORS

You should not only be obedient to some but also be obedient to your superiors. Even in society some superiors are much you're in age, or different gender, nevertheless, you should put all inferior complexes aside and obey them. You must imitate the example of Jesus; he was in position as God's appointed king and requires all others should obey him. Jesus is the one whom the obedience of the people belongs as the high priest whose instruction leads to healing and life everlasting for those hearing him in submission and obedience is proof and springs from the love of Christ-followers have for him, because God has made his Son the key figure of the outworking of all the purposes and as head of the Christian congregation. Therefore Christ Jesus delegates authority as he did to the apostles; these people convey the instructions to them are right and necessary.

OBEDIENCE TO PARENTS

The apostle Paul admonishes children to be obedient to their parents in everything. It must be remembered that his letter was addressed to Christians and hence everything cannot for obedience to commands that would result in disobedience to the word of the heavenly Father God, for this could not be well-pleasing to the Lord. As a child, Jesus shows submission to his earthly parents, so a parent has a God-given natural right to the obedience of their children. Jesus parents did not understand when he said, 'he meant about his father's house' they did not realize he was making a distinction between his early father and his heavenly father. Jesus knew that he had a unique relationship with God. Although Mary and Joseph knew he was God's on, they didn't understand what his mission would involve; besides they had to bring Jesus up alongside his brothers and sisters as a normal child. (Phil. 2:10)

HUSBAND/WIVES

The headship of the man calls for the obedience of wives to their husbands, in everything. Sarah was cited as an example to be emulated and submitting to another person is an often misunderstood concept, it does not mean becoming a doormat, no, Christ at whose name every knee should bow, in heaven and on earth and under the earth, he submitted his will to the father, we honor Christ by following his example.

When submitting to God you may be more willing to obey his command than to others that are to subordinate our rights to theirs. In a marriage relationship, both husband and wife are called to submit. For the wife, this means willingly following her husband's leadership in Christ. The husband should act by putting aside his interest to care for his wife. Sometimes submission can be a problem in the home where both husband and wife are stubbornly refusing to listen to each other, rather than building a strong relationship in Christ and have concern for the happiness of the other. (Eph. 5:20-21)

MASTER AND GOVERNMENTS

Obedience is due to the earthly government's authorities, and rulers since God allowed them to function and even to render certain services to his people. It is also required that Christians pay back what is due to Caesar since conscience is the decisive factor. For the Christian, our first allegiance is to Jesus, but we must obey government and leaders as well as obeying the civil law is only the beginning of your Christian responsibility, and also do what you can to be a good citizen and in a democratic society this means participation and willingness to serve.

The same obedience is required from slaves to render to masters in everything, not with eye service but as Christ's slaves, serving with fear of God. Since the creation, God has given us work to do, and if we all could regard our work as an act of service to God, and some of the attitudes would take some of the drudgery and boredom out of it. We could work without complaining and resentment if we would treat our job as a problem as the cost of discipleship. Master would provide what was right and fair; similarly employers such as paying fair wages and treating their employees justly.

Paul the apostle urged believers to submit to authorities, but he also thought there might be times when we should not submit to the government, for example, we should never allow the government to force us to disobey God. Jesus and his followers had never disobeyed the government for personal reasons, when they disobeyed; it was to follow their high loyalty to God. Their disobedience was not cheap, they were threatened, beaten, thrown into jails, tortured, and executed by their convictions, therefore, if you are compelled to disobey you must consider the consequences.

You taught how to conduct yourselves towards magistrates, and those that are in authority over you it is called the 'higher power' The just power which they have must be submitted to and obeyed, not that our conscience are to be submitted to the will of any man, and so it is God's prerogative to make laws immediately to bind conscience when you submit to them accordingly, because of the reproach which the Christian religion lays under in the world, as an enemy to public peace, order and government. Our Lord Jesus was so reproached, though he told them his kingdom was not of this world. Paul reminds believers that obedience to civil magistrates is one of the laws of Christ whose religion helps to make people good. (Romans 13:1)

DISOBEDIENCE DUE TO SIN AND IMPERFECTION

At the outset, God informed the man that obedience was a life or death matter, and God commanded the man, you are free to eat from any tree in the garden, but you must not eat from the tree of the knowledge of good and evil for when you eat of it you will surely die. You may ask, 'Why did God place the tree in the garden and then forbid Adam to eat from it. God wanted Adam to obey, but God gave Adam the freedom to choose, yet without choice, Adam would be like a prisoner and his obedience would have been hallowed. The two trees provided an exercise in choice, with rewards for choosing to obey, and consequences for choosing to disobey. If whenever you are faced with a choice, always chose to obey God, and the same rules do apply to God spirit sons. The willful disobedience of perfect man Adam as the responsible head over Eve and the male progenitor or life source of the human family, brought sin and death to all his offspring, by nature the men are sons of dissidence and children of wrath. They merited God's disfavor due to their violation of his righteous standards. The failure to resist this inherent inclination to disobedience is the course of ultimate destruction. God has mercifully provided the means for combating sin in the flesh and for gaining forgiveness or wrongdoing resulting from imperfection rather than from willful disobedience.

God supplied by his holy spirit the force for righteousness enabling sinful men to produce good fruitage. Forgiveness for sin comes through faith in Christ, and a healthy fear of God also has a part in obedience, because one recognizes God's all-powerfulness, and that he is not to be trifled with, nor can be mocked, for he renders to each one according to their deeds.

The scriptures set fort encouragements examples of faithful obedience in all manners of circumstances and situations, and in the face of all types of oppositions. The great and foremost example was God's son who humbled himself and became obedient as far as death, yes, death on the cross. By this obedient course, he was justified, proven righteous n his merit, and hence could provide a perfect sacrifice that would redeem mankind from sin and death. (Gen 2:16)

CHAPTER FIVE

SENSE OF THE HEART

The sense of human heart means man's innermost beings, the being of man's natural disposition, and says human hearts are desperately wicked. And he is the only one who has the power and the authority to cleanse a man's heart from sin and wickedness and apart from God's redeeming grace that is described as deceitful, crooked and desperately wicked.

God knew the degree of a man's heart and his intention from the beginning of creation, so he made provision to deal with man's heart, by sending Jesus.

Man's heart is also described as accurately sick, therefore man cannot trust in his own heart, but he must leave all to God who knows and judges the heart of all men fairly. During the process of true repentance, there has to be an initial hearing with understanding, due to a receptive heart, not only does the mind perceive and grasp what the ear hears, and the eyes see but, more importantly, the person who seeks repentance will understand the sense of what they hear and respond.

For example; people in Jesus time did not believe in him, despite various evidence, and such a result of God hardens their hearts. 'You may ask, 'does it mean God intentionally prevented these people from believing in him? The answer is, no, God simply confirm their own choices, after a lifetime people deliberately resisting God, they had become set in their ways sadly they would not even try to understand the message of Jesus, and although Jesus had performed various signs in the presence of the people, yet, they still did not believe in him, but this was the fulfillment of the word from Isaiah the prophet, he said, the reason why they could not believe, because, he would blind their eyes and harden their hearts so that they can neither see with their eyes nor understand with their hearts nor turn and he would save them'.

Although the people saw Christ miracles, yet, they did not see the arm of the Lord revealed in them, they could not believe because, Isaiah said, 'He hath blinded their eyes.'

For God has blinded their eyes and harden their heart and benumbed their callous heart, he has made their minds dull, to keep them from seeing and understanding with their hearts and minds and repenting and turning to him to heal them. We are confident that God is not the author of sin; however, there is a righteous hand of God sometimes to be acknowledged in the blindness of those who persist in impenitency and unbelief, they were justly punished for the former resistance of the divine light, and sinners are brought to see with their eyes, to discern, the reality of divine things, and to understand with their hearts is not only to assent and approve, but to consent and accept, to be converted to effectually turn from sin to Christ. Then God would pardon their sins and mortify their corruptions which are lurking diseases, and after a life of resisting God, they had become set in their ways that never try to understand the message of Jesus.

The word of God described the heart of human's as the soil which like a seed sown; the seed is the word of God, here called the word of the kingdom of heaven. The word is the seed sown, which seems a dead, dry thing, but all the produce is virtually an incorruptible seed. The Lord Jesus Christ is the sower that scattered the seed, either by himself or by his ministers. The sower went out to sow seeds, some seed fell by the wayside, and the birds came and devoured them.

Some seeds fell on stony places where there was not much earth and they immediately sprang up because they had no depth of earth. There is not merely an intellectual recognition of the wrongness of their way, but a heart acceptance of the fact. A multitude of people is similar to a sower sowing corn; we might never know where it falls. The ground in which the seed is sown in the heart of men, which are differently qualified and disperse. For, instance when the word as the seed falls in the heart of men they are regenerated, born again, not from a mortal origin seed as sperm, but from one which is immortal by the ever-living and lasting word of God. (1 Peter 1:23)

Those who profess repentance and are baptized must be as penitent, and who are already knowledgeable of God, maybe a case of falling back to their heart own desires, and having such knowledge of God and his commandments, need to ask God for his forgiveness to go forward in the right direction.

With the right motivation, the minds can be remade over and proving to themselves the good, acceptable and perfect will of God, and if there is faith and love in the heart, then there will be sincere regret, sadness over the wrong course, will show appreciation for God's goodness and greatness. Therefore it is only natural if the transgressor experiences a feeling of remorse of bringing reproach on God's name and although God permits Satan to try Job yet he does not order Satan to test him, since Satan's power is always exercised under the control of God, he was limited by the unlimited power of God. Even good people who have no gross enormities to repent must be greatly afflicted in the soul for the working and breaking out of pride, passion, peevishness and discontent and all their hasty unadvisable speeches. The more you see of the glory and majesty of God, is the more you will see the vileness and odiousness of sin in yourselves, yet, the more you should abhor yourselves for it, thus, we must leave God to govern the world, and make it your care and strength to govern yourselves. (Job 42:1-6)

A genuine demonstration of love for one's neighbor will also make them feel regret of the harm they have done to others, for instance, the bad example set, perhaps how they have sullied the reputation of God's people among outsiders, to rectify this they must seek forgiveness to honor God's name and to work for the good of one's neighbor. When a person feels repentant, he may feel broken at heart, crushed and lowly, contrite in spirit and trembles at God's word. This is the time to call oneself for repentance and in effect come quivering to God and desire his goodness.

For example, when David began acting foolishly in a matter of his census; his heart began to beat within him. He had a penitent reflection and confession of his sin in numbering the people. When the account was completed, David was thinking over the matter, and his conscience was awakened, his heart smothers and was convinced of his sin before the prophet Nathan came to see him. As Nathan talked with David using riddles that would stir the conscience of David, and it did not take long for David to be convicted of his sin. He did not hesitate to take ownership and repented and confessed his sin to God and begged his forgiveness. He owned that he had done foolishly because he had done it in the pride of his heart, David suffers just unnecessary correction, while he was tossing to and fro all night under the sense of his sin, as a rose in the morning he made a decision to speak with God and God directed the prophet Nathan to go and speak with David since he repented and was willing to confess and turn from his sin, and acknowledged God, yet, God must correct David for his fault; the punishment must answer to the sin. (1 Sam. 24:10)

HUMILITY

Humility means to be bowed down, afflicted, to be humbled, to be lowly, humility is described as the quality of being humble and putting the needs of the other person before your own, and thinking of others before yourself. It also means not drawing attention to yourself, and it can mean acknowledging that you are not always right, and that, *'God is always right*! We all need the spirit of humility, it does not mean a humble person is a weak individual, but rather strong to be humble and humility also means freedom from pride or arrogance. A person who has true humility will be meek and lowly in spirit.

You can achieve a state of humility by reasoning on your relationship with God and fellowmen. Going humble is to throw away our pride and acknowledge our mistakes, and set matters straight and seek forgiveness. Jesus admonished a person to humble before God, instead of trying to be prominent ministering or to serve others. Even those in the past who practiced very bad wrongs, yet if they truly humble themselves before God, and beseech him for his mercy he will hear them; therefore, humbling before God is the key to God's guidance. Humility will guide a person in the proper path, for it is God who exalts a person and put down another, before a crash the heart of a man is lofty, and before glory there is humility.

Paul urges believers as God's chosen people, he addresses them as holy, and dearly beloved, and urged them to be clothed with you with compassion, kindness, humility, gentleness and patience. Paul offers a strategy to help in living for God and said to imitate Christ's compassion, having a forgiving attitude, letting love guide our life, and allowing the peace of Christ rule our heart, always be thankful, keeping God's word in our heart at all times and live as Jesus Christ's representatives. Both young and old can benefit from Peter's instruction, for instance, pride always keep older people from understanding younger people and keep them from listening to those who are older. His advice was to both young and old to be humble and to serve each other; young men should follow the leadership of the older men who should lead by example. Respecting older folks than you, and be humble enough to admit that you can learn from each other, since God has chosen us to be Christ representatives on earth, in the light of this truth.

True humility means seeing yourselves as you are from God's perspective, and acting accordingly, though many may feel comfortable in their false humility, boasting about themselves and hoping that others may believe them as spiritual. On the other hand, some may think too little of themselves, while others over-estimating them. The key is having an honest and accurate evaluation knowing the basis of your self-worth, your identity is in Christ. True humility will cause you to understand that apart from Christ a person is not capable of worthy service, and if you should evaluate yourselves by the worldly standard, success and achievements, you will not think too much about your worth in the eyes of others or your true value in God's eyes.

How can we humble ourselves? the word of God give ample warnings regarding humility, For everyone who exalts themselves will be humbled, and he who humbles himself will be exalted, for instance, while some people try to give an appearance of humility to manipulate others some have a strong belief that humility means to put one self-down, but in truth, humble people should compare themselves only with Christ, and realize their sinfulness, and understand their limitations. They will also realize their gifts and strengths comes from God and must be used as Christ service helping others, therefore, humility is not self-degradation; rather, it is a realistic assessment and commitment to service. God is always right, he brings out the truth and exposes what is false.

FALSE HUMILITY

False humility is like wearing a mask to cover up their true identity, thus Christians should never allowed false humility and letting their humility be on the surface, such as when a person becomes puffed up without proper cause by his fleshy frame of mind. The action of false humility can result in developing haughtiness in the individual for he may tend to think he is righteous on his merit, or he may feel he is accomplishing more than others and if haughtiness should develop, he will in time be humbled in a way he will not enjoy, he will be brought low and recognize that it is God who lifts one and put down another. There is a parable regarding some people who enjoy having high seats, and also those who are full of pride will have shame when someone more honorable than they are promoted to the highest seat. Those who were contented to the lowest seat will be asked to move higher this lesson must be applied not to mind high things, because pride and ambition are disgraceful before men, for whosoever exalts himself shall be abased, but humility and self-denial are honorable. (Luke 14:11)

Many bible characters showed their humility, for example, David, a man after God's own heart, yet, he was not all right at times, but he has always shown his deep humility in areas that otherwise expressed pride. Comparing Saul's popularity, he was proud and arrogant, once the spirit of pride enters Saul, he was on his way to a mighty downfall because pride goes before destruction and a haughty spirit before a fall. Although David was a king, yet, he chose to remain humble, even when the entire nation was praising David had a humble spirit and succeeded in almost everything he did, he became famous throughout the land, yet he refused to use his popularity to support his advantage against Saul.

David's prayer shows the humble heart, he prayed; 'Oh Lord, our God, how majestic is your name in all the earth!' You have set your glory above the heavens when I consider your heavens, and the work of your fingers, the moon and the stars which you have set in place, what is a man that you are mindful of him, the sons of man that he cares for him? 'You have made a little lower than the heavenly being's and crowned him with glory and honor, you made him ruler over the work of your hands, you put everything under your feet, all the flocks, and herds, and all the beats of the field, the birds of the air, and the fish of the sea, all that swim that part of the sea, 'Oh Lord, our Lord, how excellent is your name in all the earth!

Thus, you should never allow popularity to twist the perception of your importance. It is comparatively easy to be humble when at a certain stage when others are praising and applauding you, but how will you react when you receive criticism regarding your best performance? Rather, some people thrive on the praises of men, rather than saying, no, praises belong to God, they become an abscess and demand some part of the praise.

When you examine the humility of Jesus our Lord in his sufferings, was rejected as a bad man; he humbled himself to which he became obedient to the death of the cross. He had grief and sorrow, he bore them and did not blame his lot, he did neither shrink from them, nor sink under them, but persevered to the end, till he said, 'It is finished. It was natural to ask with amazement 'What evil had Jesus done?' That causes his enemies to afflict him stricken, smitten of God, and afflicted because they hated and persecuted him; they thought that God did hate his son as they did.

Thus, humility will promote peace, for example, a humble person does not fight his Christian brother or sisters to establish his rights, although he might have the freedom to all things, yet he would only do what is necessary for up building, and if anyone's conscience was bothered by his actions, it is right to refrain from that practice. Humility demands keeping the peace by putting into practice Jesus counsel to forgive others their sins against us, and when one offends another, it tests his humility to obey the command to go to the other person and admit the wrongs and asking forgiveness, or when the offended person approaches him, only love coupled with humility will prompt one to acknowledge the wrong and set immediately to set matters straight.

CHAPTER SIX

WORLDLY SADNESS

The sadness of the world is born out of failure, disappointment, loss, punishment for wrongdoings and shame. The word of God warns us to be aware of people who use flattery and smote speech, like lips that drip honey that leads others to sin. The best advice is to take a detour and even avoid having a conversation with such a person. These people can be found in places of work, in communities, schools, our homes, even in churches.

The sadness was about the state of how people lived their lives without having regard to the needs of their fellowmen. Each person seems to escape in a world to themselves, just enough to contain themselves, and how they think of doing all they can and pleasing their agues for what they think is right. When human desires are fully activated, they do not desire taking advice, they desire satisfaction, indulging their minds in foolishness, and taking part in forbidden sex or anything harmful, these ungodly feelings will arrive long before the temptation comes.

Therefore, resistance is easier if the decision is already been made, never wait to see what will happen, just prepare yourself for temptation by deciding how you will act when you face it. Worldly sadness will mourn for the unpleasant consequences of sin, but not the sin itself, or the reproach it constitutes towards God. Thus, the apostle Paul wrote sternly to the Corinthians for the things that caused them pain, but they ceased to feel any regret of their sadness, instead, it was the sadness they felt from his rebuke that produces a godly sort leading to earnest repentance for their wrong attitude.

Paul knew that the pain would cause them no damage for their good, and he knew sadness would lead to repentance was not something they should regret either, for it keeps them on the way to salvation, and saving them from backsliding or apostasy, and giving hope of life everlasting. God contrasted this sadness with the sadness of the world that produces death. Such does not stem from faith and love for God and righteousness, but, for example, the amazing story of Cain one of Adam's sons; Cain was the first one whom God called to repentance. Cain was divinely warned to turn to do well so that sin should not win him over, rather, Cain chooses not to repent of his murderous, hatred; he allows it to motivate him to kill his brother. When God questioned Cain and he gave a devious reply, and only when his sentence was pronounced on him, yet, he did not express any regret. Cain showed deep regret over the severity of the punishment, but not over the wrongs committed, thus, he showed the originated with the wicked one.

Worldly sadness was also displayed by Esau when he learned that his brother Jacob had received the blessing of the firstborn, a right that Esau had callously sold to Jacob. Thus, Esau impetuously forfeited his important rights, responsibilities and honors as unimportant, or he was uninterested in them. This agreement was solidified by a form of oath unhallowed, something sacred made common. Esau took what God considered sacred and made it common. Esau being was totally concerned with his temporary and material needs, which he gave priority over his rights as the firstborn son and his responsibilities as heir to the blessing of Abrahamic covenant.

Therefore, every Christian must beware lest he counts as unimportant what God considers sacred. Esau cried out in an extremely loud and bitter manner with tears seeking repentance, not his own but a change of mind, on the part of his father. Esau regretted his loss rather than the materialistic attitude that caused him to despise the birthright, which was a special honor given to the firstborn son, it includes a double portion of the family inheritance along with the honor of the day becoming the family leader. Esau was the oldest son who could sell his birthright or give it away if he chooses, but in so doing he might lose material goods and his leadership position, by trading his birthright Esau showed complete disregard for the spiritual blessings that would have come his way if he had kept it in effect.

Repentance was hidden from Esau's eyes, and causing him neither eating nor drinking to please his palate, then he carelessly rose and went his way without showing any sort of regret. Esau despised his birthright, his life was filled with choices, he must have regretted bitterly. He appears to be a person who found it hard to consider consequences, by reacting to the needs of the moment without realizing what he was giving up to meet his ravenous need. Esau choice to exchange his birthright for a bowl of stew was a clear example of his weakness. (Gen 25:34)

Nevertheless, having regret, remorse and tears, these were not a certain measure of genuine repentance. The motives of the heart can be determinative, for instance, the prophet Hosea voices God's denunciation of Israel, when they were under personal troubles, yet they did not call on God for aid with all their heart, although they kept howling on their beds.

The people groan in times of calamity, they were selfishly motivated, and if they were granted relief, they did not use the opportunity to improve their relationship with God, by closer adherence to the high standards. God was far from approving their prayers that he calls it howling, some made loud noises and praying loudly as they use to crying to dead Baal, whom they worshipped. These people did not pray for the grace of God, that he would pardon their sins, but prayed that he would not take away their corn and wine. Thus, God said, 'If you will return, 'Oh Israel, do not only turn towards me but return to me.

When God brought Israel out of Egypt and gave liberty, but when they rebelled their liberty was forfeited against them. God is a God of justice, he gives clear guidance regarding obeying him, and if by any chance they disobeyed, he has even provided a way they can choose to return to him. What more could God do to these rebellious people? But, saying this all human tends to disobey God from time to time, but even so, God is still calling, 'Return to me you backsliding children, come let us reason together, though your sins are as scarlet, I will wash them white as snow.

The church is in a similar situation, believers have liberty, but could lose it, it is like being redeemed but still at risk, believers have been brought out of bondage, but continues to battle temptation, still as Christians, but the enemy pursues after them rigorously and trying to gain control to kill and destroy, he is said to be like, 'A roaring lion, seeking whom he may devour, he seeks to kill and destroy; by enforcing us to return to a deadly lifestyle of sin' We must be reminded he is not a real lion, but like one, yet, he is capable of doing serious damage to the believer's mind, be warned, never spend your time listening to the voice of the roaring lion, but use your time to evaluate how to overcome secret sinful thoughts and pursuits, such as internet pornography, which has become a serious problem in today's churches, where do we find an escape route, we may ask?

Having such an attitude, the people acted like a loose bow that never hits the mark, as a faulty bow is unreliable, so is life without God is unreliable. Without God's direction, our thoughts are filled with lust, lust cheating and selfishness and deceit. Sometimes people will look everywhere except to God for happiness, fulfillers pursing possessions and activities and relationships. In truth only God will satisfy the longing of the soul, he promises to meet our needs and grant our material needs.

Instances, when the children of Israel realize their folly, and cried out to the Lord, thus, it was a recurring expression, to cry out means to call to the Lord in repentance. For, the Lord is great in mercy; he will hear when we call on his name and repent of our sins. God is our father in heaven and we are his children, he loves us and wants to take care of us, therefore, fasting weeping and walling were proper, but only if the repentant ripped apart their hearts and not simply their garments.

Therefore, says the Lord, 'turn and weep and come to me with all your heart, with fasting, with weeping, and with mourning, until every hindrance is removed, and the broken fellowship is restored' 'Rend your hearts and not your garments, and return to the Lord, your God, for he is gracious and merciful, slow to anger, and abounding in loving-kindness, and He revokes His sentence of evil when his conditions are met' deep remorse was often shown by tearing or rending one's clothes.

'What does the holy God require?' God requires no outward display from penitents without true inward repentance, we must be sure that our attitude towards God is correct, and not just our outward actions. God told the people to turn to him while there is still time, if not destruction will soon be upon them.

The time of listening to God's calling is running out for everyone because we don't know when our lives will come to an end. We are urged to trust and obey God at all times, and not allowing anything or anyone to hold us back from turning to God. We should not harden our heart when we know it's the voice of the Lord urging, and calling to repentance.

God is always right urging his people to hear his voice and heed, he graciously urged, 'If my people who are called by my name would humble themselves and pray and seek His face, and turn from their evil ways, then I will hear from heaven, and will forgive their sins and heal their land' This was a call for God's people who were redeemed by the blood of Jesus, and not for the ungodly, the ungodly must repent and be born again then they will be addressed as 'My people' In this context, there is a call to first humble oneself, and then pray to God for his forgiveness and seeking His face, and turn from the wicked ways.

CHAPTER SEVEN

REGRETTING

Regretting is the opposite of pleasurable, satisfaction and rejoicing. God is a God of truth whose word we may take and rely on, for he cannot despise those who are faithful to all His promises, nor will his threatening falls to the ground.

The Lord said the people have forsaken him, he asks, 'are you gone backwards?' Therefore, I will stretch out my hand against you, and destroy you; 'I am weary with your repenting' Thus, God repenting is anthropomorphic language; from a human point of view, God's relenting of the threatened calamities against Judah may be seen as a change of mind, however, the hand of God will stretch out in judgment against them.

God has resented man's wickedness, he did not see it as any spectator as one injure and affront by it. He saw it as a tender father who sees the folly and stubbornness of a rebellious and disobedient child, which not only angered him but grieves him. The language does not imply any passive or uneasiness in God, because nothing can disturb the eternal mind, but express his just and holy displeasure against sin, and sinners. Does God thus hate sin? And should you hate it also?

We may wonder if your sin grieves God, yet you not grieve and pricked to your heart? Although it does not imply any changes in God's mind, it expresses the change in his way, and the change should also be in man, and not God. God solution is to destroy man for his wickedness, and we do not mock God in saying we are sorry for our sins, and that it grieves you to the heart if you should continue to indulge in it.

It is very significant what God said, 'I will wipe man from the face of the earth, as dust, or filth is wiped off from a place which should be cleaned. God took up this resolution after his Spirit had been long striving with humans in vain and there is only one outcome by the justice of God to those that hate to be reformed by the grace of God.

God is the Rock, his work is perfect, for all his ways are law and justice, he a God of faithfulness without breach or deviation, just and right, he is always right. An instant when Moses spoke in the hearing of all the people and reminding them of whom they are contending with, he said, 'I will proclaim the name and presence of the Lord, and concede and ascribe greatness to our God;

When the people heard the words from Moses, they mourned for the sins that provoked God to withdraw His presence from them, and also they mourned for the punishment of their sin, they mourn for all the bitter fruit and consequences of their sin for which the true penitent would most lament and dreaded that God has departed from them. In a token of great shame and humiliation, those who were underdressed did not put on their ornament, and those that were dressed stripped themselves of their ornament. (Due.32:4)

When God saw the people pinning away in their iniquity, then God sent the prophet to them, with all speed, because God has no delight in the ruin of sinners. The people question whether they could live knowing the wrath of God, though they did not repent and reform, yet God sends the prophet Ezekiel, to say to them, 'As 'I live says the Lord God, 'I have no pleasure in the death of the wicked, but that the wicked turn from his way and live, turn you, turn from your evil ways, for why will you die Oh house of Israel?' (Ezek. 33:11)

God himself is said to repent, and feeling regret, but this can only be understood as altering his conduct towards his creatures, either in the bestowing of good or infliction of evil- which changes in the divine conduct and if founded on a change in the creatures; thus speaking after the manner of men. God is said to repent, but his righteous standard remains constant, stable, unchanging and free from fluctuation, and though God tries the saints he never tries with evil intent to tempt them. (James 1:17)

No circumstance can change God's mind towards those who turn from him or abandon them, however, the attitude and reactions of his intelligent creatures towards his perfect standards and towards God's application can be good or evil if it is good and pleasing to God. On the other hand, if it is bad, it might cause regret, but since God does not change his standards to accommodate men his judgment and decision are free from caprice, fickleness, unreal liability or error, hence he is free, and erratic or eccentric conduct.

For example, a potter placing the shapeless clay on the wheel, the potter used his hands to form a vessel as the wheel is turned, the utensil would then be dried in the sun and again put on the wheel where the potter might employ pebbles shells or something to smooth and burnish it and to impart a design to its surface, some methods are varying; occasionally things were molded by hand without using the wheels when making toys and household ovens.

This example, demonstrated that God is like a human potter in making earthen vessels, by his hand, but rather, he has divine authority over mankind, and his authority to adjust his dealings with humans is according to the way they respond, or fail to respond to his righteousness and mercy. God can be feeling regret over the calamity he thought to execute upon the nation, or feeling regret over the good that he said to himself to do depending on the reaction of the nation to his prior dealings with them.

Thus, as the human clay undergoes a metamorphosis, change of form or composition, and as the heart of man condition can produce a change of feeling on God's part, this is true of individuals as well as the nations. The very fact that God speaks of his feeling of regret over certain of his servants, such as King Saul, who turned away from his righteousness, shows that he does not predestinate the future. Of such individuals as Saul, God's regretted over his deviation, and it could not mean that God's choice of him as the king had been erroneous; this was not to be regretted on that ground that God's regret.

It must rather be since Saul, as a free moral agent, had not made use of the splendid privilege and responsibility God offered him, and that Saul's attitude for a change to God' dealing with him was not appreciated. The same sun that makes the garden of flowers more fragrant makes the dunghill more noisome. The apostle stated, 'for sin, seizing the opportunity and getting a hold on me, and by taking its incentive from the commandments, beguiled and entrapped and cheated me, and using it as a weapon, killed me.

Therefore, where there is no law, there is no sin, because man cannot know that their action is worthless unless God's law

91

enlightens them, and the people who are sinners are doomed to die, yet the law offers no help. The way to prevent this mischief is to bow your soul to the commanding authority of God's law. For example, taking your family to the beach on a sunny day, and as you plunged into the area, suddenly you notice a large sign on the pier, saying. 'No swimming' Sharks are in the sea' what will be the first thing that would come to mind? 'Will you feel anger at the people who posted the sign?' or, should you have taken the responsibility of not looking around before jumping into the sea? Thus, the law is exactly like that sign, it is essentially important, and we are grateful for it, but it does not get rid of the *Sharks.*

If anyone decides to work for sin, sin is a cruel taskmaster, when it pays; its wages is death, separation from God forever. In contrast, God does not pay wages; he has offered a gift to all who accepted his invitation, which is eternal life. There is nothing that one can do to gain this gift if one could earn it, otherwise, it could not be a gift, and it would be waged, receiving and accepting the gift of God, believing in Jesus as Savior, and even the people who have returned to God, he will return to them. (Romans 7:11)

In the same way, God can feel regrettable and turning back from carrying out some punishment because his warning of such action produces a change. When we recognized that life is short it will help to utilized the little time we have more wisely and for eternal good. As we take time to number our days, someone might be asked, 'what would you most want to happen in your life, because times are irretrievable and days are numbered, we would like to know our work is valuable, effective and productive, leaving a declaration of faith in God, 'I've trusted in God'.

Instead of God regretting, he now rejoices, for he finds no delight in bringing death to sinners and while God is never shifting away from his righteous standards, he extends help so that persons can return to him, and they are encouraged to do so and kindly invites them to do so by his representatives, and gives amply time for change and shows great patience and forbearance since he does not desire any to be destroyed.

God has kindly accompanied his message on occasion by powerful works, and miracles that establish the divine commission of his messengers and help strengthen faith in those hearing. (Acts 9:32)

Where the message of Christ is received with no response, he employed discipline, and he then withdraws his favor and protection, thereby allowing the unrepentant to undergo privations, famine, the suffering of oppression from their enemies. This approach may bring them to their senses, and restore their proper fear of God, or it may cause them to realize their course was stupid, and their set of values was wrong. For instance, how God warned the people, sometimes through famine, drought, blight, locusts, plagues, or war, they still ignored him. God repeated several times, 'You have not rerun unto me'.

God's design in his entire rebuke was to influence the people to return to him. If they had returned, God, they would be accepted, because Almighty God takes no pleasure in afflicting his people. The people persisted in their wicked course of presumption thinking they would never be called to account, and indulged themselves in all kinds of pleasures and delights, these were not the case if they were soberly and moderately used, but they place their gratification of carnal appetites. The people were extravagant and lazy, and some were found guilty, however, God's patience has its limit and when they are reached he gets tired of feeling regret, and then his decision to render punishment is unchangeable, and no longer thinking or forming a calamity but reached an irreversible decision.

God is from eternity and has infinite power before there was neither idols, nor idolatry, he says, 'I, even the Lord the great Jehovah, who is, and was, and is to come, and beside me, there was no Savior' and God has an infinite infallible knowledge and is evident from the prediction of his word, 'I have declared, from the ancient of days, I am he, and no one can deliver out of my hand, when I act, who can reverse it and I have shown without fail come to pass' However, God's willingness to forgive repentant ones, and mercifully opening to such forgiveness, even in the face of repeated offences, so God set examples for all his servants. (Isa 43:13)

For an example of when Peter came to Jesus and asked, 'Lord how many times shall I forgive my brother when he sins against me?' 'Up to seventy times seven' Jesus answered 'I tell you not seven times but seventy times seven' meaning we should not be keeping track of how many times we forgive others; instead, we should forgive those who are truly repentant no matter how many times they asked. God multiplies his pardon towards us, and so we should towards each other. It does not look well for us to keep count of the offences done against us by our brethren.

There is something about ill-nature in scoring injuries as if you were to allow yourselves to be avenged when the measure is full. It is necessary to pass by injuries, without reckoning how often; to forgive, to forget. God multiplies his pardon, and so you should and make it your constant practice to forgive injuries, and practice until it becomes habitual.

No circumstance can allow God to change his mind, like a potter who begins to make a style of vessel, and then changes his mind to another style if the vessel is spoiled in his hand. By this example, God illustrates he is not like the human potter, he is Creator who forms man in his image and has divine authority over mankind. His authority is adjusted his dealing with man and according to the way they respond to his righteousness and his mercy.

Every sin that is committed by man becomes a debt to God; it is not like a debt to a business person or a contractor, but a superior, like a prince, when a recognizance is forfeited or a penalty accrued by a breach of the law. In truth we are debtors, we owe satisfaction, and are liable to proceed of the law, and there is an account kept in these debts. Thus, God will reckon us through our conscience, while not shifting away from his righteousness standard. God extends help to those who return to him; they are encouraged to do so. He kindly encouraged doing so by spreading out his hand, and saying through his representatives, 'Return please, that I may not cause calamity to you" do not do this detestable sin that I have hated'.

God gives ample time for man to change their sinful behavior against one another, and God was found of those who were far off, and those who did not enquire after him, those who have long been in the world will be seeking after God. We should never quarrel with God, 'Shall the clay say to him that form it or why makes thou?' 'Why do you make me of this shape, and not that?'

We cannot impeach God's wisdom, or question his powers, we are so wonderfully made? It is unnatural for the child to find fault with the parent and ask why this are that, why wasn't I born as an angel? or why was I not born looking like my friend? God understands all these inner reasons, he sees and waits on us to accept ourselves and be thankful for making us like in his image.

Humans have no answers to these questions, but rather giving thanks to the Father of our Lord Jesus Christ for his life in us. So, must the ministers of the gospel, and endeavoring to preach the word of Christ faithfully, in their government of the church, strictly adhere to his laws, and then they can be assured that Christ will own them and stand by them. In suspension; whatever you shall bind on earth shall be bound in heaven. If the censures of the church duly follow the institution of Christ, his judgment will follow the censures of the church, and Christ will graciously find those who are cast out. What the glory the spirit of God imparts to the believer, it is more excellent and lasting longer than the glory that Moses experienced, while he gauzes in amazement of the nature of God with unveiled face.

You can also be in the same attitude, and mind when you have stretched your spiritual imagination to be like Jesus, and yes you can become more like him. For instance, in the gospel, there is the naked truth about Christ how he transforms humans with a new understanding that can be applied through learning about his life, it gives a new experience of how wonderful God is yet your knowledge of the changes will deepen on the work of the Holy Spirit 'and becoming Christ-like is a progressive's experience, you will also discover that all things work together for good to those who love him, God's ultimate goal is to make you like Christ, to become more a more like him, you must discover your true self, that you are created in the image of God. (Romans 8: 29)

Thus, humans have many regrettable actions that they have taken on and although years have passed yet, the shame, the memory, and the consequences seem to live on. Many people who have to end up in jail cells doing time for the things they have done, even more than once, it seems as if they have not learned lessons from the first mistakes, and why it continues going downhill without a conscience to apply the brakes. The conscience might be dead, snared, or totally out of touch, but God is willing to awake dead situations back to life if men would do themselves justice and call for help.

There is a common word that is constantly used when things have caught up, 'if I' had known, even after this life has come to an end the same word will come into force, 'If I had known I would pray, do things differently, never come out of my house, never said the wrong word to mum' this list goes on a mile. One should never allow a life of regret to dominate our lives, therefore, stand up and be counted and do the right thing then it will become a right principle in days to come.

CHAPTER EIGHT

BEYOND REPENTANCE

A person who is devoted in willfully practicing what they know is wrong, after they have received the accurate knowledge of the truth has gone beyond repentance, for in truth they have rejected the very purpose for which God's Son died, and have joined themselves to the rank of those who sentenced Christ to death, in effect impaling the Son of God afresh for themselves and exposing him in public shame.

In such case, it is also impossible for those who have once been enlightened, who have tasted the goodness of the word of God and the powers of the coming age, and have fallen away to be brought back to repentance, to their loss they are crucifying the Son of God all over again and subjecting him to public disgrace, 'This is then an unpardonable sin'.

The lack of genuine repentance will lead to destruction. In the past, it had led God's people Israel and Judah into exile and finally to complete rejection of the nation by God. When the people were reproved they did not really return to God wholeheartedly but kept going back into the popular course, like a horse that is dashing into battle. In their heart, they did not want to repent and turn back to God. Although God's prophets were warning day and night yet, what they heard and saw brought no understanding and knowledge, it seems as a veil was laid on their hearts. In such times there were unfaithful religious leaders and prophets, and also prophetesses that contributed to this by strengthening the people in their wrongdoings.

God spoke to his prophet Isaiah to speak to the people, since they refuse to listen, they could not learn from his message because their hearts had become callous and hardened beyond repentance. God's patience with their critical rebelliousness was finally exhausted, and his judgment was to abandon them to their rebellion and hardness of heart. For such behavior, the people may only listen when they come to the end and had nowhere to turn, but to God. Although God dealt kindly with the Israelites, they stubbornly continued to worship idols, even when God's prophets called them to repentance, they refused to return to God again and again, and because of man's unrepentant attitude, therefore, the sword of foreign people would be unleashed against them.

Sometimes God uses the method of allowing the enemy to chastise his people because of their stubbornness and bad behavior against him. This was exactly what was now taking place with the people; the enemy was now attacking them. This attack from the enemy was more than an overnight incursion; it was to be a lasting war for years, it was dreadful when the sword abides on the people. In this, because of the Israelites own counsel, they followed their own ways instead of God's design; this resulted in their being taken captive by the Assyrians, who were a proud and cruel people. Yet, the people were still determined to walk in their backslidden ways; they refuse to turn to God from their waywardness.

This action of the people grieved God for his own people to turn away from him and follow the course of displeasing him. Examples, how many times the Israelites said, '*goodbye to God*' but God would not let them go, he still remains faithful in spite of their unfaithfulness. God commissioned his prophet to say to his people,' shall men fall and not rise up again? Shall one turn away from God and not return again to him? 'Why then are these people of Jerusalem turning away from me? These were heart-stirring questions that should have reached the very heart of the people to return to God.

Rather the people held fast to deceit, and idolatry, and refuse to repent and turn to God, yet, they professed. 'I've listened and heard but they have not spoken aright, no man repents of his wickedness, and asking, 'What have we done?' Everyone turns to his individual course as a horse rushes like a torrent into battle thus; Jeremiah gave the word from the Lord to the people in a question form. 'When men fall down, do they not get up? When a man turns away, 'does he not return?' When people fall and realize they are heading in the wrong direction, it will only make sense to get up or to change direction.

God watches over the nation, and saw people were living sinful lives by their own choice, and deceive themselves that there will be no consequences, they had lost their perspective concerning God's will for their lives and trying hard to minimized their sins. We should examine ourselves against the word of God and get up and turn to him he will have mercy and forgive our sins, as we turn from our evil ways. Christian's prophecies foretold the future of divine action reproving and calling men to repentance would be similarly be rejected by many and would suffering will only harden and embitter and point of blaspheming God. They believe it is by their own rejecting of God's righteous ways that form the root and generative cause of all their troubles and plagues, yet, these people were so hard-hearted that even plagues did not drive them to God.

People normally don't usually fall into immorality and evil suddenly, they slip into it little by little, until it is hardly realized what had happened until they are irrevocably mired in their wicked ways. Sin has its consequences, and the unrepentant will face the judgment of God's wrath, and sometimes it is felt in this life; its full impact will be manifest in salvation through judgment, but there is a remedy provided by Jesus's death on the cross. His subsequent resurrection provided redemption for those who will turn from their sin, and put their faith in him, trusting God will lead to a life of abundant joy in this world and a home in heaven next.

The person who allows sin to take root in his or her life will end up in this predicament; it is a true fact that temptation and entertainment today becomes sin tomorrow and a habit the next day, then death and separation from God forever, therefore, it is important to acknowledge your need, confess your sin before God while you have the opportunity doing so. (Je 8:4-6)

The unpardonable sin is the deliberate refusal to acknowledge God's power in Christ; it indicates a deliberate and irreversible hardness of heart. Sometimes people worry if they have committed this unpardonable sin of blasphemy, but it is only those who have turned their backs on God and rejected all faith need to worry about their fate; Jesus say that they can't be forgiven, it is not because their sin is worse than any other, but because they will never ask forgiveness.

Therefore, whoever rejects the prompting of the Holy Spirit actually remove him or herself from the only force that can lead him or her to repentance and restoration to God. This then, is unforgivable blasphemy against the spirit, since it is only by God's spirit that one can come to the accurate knowledge of the truth. The apostle spoke about a person who has once learned about Christ and how to be saved and has been positively influenced by other Christians, but afterwards, they reject the truth and returns to his or her sin. This person will be worse off than before, because they have rejected the only way out of sin, and the very way for salvation, he or she will be described as a person who is sinking in quicksand and refuses to grab the rope thrown to him or her. (Matt 12:31)

The person who turns away from Christ should realize that he has cast away the only means of escape from hell and destruction, and it would be better for such, not to have accurately known the path of righteousness than after knowing it accurately to turn away from the holy commandments delivered to them, their last condition would be worse than the first. (2 Peter 2:20)

Since Adam and Eve were perfect creatures, and God's command to them was explicit and understood by both, it is evident that their sinning was willful and not excusable on the basis of any human weakness or imperfection. Hence, God's words to them offer no invitation to repentance, so too, the spirit creature who had induced them into rebellion, his end and the end of other angelic creatures that joined them is everlasting destruction. Adam and Eve chose their action of disobedience and then God chose his, as a holy God he could respond in a way consistent with his perfect moral nature, but he could not allow sin to go unchecked, he had to punish it.

If the consequence of Adam sin seems extreme, sin was set in motion in the world tendency towards disobeying God; this is one of the reasons why men sin today. Every human that is every born with the exception of Jesus, has inherited the sinful nature of Adam and Eve. The punishment of both Adam and his wife Eve reflects how seriously God views sin of any kind.

Adam and Eve learnt by painful experience because God is holy and he hates sin, therefore, he must punish sinners.

After some forty years in the Judean wilderness, Jesus was baptized and was confronted by this principle opponent of God's sovereignty. By some means, the spirit adversary conveyed to Jesus certain subtle suggestions designed to draw Jesus into acts violating God's expressed will and word. Satan has even offered to give the anointed Jesus who has dominion over all earthly kingdoms without a struggle and without any end for suffering on Jesus's part, in exchange for one act of worship towards himself. Jesus refused Satan's offer and acknowledge God as the one only true Sovereign from which authority rightly proceed and to who worship goes. God's adversary began to draw up other plans of war strategy against God representatives, resorting to the use of human agents in various ways as he had done before in the case of Job.

The story is told that Job was a model of trust and obedience, yet God allow Satan to attack Job in an especially harsh manner, and although God loves us, sad to say, believing and obeying his still does not shelter us from life's calamities. God knew he could trust his servant Job not to give in to the enemy's harsh critics and mocking regarding his integrity. For example, when we face setbacks, tragedies, and sorrow, these strike Christian and non-Christian alike, but in our test and trail, God expects us to express our faith in the world, remembering that we are light and salt in the world no matter what.

God gave Satan a close character of his servant Job, God inform Satan, 'Job is my faithful servant, and there is none like him' and Satan could not deny that Job feared God, but suggested that he was mercenary in his religion and therefore a hypocrite. Satan was impatient to hear Job's praised, though it was God himself that praised him. God special people are under God's protection, and all that belongs to them, divine grace makes a hedge about their spiritual life and divine providence about their natural life.

God had prospered Job, not in idleness or justice, but in the way of honest diligence, he has blessed the work of hands, was the devil's complaint, he speaks of it with vexation, after a while. Satan departed from the meeting of the sons of God. He went forth to go to and fro, rambling through the earth, but with a direct course to fall on Job, the Lord God said to the serpent, 'Because you have done this, you are cursed above all domestic animals, and above every wild beast of the field, upon your belly, you shall go and you shall eat dust and what it contains all the days of your life.

The stories of Genesis reports the painful stories of lives ruined as a result of the fall of disobedience, thus, disobedience is sin, and sin breaks our fellowship with God, rather, when we obey, God is willing to forgive us and to restore our fellowship with him. Judas, though imperfect, yet, had he lived in intimate association with God's own Son, and still, he becomes a traitor. Jesus himself refers to Judas as the son of destruction.

The apostate man of lawlessness is also called the son of destruction, this action can be compared to the dividing between the sheep from the goats, and these are classed as fulgurate goats that will be cast into everlasting cutting-off, and there is no invitation to repentance being extended to them. This is the judgment of separation; for example, Christ will call the sheep to stand at his right and the goats on the left. Jesus is Christ Shepherd; he feeds his flock like a good shepherd and will shortly be distinguished between those that are his, and those that are not.

The Godly are compared like sheep, innocent, mild, patient, useful, while the wicked sheep and goats are a baser kind of animal, unsavory and unruly. The sheep and goats were fed all day in the same pasture, but will be counted at night in different folds, he will divide, and he will set the sheep on his right hand and the goats on his left. Christ puts honor upon the Godly, and therefore showing respect to those we set on our right hand, all other divisions will then be abolished, but the great distinction of men is becoming saints out of sinners, the sanctified and un-sanctified, will remain forever. (Matt 25:33)

CHAPTER NINE

GODLY SORROW FOR SIN

Repentance is a Godly sorrow for sins, and repentance comes to humans in various forms, for instance, there is national repentance that suggests that the world have sinned and must repent. The cause of making repentance usually is sin, a failure to meet God's righteous requirements. Since all things created were sold into sin by Adam all his descendants have required repentance. A repented person is asking God to forgive and then abandoning sinful ways, but we cannot do this sincerely unless we are truly sorry for our sinful actions. When we are aware that we have done wrong, we should admit to God, rather than trying to cover up or hoping to get away with it.

Repentance may be towards one whole life course that has been in harmony with the world under the control of God's adversary. It may have been concerning a particular aspect of one's life, for instance, a wrong practice marrying, and staining and otherwise acceptable course, a wrong tendency, or even inclination or attitude, there might be a wide range of faults, why, and how. (Psalms 38:18)

Repentance involves both mind and heart. All wrongdoings of actions must be recognized and this requires an acknowledgement that God's standards and will are righteous.

Ignorance and forgetfulness of God's will and standards is a barrier to repentance. For this reason, God has mercifully sent prophets and preachers calling persons to repentance, through the publishing of the good news through the Christian congregation, and particularly from the time of Cornelius conversion forward, God has been telling mankind everywhere that they should all repent. However, God's word is written as a means for persuading, convincing them of the righteous of God's way, and the wrongness of their way.

God's law is perfect, bringing back the soul (Psalms 19:7) King David speaks of teaching transgressors God's ways so that they may turn back to him, these sinners doubtless being fellow Israelites. The apostle Paul instructed Timothy not to fight them when dealing with Christians in the congregation whom he served, but to instruct with mildness those who are not favorable disposed of as God might give them repentance leading to an accurate knowledge of the truth, and they may come back to their proper senses out from the snare of the Devil. (2Tim 2:23-26)

The person must realize his sin against God, for an instant, vocal misused of God's name, or worshipping other gods, as using idol images, involving and even in private matters, or something between himself and another human, any wrongs that are committed must be recognized as sins against God. Even wrongs that are committed in ignorance or by mistake must be recognized, making one guilty before the Sovereign Ruler, Jehovah God. The message of John the Baptist and that of Jesus were calling men to repentance on the part of the Jews. John and Jesus stripped away from the people and their religious leaders the cloak of self-righteousness and the observance of man-made traditions and hypocrisy and exposing their sinful state. (Matt 1:1-9)

COLLECTIVE REPENTANCE

Repentance may be on a collective basis as well as an individual basis. For instance, Jonah's preaching caused the entire city of Nineveh, from the king down to the least of them, to repent, for in God's eyes they were all sharers in the wrong so the people of Nineveh believed in God and proclaimed a fast and put on sackcloth in penitent mourning from the greatest to the least of them. Repentance may be on a collective basis as well as an individual, for example, Jonah's preaching that caused the entire city of Nineveh, from the king down to the least to repent, for in God's eyes they were all sinners in wrongs doings. For an instant, when the entire congregation of Israel returned under Ezra's promptings, they acknowledge community guilt before God expressing their repentance through their princely representatives.

The people were in a deep panic about the preaching of Jonah, it brought word came to the king of all that was said his terrifying message from God. (Acts 11:18)

The king was also terrified and immediately rose from his throne and laid his robe aside, and covered himself with sackcloth's and sat in ashes that were the sign of great distress at that time. The Nivevehites believed God, and they declared a fast and all men even the king made a proclamation and published it throughout Nineveh, by a decree to all his nobles, he said, 'By the decree by the king and his nobles 'Let neither man, nor beast herds, nor flocks, taste anything, let them not feed or drink water

The king of Nineveh orders was so severe that even the beast in Nineveh was to be covered with sackcloth and cried mightily to God, 'Let them turn from his evil ways, and from the violence

that is in his hands.' Who can tell God may turn and revoke His sentence against us when we have met his terms, and turn away from his fierce anger so that we perish not. It seems a positive action to take for being
sorry for sin. In this moment of outcry, the king as head of the people commands this action and the people were obedient to obey.

The pagan people of Nineveh believed Jonah's message and repented, for God take no pleasure to quickly destroy his people, he always sends his prophets to give warning before his final actions.

SELF ABASEMENT

Self-abasement is described as someone who displays self above others; it acts as degrading humility; 'Whoever shall exalt himself shall be abased, but he who humbles himself shall be exalted' For example, a person who exalts himself above others, and express that they are better than others, they are only deceiving themselves. In this life, there are many such people in society, in work environments, homes, churches and other places where people crave platforms to be elevated exalted. People are not contented taking the lower seats or place until they are asks to come up higher to a well-earned seat, or place of exalting.

Some people can be seen as front-up by others, they cry inwardly for attention, for others to speak well of them without doing any acts of deserving such accolade. These people will find it pleasing to give their opinion of the faults of others while the bean stands tall in their own eyes. Considering the exemplary life of Jesus Christ, he had all rights to exalt himself among men, and above other men, but no, he chose to humble himself even to the death on the cross, there, God had elevated him to the highest position to be seated at his right hand far above principles and powers and rules of darkness of this world, and God his father has given him a name that is above every name that at the name of Jesus every knee must bow and every tongue confess that he is Lord.

For such a case Jesus warned his disciples of the importance of humility and mutual submission, he said, 'He that is greatest among you shall be your servant'.

He that is advance to any place should be the greatest among you, but in truth, they shall be your servant, that greatest is not a Lord, as a matter, the preference is intended for those who are humble, be 'exalted' The people who are humbled shall be honored and be accepted with the holy God, and also be respected by wise men that are qualified to be called out to special services among honorable services. Considering the life of Paul, he was exalted so many different times, and he was highly favored with the sight of Christ resurrection from the dead. When the Lord Jesus appeared to Paul by the way to Damascus road, Paul was highly favored by God but he always endeavors to keep up a mean opinion of himself; he said, 'He was the least and not worthy to be called an apostle, because he had been a persecutor of the church of God, and having a humble spirit, amid high attainments as a great ornament to any man. What kept Paul low was the remembrance of his past wickedness, his raging against God and his members.

Nevertheless, God can cause a man to become humble, diligent, and faithful by ascribing all that was valuable in him to divine grace. God was gracious to his people all through history, he wanted the best for them, even when they turned away from him, and he remembers them as his children.

God's message is, 'Return, you, backsliding children.
Here God calls them children, in tenderness and compassion, as parents he correcting their children, although they don't listen, yet, he will not disinhibit, he bears with them, the people gave consent to his invitation, to God's call, their cry was described as a voice returning from broken walls, and their hearts were broken. (Matt.26:68-75)

Time and time God warns, 'Return,' then they gave an immediate answer; they came devoting themselves to God as theirs, as to say, 'Thou are the Lord our God' the people are used to worshipping their gods on the hill and mountains, but now they will have nothing more to do with them. The people became very ashamed of their sin and folly, they say, 'We lie down in our shame and our disgrace cover us, both our penal and our penitential shame, for we sinners by descent, we and our fathers have sinned, we have sinned from our youth, we have continued to sin, even until this day, though often call to repent and forsake our sins sinned against the Lord our God, both we and our fathers, sadly from our youth till this day and we have not obeyed the Lord our God.

The people lamented, 'we are sinners by descent, we and our father have sinned, we have sinned from our youth, we have continued in sin, and have sinned even to this day, though often called to repentance and to forsake our sins, we have not obeyed the voice of the Lord our God who has commanding us to repent. The people confess, and say, 'we have not obeyed the voice of the Lord commanding us, when we have sinned, to repent. The prophet Jeremiah lamented, 'this seems to be the

111

language of the penitents of the house of Israel; even though they talk about their condition, yet, they refused to do the right thing and repent'. (Jeremiah 3.25)

Humans must be conscious and having Godly sorrow for sin and wrong behavior, with a right desire to turn with a right attitude. The antecedent of true repentance is Godly sorrow for sin. Godly sorrow will proceed in salvation; and rather worldly sorrow works death, the sorrow of worldly living eventually will bring down grey hairs and will sooner to the grave.

Many people are only feeling sorrowful for the effect of their sins, or when they are caught, otherwise, they will continue to ignore the warning to change and repent. Example of Peter's behavior when he committed his sin by denying Christ, he was devastated when he remembered the words of the Lord, he brought it to himself, as a sense of his ingratitude to Christ. Peter wept bitterly, his sorrow was secret, sorrow for sin must not be slighted, but great and deep, those that have sinned must weep bitterly, for sooner or later sin will be bitterness. The deep sorrow is requisite to evidence of a real change of mind has taken place within.

Peter wept very bitterly for denying Christ, and surely he will never deny Christ again but confessed him often and openly. Sin was the turning aside to crooked ways, and forgetting the Lord God is the bottom of all this, yet, God still gives an invitation to return to him.

Humiliation and godly sorrow are previously necessary to repentance and both are of God, the giver of all graces. When the heart of man has changed from his sinfulness, his life and actions will be changed also, his conscience will work indignation of sin, fear of reverence, and a jealous fear of themselves. What comes from God has the sign to preserve the soul from the lust and passion of which the increase of riches is commonly the incentive.

Godly sorrow and confession of sin should normally involve only those who have an acknowledgement of the sin, this means that private sin should be confessed privately, and others who desire to make an open confession. A person who chose to repent will make a halt of their wrong course, repentance is rejection in the wrong way and the determination to take the right course. When the people of Israel knew they had sinned, and wept loudly, and responding with deep sorrow. Since all humans tend to sin, thus, repentance is the true measure of spiritual sensitivity.

The English word for *repent;* is to change one's mind concerning past action, conduct, on account of regret, or disaffection, or to feel regret, contrition for what one has done, or omitted to do, It may also mean to comfort one's self, be relieved of one's enemies, whether having serious regret or comfort it can be seen that a change of mind or a feeling is revolved. All human needs to repent, whether saved or unsaved, Jews, or Gentiles, young or old, every nationality under the sun needs to repent of sins or wrongdoing. It is best to repent while the opportunities exist since there can be no repentance in the grave.

Similar the extent to which a person deviates from righteousness may be major or minor and the degree will, logically, be commensurate with the degree of deviation. For example when the Israelites were deep in revolt against God and were rotting away in their transgressions. The apostle Paul speaks of the man who takes some false step before he is aware of it. Paul counsels that those with spiritual qualifications should try to readjust such a man in a spirit of mildness.

Since God mercifully considers the fleshy weakness of his servants, thus, man needs not to be in a constant state of remorse due to their errors resulting from their inherent imperfections, when they are conscientiously walking in Gods way, they must be joyful that the light has come, and the darkness has faded away. For those who have not previously enjoyed such a relationship with God, such as the pagan peoples of the non-Israelite nations as when God's covenant was in force with Israel, and also those persons of whatever race or nationality who were outside the Christian congregation, repentance is a primary and essential step forward being brought into right standing before God with life everlasting in view.

Some people repent based on already having enjoyed a favorable relationship with God, but have strayed away and suffered the loss of God's favor and blessings. For example, when Israel was in covenant with them, they were a holy people chosen from all the other nations. So, then the Christian also comes into righteous standing before God through the new covenant mediated by Christ. In the case of such who strayed, repentance will lead to restoration of the right relationship with God. (Jeremiah 15:19-21)

The apostle cautions with an awful example of Esau's sin which He profanely despised and sold the birthright, and all the advantages that were attached, Esau's punishment was through his conscience, he was convinced of his sin and folly when it was too late, and he now saw the blessings he had made so light of he was worth having. Esau was rejected by God, and he found no place for repentance. Esau in his great wickedness had made the bargain, and God in his righteous judgment, ratified it. Esau shows that mistakes and sins sometimes have lasting consequences. Although he sought to solve his mistake with tears, yet he could not bring any changes. Therefore, repentance and forgiveness do not always eliminate sin's consequences. Sometimes we make decisions on what we want now, rather than what we need in the long run, it is useful to always evaluate all long-term effects when making decisions. (He 12:16-17)

TRUE REPENTANCE

Truth must be the main ingredient in man's repentance since repentance is a lasting lifelong product of God's gift to man. The truth will set men free, and true repentance for any sin will be the best evidence by abounding on the contrary grace and duty; some may say as long as Peter lived he will never hear the crowing of a cock. Those who are truly sorrowful for sin will sorrow on every remembrance of it. He went out of the High Priest hall, and he was vexed with himself and what he had done. The people of Israel went backsliding, some voices were heard weeping and praying, and humbling themselves before the God of their fathers, that they have perverted their way and forgotten the Lord their God.

Sometimes God unusually breaks into life, especially for those in need of salvation. Conviction of sins when the heart of man is deeply touched by their sin, it hits home with power upon the conscience and silent all excuses and self-justification. Conviction should drive us to prayer, Christ although in heaven yet he knows to find those who are his, under their conviction, they have a friend in heaven that knows in what street they live, and in what frame of mind they are in. Thus, the fear of God means hating bad actions, including self-exalting, pride, the bad way and the perverse mouth. The more a person fears and respect God, the more he or she will hate evil, and having a love for God and love for sin cannot coexist, by harboring secret sins mean that you are tolerating evil within yourself.

The person who turns to God through faith in Christ Jesus must genuinely repent from all works rightly classed as dead works and after avoids them once for all, 'touch not, handle not, stay away from dead works to serve the living God. If a person's conscience thereby becomes cleansed from dead works of sin, how much more surely shall the blood of Christ, who then through his eternal spirit, be made completely clean? Thus, Christ owns preexistent divine personality has offered himself as an unblemished sacrifice to God; we should purify our conscience from dead works and lifeless observances to serve the living God.

A person can profess repentance that is unreal, untrue, pretend, half-hearted, and that attitude will pay serious consequences in the long run. We cannot pretend to be what we are not for long, because our conscience will speak louder than any trumpet. Anything unreal is untrue, and only the truth will set men free. After Pharaoh promised to let the Hebrews go, he immediately broke his promise and brought even more trouble upon the land. His actions reveal that his repentance was not real. We will only damage ourselves and others if we pretend to change but don't mean it.

For instance, when Moses left Pharaoh presence he went out of the city and spread out his hands towards the Lord, then there was thunder and lightning stopped on the land, when Pharaoh saw that the thunder and lightning Pharaoh says he sinned again, he and his official hearts were hardened, so he would not let the Israelites go, just as the Lord had said to Moses. God gave Pharaoh many opportunities to heed Moses warnings' 'let the people go' when he continually refused, finally God seems to say ok Pharaoh have it your way, and God hardened his heart that it became prenatally hardened. The person who desires to mend his rebellious behavior that person must seek to make a clean break from old habits and commit all in God's hands.

Along this line, there must be a love of righteousness and a firm determination to adhere to a righteous course thenceforth. Therefore, without hatred of the bad, and begin loving righteousness there will be no genuine force to repentance, and no follow through with a true conversion.

Repentance may be regarded to a person whole life course, has been contrary to God's purpose and will, and instead has been in harmony with the world under the control of God's adversary. A person whose life has radically changed at conversion may experience contempt from old friends, he may be scorn not only because he refuses to participate in certain activities, but also because his priorities have changed and he is now heading in the opposite direction, The more a person fears and respect God the more he or she will hate evil., therefore love for God and love for sin cannot coexist. When you harboring secret sins means that you are tolerating evil within yourself, it may be better to make a clean break from sin and serve God wholehearted. (Pro.8:13)

INTERNAL REPENTANCE

Internal repentance is the private work of the heart but it must be manifested outwardly to be effective, David manifested his inward repentance in prayer, 'Creates in me a clean heart, 'O God, and renew a right spirit within me.

We were born sinners and the natural inclination is to please ourselves, rather than God. David followed that inclination when he took another man's wife. We also follow it when we sin in any way; we must ask God to cleanse us from within, cleansing our hearts and spirit for new thoughts, and desires, knowing that right conduct can only come from a clean heart.

Is there a time in your Christian faith life when you feel stagnant as though you are just going through the motions? Any sin that comes between you and God and has driven a wedge between must be removed. David in his prayer he cried, 'Restore to me the joy of thy salvation. We must be real to ourselves and others. From time to time in our lifetime, we might commit wrong either against one another or against God, it is of no use fooling ourselves; because our sin will find us out, it is advisable to be real and confess to God and ask his forgiveness. (Exodus 9:27-35)

God wants us to be close to him and to experience his complete life. If sin remains unconfused makes intimacy impossible. You must confess your sins to God even though you may still have to face some earthly consequences as David did, but God will restore the joy to your relationship with him. When God forgives our sin and restores us to a relationship with him, he wants to us reach out to others who need this forgiveness and reconciliation. God desire a broken spirit, a broken and contrite heart, he will not despise. You can never please God by outward actions, no matter how good you are, if your inward attitude is not right, it cannot be accepted in God's sight, and there must also be a rejection of bad courses, and having a heart hating of it and repenting for it, and a sincere desire to please God. All things will result in the alignment of your desire with God's desire, and you will desire to love what God loves and hate what God hates.

If you truly love the Lord you will dislike evil and must despise the action of people who takes advantage of others, and admire people who only look out for themselves, then we ought to agree with God by complying with his desires for all people. Thus, God declares over his Son Jesus, 'Your throne O God, will last forever, a scepter of justice will be the scepter of your kingdom, 'You have loved righteousness and hated wickedness; therefore God, your God has set you above your companions by anointing you with the oil of joy'.

Since the authority of Jesus was established over all the entire creation, we dear not treat any created object of earthly resource as more important than he is. Christ is our security in a changing world; whatever may happen in this world, and Christ remains forever changeless, meaning that Christ's character will never change; He persistently shows his love to us, he is always fair and merciful to us who are so undeserving. Christ loved righteousness and hates wickedness; therefore God has set you above your companions, by anointing you with oil. (Hebrews 1:9)

INTERNATIONAL REPENTANCE

National sins bring national disorders, for the regression of land, and general defection from God, and religion, idolatry, profaneness, or immorality, many are the princes thereof, and may at the same time pretending to the sovereignty by which the people are crumbled into parties and factions, one cutting off another, or soon cut off by the hand of God, or of a foreign enemy. The government sometimes suffers for the sins of the people, only wisdom will prevent or redress the grievances, by a man or a people of understanding that comes again to their right mind, things are kept in good order.

Imagine what a great deal of service one wise man may do to a nation in a critical juncture, by calling the entire world to repentance; this kind of repentance is belonging to all humans. Repentance can be individual, personal, or international. Surely everyone needs to repent because all mankind has sinned and come short of the glory of God. One would wonder in amazement if it was ever possible if the entire world repents; what a wonderful world that would be. For example, there was a prime example of how a whole city could repent when they heard the gospel of the prophet Jonah's warning what God intended to do if men would not turn from their wicked ways and repent.

The people were very scared of the word from God through his prophet Jonah and the people followed the example of their king and also decided to repent. Every born again individual should be actively engaged in evangelism that the world might come to realize Jesus love them and gave his Son Jesus to die to redeem them from the curse of sin and death. This was an active work of evangelism, doing and spreading the gospel of Jesus Christ across the whole world.

A Christian who desire to be trained in evangelism is a very good ambition because Jesus equipped his disciples for this cause, they were to go into all the world and spread the Good News to every person they come into contact, starting with their household, the community, telling and living a Christian life that the world may see your good works and be led to glorify the Father in heaven.

Since sin is a deadly virus and can easily develop into a worldwide epidemic, therefore the whole world needs the solution and the cure for sin. Some virus is so deadly that there is no cure for such, but Jesus offers a cure, if men would forget their helplessness and call on his name for his help, it will make the difference.

It would take lively workers whom the Spirit of the Lord has touched; to carry out the work of winning all men to Christ, they must go with the word of God and be depended on the Holy Spirit for directions. You don't have to go as far as Jonah, you can begin where you are, and the time is now.

CHAPTER TEN

CONFESSION

Confession must proceed with forgiveness and will pave the way for God to work. The willingness of confession to God for you to be forgiven; will be manifested by repentance. Confession proceeds worshipping God in spirit and truth. Everyone has something to confess to God about. When was the last time you honestly confessed to God about anything? It is useful and healthy to empty our minds of the things we are unable to deal with. We are invited to take our confession to God in prayer and leave them with him and walk away. Humans have sinned and need to confess to God and ask his forgiveness. True confession from a heart that is broken by sin will result in pardon.

The story of David's confession has always been a reminder as soon as the subject comes up about confession. It is a very important example of true repentance and confession of a person who sinned against God. Even people who might be in the same situation will preach sermons on this man's sin and failure, but we should be honest and examine our hearts and identify the sins of all sorts that need to confess to God and sometimes to others. David sin was against God also against Uriah, and even against his conscience, that seems a lot to deal with, when it all adds up, it is worrying, deadly but not unto death. God can deal with it.

David was honest and open not to balance his good deeds with his evil deeds, neither did he think his services could atone for his offences, rather, he flies to God's infinite mercy, and depend on him for pardon and peace. David cried for God's mercy, he had nothing to plea except mercy. Mercy is the goodness of God's mercy, and the pardon of sin, he begs, 'blot out my transgression as debt is blotted, or crossed out of a book when either the debt was paid or the creditor has remitted it. David continued his penitent prayer; 'wash me thoroughly from my iniquity, and cleanse me from my sin.' Nathan the prophet first assured David upon his profession of repentance, that his sin was pardon, by saying, the Lord has taken away your sin, thou shall not die, yet it was not enough for David, he improved his prayers by asking God to, 'Wash me, cleanse me, and blot out my transgressions.

Though God has forgiven David, yet, he could not forgive himself, and therefore he was thus importunate for pardon. His penitent confessions; he was very free to own his guilt before God, he said, 'I have acknowledged my transgressions' he honestly owns his sin, it bothers him day and night, sin is tormenting, it's annoying, it will not easily go away as it comes.

Confession is the only way of easing his conscience, when the prophet said to David, 'Thou are the man" David could not deny it said, 'I have sinned, how many times David repeated the same words to himself and confessed it to God. Godly sorrow for sin has led him to repentance. He had a deep sense of his sin because he was continually thinking of it with sorrow and shame, he sighed, and 'my sin is ever before me'.

David actual confession 'Against thee, thee only, have I sinned?' When the best men sin they should give the best example of repentance, like David made no excuse of his sins, but he publicly made confession of sin, that hereafter no one could blame God for doing him any wrong, because the Lord is righteous and just towards everyone, he also confesses his original corruption, He says, 'Behold I sharpened in iniquity' While he speaks elsewhere of the admirable structure of his body, he says, it was curiously wrought, and yet, here he says, it was sharpened in iniquity.

Sin was twisted within, it might be sad with all humans who came out into the world with a corrupt nature, wretched and degenerated from its primitive purity and rectitude, that is what can be called original sin, nevertheless, David prays and acknowledgement of God's grace and goodwill towards him, he said, 'God, you desires truth in the parts of the inner ward, thou will have us, to be honest, sincere, and truth to be our profession. In the hidden part thou hast made me know wisdom because truth and wisdom will go very far in making a good man.

David was conscious of his unrighteous heart towards God in his repentance, and therefore, he doubted if God would accept him, hoping that God would enable him to make good of his resolutions, that in the hidden part, in the new man, which is called the hidden man of the heart, he would make him to know wisdom, to discern and avoid sin since the cause for one's repentance is usually a sin, and failure to meet God's righteous requirements of all wrongdoing.

Some persons rejected the only way of salvation, and also those who were putting themselves out of the reach of prayer. They were making themselves available for the enemy to take them into his clutches as prey. We may not fully understand how deadly sin is; therefore we must continue praying for our loved ones and our Christian's brothers and sisters and leaving the judgment up to God, remember what John says, 'we should pray about it, and rather than not praying about it' Since repentance involves both mind and heart, the wrongness of the course or act must be recognized, it and required an acknowledgement that God standard and his will are righteous.

Therefore, the ignorance of man or the forgetfulness of God's will, and standards might stand as a barrier to repentance. The reason for repenting is that man has turned from God and followed his sinful ways from the beginning of time when none was created as a sinner, yet, all men were born as sinners.

In the time of the flood in the days of Noah, when God shut the door of the Ark after men ignored the warning of Noah until the flood came, and the door was eventually shut for good, and no man was strong enough to open the door once it was shut by God. Those who were left outside the Ark were destroyed by water both man and beast. This will never be repeated, the door of repentance to salvation is made available to mankind all over the world.

Each human has the opportunity to accept Jesus on his terms and be saved from their sins or be shut out of God's presence forever. The first part of man is the body, which is given as soul and spirit. The soul of man is the temple of the human race' the body of man is the cover or house of the soul and the breath of man. The spirit brings man to life, and he becomes a living soul, for instance, the physical man was not created to die, but because of the sin of disobedience comes, the punishment of death, and because of sin the body of man became corrupted and limited to short life, and at the death of a man the soul then returns to the giver (God).

Who would describe themselves as a penitent? One who realizes his predicament, the result of sin and expresses sorrow over it, and demonstrate fresh committeemen to remain close to God. In some Orthotic churches penitence, confession is seen as repentance of sins, as well as the sacrament of reconciliation, or confession. It also plays a part in the Methodists, as a rite. For instance, if the penitent forgets to confess a mortal sin in confession, then, the sacrament would still be valid and their sin is forgiven, but they must tell the mortal of their sin in the next time of confession. In some religions, the practice of confession is only through prayer to God, and a person should never condemn what method others chose in confessing their sins, in the end, only God can forgive man's sin, and the seeking penitent must call on the name of the Lord in prayer to be saved.

Therefore, the penitent must seek God in prayer. Prayer is a conversation between mankind and God, using the medium of prayer is a very effective tool in reaching God through the name of Jesus God's son. God is prayer-hearing; therefore prayer must be prayed in faith believing that although you cannot see God, yet he hears your prayers. The penitent must pray to God asking for forgiveness based on Christ ransom sacrifice. Through Christ we have redemption deliverance and salvation through his blood, the forgiveness of our offences, shortcomings and trespasses avail the riches and the generosity of his gracious favor; therefore, there can be no remission of sin without redemption. Thus Christians can take examples, from when Paul was accused by the Jews for preaching Jesus; he knew he was innocent of doing no wrong, He declares 'Men and brethren, I have lived in all good conscience unto this day' city' The penitent should treat those who despitefully you and persecute him, and take the opportunity to feed the enemy, as you would do for your children, friends, or sick people with most tenderness, and considering that you are expressing your love, if the enemy thirsty give him a drink, in token of reconciliation and friendship to confirm your love to him. The guilt and the stain of sin could not be otherwise removed by the blood of Jesus, therefore, all our spiritual blessing flows down in that stream; it is according to the riches of God's grace.

It was rich grace that provides such a surety as his own Son when nothing of the nature could have entered into our thoughts, nor otherwise found for us. Persecution is one of the tools that the enemies of Jesus often used on his followers. When a Christian decided to follow Christ, he or she should be expecting persecution by the world, as Jesus was. Persecution comes in various ways and among various people for their faith in Jesus Christ; some receive severe persecution and sometimes death, imprisonment, tortures, starvation, ridicules, exempted from church gathering, and more.

The Christian must be aware of all these hard times that are predicated and develop patience and endurance to cope effectively during such times. God has promised never to leave or forsake, he knows what you will experience persecution for his sake, so be of good cheer. It has been the common test for God's people to be persecuted, therefore, Jesus advises his disciples to bless the persecutors, speak well of them, speak respectfully to them and render not railing for railing, but wishing them well and offer them up to God in prayer, and not curse them. In the meantime, even if we are in a hurry, we must show kindness, by doing good to all our enemies, if they are hungry, do not say how it is God who is avenging, for your sake, find food and feed him.

This statement can be a hard saying, especially when you are a gentle person and other people takes a dislike to you for no particular reason, I tell you it is not a humble pie, to swallow, but since it's a command, God will give the ability to stay strong under such challenges and leave the matter in his hands. There is a reason for doing so, *one*, is to heap up coals of fire on his head, to bring him to repentance, and friendship. We must abhor that which is evil, but cling to that which is good, by hating sin with utter irreconcilable hatred; it will denote a deliberate choice, and not a sincere affection, and constant perseverance to that which is good. Jesus wanted us to follow him rather than leading a life of sin and self-satisfaction, he wants us to stop controlling our destiny and allowing him to direct us.

CONFESSING ONE TO ANOTHER

It is important to confess sin to one another; Christ made it possible to go directly to God for forgiveness, confessing our sin to each other still has an important place in the life of the church. For instance, if we have sinned against an individual, we must ask him or her to forgive us. Secondly, if our sin has affected the church, we must confess it publicly, if we need loving support as we struggle with sin, we should confess to those who can support us. Fourth, if after confessing a private sin to god, we might still don't feel his forgiveness, we may wish to confess that sin to a fellow believer and hear him or her, assure us of God's pardon because in Christ kingdom everyone is a priest of other believers. (1 Peter 2:9)

God must recognize that Christ alone to be as a human mediator, or helper for a man with God. Since Christ alone this role by his propitiatory sacrifice, sadly by ourselves we cannot right the wrong towards God on our behalf, or behalf of others, because man is unable to provide the needed atonement, and since the love of the world is a disease that runs in the blood, men have it, and only the grace of God can cure it. With all their wealth man cannot save the life of his dearest friend in the world, nor purchase a reprieve when they are under the arrest of death. (1 Tim.2:5, 6)

The confession of all sins must be to God because confession means agreeing with God regarding our sins; this involves much more than simply acknowledging the sin. Confession is required as an attitude of sorrow for the sin, and a willingness to turn from it, and never committing the same sin again, therefore, the attitude of repentance should be always be confessed the moment the person becomes aware of it. Apart from this rule, the Scripture mention *two specific* times for confession, the first one is before the close of the day, and the other, before participation in the Lord Super; the failure to do the latter is a special cause for discipline from the Lord.

Confession of sin is told to God in prayer and praise, confession to men is by owning the ways of God before others, and this is said unto salvation, also, because it is the performance of the condition of that promise. Therefore, justification by faith lays the foundation of our title to salvation, and by profession, we build on that foundation, 'that whosoever believes in Jesus, shall not be ashamed'. (Romans 10:9)

God has promised everlasting life, it has two great values; it cannot be purchase by the wealth of the world, or by those who trust in their wealth, and boast of their great riches, no one can redeem the life of another, or give to God a ransom for them. Thus, the ransom for a life is costly, no payment is ever enough, yet, God will redeem from the realm of the dead. Since there is no way for a person to buy eternal life with God, only God has the power to redeem a soul. The rich and the poor are empty and naked before God; therefore, we are not redeemed by corruptible things as silver and gold, Christ did that for us that all the riches of the world could not do, neither a brother nor a friend could not do for us. (Psalms. 49:7-8).

Christians are encouraged to help one another through praying on behalf of their needs, while not affecting God's application of justice, since only Christ ransom alone is necessary to bring remission of sins. We must trust God with petitioning, by giving prayer and encouraging words to strengthen the one who has sinned and seeking aid. The repentant person should humble himself and seeks God's face, and make supplication for his forgiveness. It is required that the repentant person humbles himself and seeks God's face, supplicating his forgiveness; also his attitude should not be like as the self-righteous Pharisee. In contrast, the Pharisees would not go to the temple to pray to God, but would rather announce to all within an earshot how good he was. In contrast to the tax collector, recognizing his sin and begged God for mercy.

Therefore, self-righteousness is dangerous; it leads to the pride that causes a person to despise others, and prevents others from learning anything from God. In contrast, the prayer of the tax collector should be our prayer, because we all need God's mercy every day. If we should make this statement, saying, 'we have no sin" we are misleading ourselves and the truth is not in us, 'If we confess our sins, he is faithful and righteous to forgive us of our sins and to cleanse us from all righteousness.

In Jesus illustration, in contrast, of the tax collector, whom Jesus portrayed as beating his breast and saying, "O God, be gracious to me a sinner" It sends out a warning that the person who covers his faults will not succeed, but when we share it the battle is half. Everyone needs a good buddy to share their fault with, my special buddy is a girl we both knew from school days. We grew up loving and sharing our faults and sometimes we both converse about what to do if things get out of hand, for example, if one of us should move away, perhaps transported to another world, but we always find a way to talk to each other daily. We share our joys and share our sorrows, and sometimes we even decide to go on holiday together, we help out each other financially and payback when possible. (*We all need a buddy.*)

Sometimes we tend to criticize each other constructively, other times we could become cynical, but we are friends so it does not matter too tough. It is human nature to hide their sins, or overlook mistakes, but it is a waste of time not learning anything from making mistakes if you don't acknowledge making it in the first place. We must learn and gain some sort of experience from each mistake. The benefit of learning from an error in admitting it, confess it analyses it, and make the necessary adjustments so that it does not happen again.

It is believed that everyone makes mistakes, but it is only fools who repeat them. We can develop a prideful attitude regarding acknowledging and this is in each of us that strongly resist admitting when we are wrong, we admire people who openly and graciously admitting mistakes and their sins. It is a fact that these people portray a positively strong self-image, even though they are not always right to be feeling good about themselves, nevertheless, they are willing to reconsider when they are wrong and make positive changes.

PENITENT CONFESSION

1. The plea of the prodigal son to his father was in heartfelt regret, he said, 'Father I have sinned against heaven and before thee' the magnitude of his sin aims high, and it was against heaven, and he acknowledges himself to forfeit all the privileges of the family, he pleads with his father, 'I am no more worthy to be called your son' make me one of your hired servants' It becomes sinners to acknowledge their unworthiness to receive any favor from God, but the prodigal request to his father, 'Make me one of your hired servants' It's good enough for me; that I may show that I love my father's house as much as I slighted it, but sincere repentant will honestly raise their heart as well as the palm of their hands to God and honestly confessing their transgressions.

2. This title speaks of a very sad story of David's fall. The sin that is mention in this Palms which he laments was the folly and wickedness he committed with his neighbor's wife. This sin of David speaks for the whole human race to take heed lest they fall. The repentance which he expresses was brought to his attention by Nathan, who was sent by God to convince him of his sin. David was convinced of his sin, and in distress, he poured his soul to God in prayer for mercy and grace, and by divine inspiration, he drew up all that was within him to God who sees and knows everything. David affirms that God desires truth, honesty, and sincerity in the inwards parts, he also acknowledged that trust and wisdom will go very far in making a man wise by enlightening the mind and so gaining God's will.

It is not surprising if those who once knew God will still experience a conscientious sense of the righteousness of their heart towards God in his and doubted if God would accept them. But, further along, the person will experience to understand God's overwhelming ability to forgive anyone who comes to Him in repentance. For such reasons we must never doubt God's ability to forgive when we confess our sins to him, truly God is willing and just to forgive our sins, and to cleanse us from all unrighteousness, thus, we must believe in the Lord Jesus and we shall be saved.

3. In the parable, the Publican cry was, 'God be merciful to me a sinner' the publican gives himself no other character than that of a sinner. He had no dependence but on the mercies of God, he thought, justice condemns me, and nothing will save me but the mercy, and he earnestly pray for the benefit of that mercy. He comes as a beggar for alms as if he is ready to perish for hungry. Others may have contempt on the sneaking whining publican, but our Lord Jesus assures us, that this poor, penitent, broken-hearted publican went to his house justified rather than others. (Luke 18:13)

For those alive on this planet, the door of opportunity for repentance is still left open. Many people go through life and merely look at the sign on the door, 'come in', and accept forgiveness. They believe that the door will be kept open by the doorkeeper forever, or there is plenty of time to walk, through at their own pace, but ah, the keeper of that door has plans for the duration of time when the door should be left open, or closed. Once the door of our life is shut, that's final no wrongs cannot be made right after death, and of course, true repentance cannot be achieved through any human effort' Therefore, people must do the right and only thing, repent and accept the Lord Jesus that your sins might be blotted out.

CONFESSING CHRIST

Confessing Christ is necessary for salvation; men's confession of Christ is a necessity to obtain salvation; this statement has always been the case of failure from the beginning and it is the final hallmark as a requirement to satisfy the divine justice of God. Confessing Christ is requested by God who is the author and the finisher of man's salvation; Jesus declares, 'If we confess with our mouth, 'Jesus is Lord,'' and believe in our heart that God raised Christ from the dead, we shall be saved' You might be asked, 'how can I receive salvation and inherit eternal life?' read more; this confession is required as the means of salvation. Confession to the Lord Jesus must be done

Verbally and with the heart we must believe. The Lord lays great emphasis on confessing Him before men, he said with empathy, 'those who call on the name of Lord Jesus will be saved.'

God will never fail to provide forgiveness, to those who believe, and repent of their sin, if you have accepted and confessed Christ, the next step is sharing your belief with as many people you come into contact with. God is calling each individual to take part in spreading the message of salvation in community, home, churches, and friends or wherever. Can you think of one person who needs to hear the message of the Good News? Go, tell them, and although this action might cause a stir, not everyone will be willing to listen or to believe, but you must tell others, there is always someone that needs to hear the *Good News* including, the rich, the poor and who have ears to hear.

While Jesus was on earth, he warns his followers that they would experience and be persecuted, imprisonment for speaking about him, nevertheless it was profitable for their Christian witness and a good example of sharing the gospel. The profession of Christ and Christianity creates a hazard in the world, such as the case in primitive times, men would even choose to make a sacrifice of themselves for the sake of the gospel, by all possible means who believe they must take the message of salvation and confess it to others so they will respond to the Good news. Salvation is as close as your mouth and heart, if you believe in your hearts and confess with your mouth that Christ is raised from the dead, you shall be saved. If there be no power of it in the heart, it wills just a mockery, especially concerning Christ resurrection, which is the fundamental article of the Christian faith.

CHRIST CONFESSION OF US

Jesus warns his disciples and said, therefore,' whoever acknowledges me before man, 'I will also acknowledge him before my father in heaven, and those who confess me before men, I will confess before my father in heaven, and whoever denies me before men, I will also deny him before my father who is in heaven.

Jesus was not teaching a tick for that, as to say, do to me as I do to you. But he was teaching loyalty and discipline among his followers. In the days of Christ triumph, Christ will own those who honor him, in the day of his trail, and those who deny him shall be forever being disowned and rejected by him. It is our duty and if we are faithful it will hereafter be our unspeakable honor and happiness to confess Christ before man. Therefore, it is our duty not only to believe in Christ but to profess that faith, in suffering and serving for him when we are called to do so. However this may expose us to reproach and trouble, but if we hold out we will be abundantly recompense. Christ says, he will confess and represent us before his father, and those who honor Christ, he will thus, honor them.

Those who dishonor Christ before men, it is a dangerous activity, and those who dislike Christ on these terms he may leave him at their perils. Whatever we part with for the pearl of price; we may comfort ourselves with this persuasion that it is well worth what we give for it. The terms are, we must prefer Christ, before our earnest and dearest relations, father, mother, sons and daughters. It is important for children must love their parents, and parents must love their children, but if they love them better than Christ, they are unworthy of him. Before our ease and safety we must take up our cross and we must follow Christ example, and bear it as he did. It is a great encouragement to us, when we meet with crosses, that in bearing them we still follow Christ, who has shown us the way, else we are not worthy of him.

Christ has a concern regarding his faithful minister, to his disciples, his prophets, to the poor and widows, and anyone giving them even a cup of cold water shall be rewarded. Any kindness that is shown to Christ disciples no matter how small shall be noticed and will be rewarded. We cannot merit anything as wages from the hand of God, but they shall receive a reward the gift from the hand of God. Those who showed the kindness of any kind to prophets will receive a prophet's reward, by having their prayers answered. The prophets rewards are spiritual blessings in heavenly things, and if we shall know how to value them and reckoned them good as payments.

HINDRANCES TO CONFESSION

Many contributing factors cause hindrances and prevent people from doing the right thing, for example, the fear of men, feeling shame, ridiculed, and being persecuted, these are a few, and people have always experience the deep cut of been persecuted for Jesus and his Gospel sake. Thankfully the exuberant power of the Holy Spirit gives strength for extraordinary tasks, for example, when the Spirit of the Lord came upon men like Othniel, Gideon, Jephthah, and Samson and among others, this has strengthened and expresses temporary and spontaneous increase of physical-spiritual or mental strength. There was an extraordinary and supernatural occurrence to prepare persons for a special task in the depth of any hindrances that life throws at them.

Jesus always urged his disciple when they face trials of life whether from men or whatever to rejoice and be exceedingly glad for great will be their reward in heaven, for in the same way the prophets were persecuted who were before them' Even Jesus disciples had difficulty believing in him, some were afraid to confess their faith outwardly because of the fear of men. Jesus followers were often reminded of their commitment to follow him regardless of what men would do to them, or what they will say about them, Jesus said, 'If we are afraid to confess and own me before men in this world, he will also not confess them before his father in heaven.'

Some of Jesus brothers, who denied him, had eventually become leaders in churches. James, for several years, was embarrassed by his brother Jesus, but it was not until after Jesus death and resurrection that they finally believed in him, and we too should not miss the opportunity to believe in Jesus, the Son of God. You may be feeling despondent because our efforts of bringing others to faith might yield to nothing, but take heart; Jesus sometimes found it difficult as well, yet, Jesus was already aware that people had entirely missed the real point of the feeding and miracles he performed, and he also finds the Jewish leaders unable to understand his explanation of it.

They lack understanding regarding Christ earthly existence, they did not know him, it's a scenario that's easily repeated, in some cases we might devote hours to bible reading and church activities but if we still cannot recognize and respond to God in Jesus, we betray the fact that we still don't know God, because Jesus is one with God. Once we have encountered the gospel of Christ it is impossible to talk of a relationship with God that bypasses Jesus. At the heart of the gospel, of course, is the cross, and as Jesus suggested, that the cross is not something to which he willingly gave himself.

Since the world hated Jesus, the Christians who believe and follow him can be expected to be hated also; there are times when it seems well in our home, churches, place of work, even in a troublesome community, and a sense of .peace among men, yet we must not take it for granted that all is well, rather, we should be aware that a possibility of circumstances might change at any time, therefore, watch and pray for we may know what time the enemy will be struck because we are warned that he goes about like a roaring lion seeking whom he will attack.

In the case of Jesus brothers and others who hated him, he knew exactly what was happening, so he warned his disciples what was to befall him and those who followed him. Therefore, Jesus urged his disciples to deny themselves, and take up their cross and follow him; he meant the death of self and death on the cross for him. The time of Jesus death was by a form of execution used by Rome for dangerous criminals, though Jesus was not a criminal, neither was he dangerous, but as a prisoner he must carry his cross to the place of execution, signifying submission to Rome's power. Jesus used the imagery of carrying a cross to illustrate the ultimate submission that would be required of his followers. Jesus wanted to ignite the important effort that was needed to follow him every step of the way regardless of the fear of men and other factors.

THE FEAR OF MEN

Fear is such a devastating factor that most people have fear of various things and people, places, and even fear of speaking in public, fear of sleeping alone, but the fear of men makes it more difficult to live with. Some men display great power over other people whom they believe they can manipulate and cause them grief, this power struggle behaviors have caused various sort of side effects, for instance, a mental illness where people are afraid to even leave their home to avoid meeting up with these monsters. There can be trouble in some homes among husbands and wives. Some wives sometimes become fearful of their bullying husband and it can also be the other way, some wives develop an attitude of fighting back, children become afraid of their unreasonable parents. Children can develop a fear of teachers, dinner ladies, and next-door neighbors; can you imagine a child having to live through these fears daily?

Sometimes children are afraid to share their fearful feeling with parents because parents are at war with the home, where do these children find peace? Thank God there is hope, the word of God encourage us, not to fear, for the Lord our God is with us, we should not be afraid of the terror by night, nor the arrows that pass by noonday, a thousand shall fall at our side and ten thousand at our right hand but they shall not come nigh our dwellings. We should not be afraid to stand up for what we believe is right in your heart? Or, will you see the truth steering you in the face and not defending the cause?

We should be careful not to allow world pressure to get a hold of our conscience when making serious decisions, it is important to consider the consequence of acting against our conscience. Even strong men in themselves quake and crack under undue pressure making an unreasonable decision and finding it hard not to be a people's pleaser. The world is full of a people pleaser, the church is full of such, and it can be very devastating when one refuses to please God rather than man.

This is actually how fear operates; it will allow you to do the wrong thing to the right people by compromising your character. Fear is a cruel master, it pays cruel consequences, and having a fearful attitude of something or someone always harms the minds of people making good choices, and this was Pilate decision about Jesus, his fear gripped him much harder and confused his thinking ability to give a favorable decision.

For instance, although a person may know Christ, and believe and worked hard to be good enough, yet rules and rituals seem to chase people's hearts and crippling them with fear, not to continue trusting in God. Only Jesus blood alone can cleanse our conscience, and free us from death's sting, and freedom from sin's power, to live and serve God with a clean clear conscience. If you are carrying a load of guilt because you are thinking you can't be good enough for God to use you, taking time out to consider the death and resurrection of Jesus and what it means to you. Christ can heal of deadly fear that lies in your conscience and deliver you from the frustration of trying to earn God's favor through your merit. He wants you to bring your guilt-ridden life to him, and confess your inability to clean up your conscience, and then give him thanks for his forgiveness and clearing your record.

Are you feeling afraid of losing your God-given position, or being afraid of speaking the truth? What is your conscience saying about being truthful to yourselves and then to others? Or, will you rather be a part of those who conceal the truth, rather than telling the truth in love? Feel free to reevaluate these options, or you might consider perhaps finding your own, whatever the cost, you should make wise decision listening to your conscience, to do the right thing. Humans must agree with God that he is always right, and therefore make confession of their sins, and ultimately seek his forgiveness, here is how.

Healthy fear and also a negative fear exist but a positive fear is the fear of the Lord. Submission to the Lord and his revelation require us to fear the Lord and keep his commandment which is the whole duty of man. Jesus disciples were enlightened regarding the dread and became fearful, he warns, 'And fear not them which kill the body, but are not able to kill the soul, but rather fear him which can destroy both soul and body in hell'.

Fear has many root causes and reactions that torment, fear will blow things out of proportion, blinding the truth, masking, preventive, and many more. Here fear becomes a hindrance that grips the attention of people not to make decision confessing that Jesus is Lord of their lives, Jesus already gives warning regarding the fear of men for his sake, when one is afraid of something, he either run from it, or submit to it, the latter idea is in the view here, it is a healthy fear, like fear of electrifying, or the fear a parent which causes one to act appropriately.

Jesus as a wise and considerate father always highlights his disciples regarding every area that pertains to life. They were warned to fear their enemies who may only take their physical lives, but cannot prevent their blessed resurrection to life, in another world. Jesus reminds them that it was more important to fear him who has the authority over the soul as well as over the body and who can bring both to eternal condemnation.

Fearing no evil, for God as the good shepherd is with you for his rod and staff will comfort, and his word and spirit will comfort, his rod and staff alluding to the shepherd crook or the rod under which the sheep passed when he counts his sheep the staff is used by the shepherd to drive away from the dogs that would worry the sheep causing fear, but, ah, perfect love cast out all fear and the fear of the Lord is the beginning of wisdom, the whole duty of man is to fear God and keep his commandments.

The Psalmist confidently rejoice, he says, 'Though I walk through the valley of the shadows of death, meaning though, I'm in the peril of death, and amid danger, deep as a valley, yet I'm easy, in the shadow of death, there is no substantial fear, there is no evil in it for a child of God, and death cannot separate us from the love of God, they might kill the body but cannot touch the soul. Psalms 23. When we allow God our shepherd to guide us we will experience his contentment, our shepherd knows the green pastures, and quiet waters, that will restore and refreshes us. We can reach these places by following Christ obediently if we rebel against our shepherd's leading is rebelling against our own best interest.

FEAR OF FALSE TEACHERS

Anything or anyone false is further from the truth, and without any doubt will be exposed by the truth. False teachers and false teachers are gone widely into our world with a reason of gaining more people like themselves, and ordinary, Christians may not easily discern them. If you are wondering who they are, what is their belief, here is a description by the apostle Paul, he gives us the insight to enlighten our understanding to discern whether or not false teachers who claim to speak for God as a messenger is really from God or not.

He stated that, 'the messenger who confesses Christ is Lord, you can listen to him, if not, be aware, don't naively ready to accept the words of all who claim to speak for God. We should test their credentials by finding out whether they teach about Christ, or not, because, the truth is, no messenger can preach Christ unless the Holy Spirit is with that messenger. Before accepting the teachings of religious teachers about the topic, especially about our Lord Jesus, listen carefully to what they believe about Jesus, and if they deny either his divinity or his humanity, they might be willfully considering him less than Christ, the Savior.

The apostle Paul also warned that false teachers should not be allowed to invade the church to spread their teaching, because, they take delight and refuse to believe that God of Creation was good, and his very contact with the physical would soil himself. These influences honored Jesus but they could not believe he was truly man. Paul knew if these teachings were left unclear it would greatly distort the Christian truth. It is not enough that a teacher appears to know what he is talking about, but his discipline and morals must be recognized whether or not he is speaking for God, if his teachings contradict the bible, his teaching is false.

The apostle Paul warns Timothy to be aware and guard against these teachings that cause believers to dilute any aspect of their faith. Thus, false teachers can be very direct or extremely subtle, as wolfs in sheep clothing, the apostle warns Timothy as a young minister, to be aware that in the last days; there will be bad men in the church, for the net of the gospel was to enclose both good and the bad. False teachers are men who are lovers of themselves they are covetous and no good can be expected of them as those who love God because every man is for what he can get and for keeping what he has. These men are dangerous to one another.

It is perilous times when pride and vain-glory when men are boasters and blasphemers when men do not fear of God or have any regard for other men. When children are disobedient to parents, unthankful and unholy and without the fear of God, and are unthankful for the grace of God? When men are without natural affection and truce-breakers, false accusers of one another, devils one to another, when men have no government of themselves and their appetites are inconsistent, they are fierce. When men are generally treacherous, willful and haughty, when are puffed and behaving scornfully to all about them, then the times are perilous.

In the last days, men will be generally lovers of pleasure more than lovers of God that are carnal minded, and we can notice these behaviors playing out when concert halls are overflowing, but the place of prayer is almost empty. They are full of enmity against God, can a mortal man hates God? When men have a form of godliness they are having just the shadow but not the real, they are in the class as pretenders it is a very different thing from the power of it, men may have the one and be wholly distant from the other.

In perilous times is not so much of persecution from without as account of the corruption within. Perilous when men shall be wicked because it is sin that makes the perilous times. Paul told Timothy to expose them so they will be known to others. False teachers are people who demonstrate self-love, they love themselves above average and decorate every part of their body to show the Devils as head of their lives, instead, the Christians charity, which takes care of the good of others, yet, these will mind only their own.

CHAPTER ELEVEN

THE AUTHOR OF CHANGE

The naked truth is Christ is the author of the change; he has the ultimate ability to change man's heart from a life of sinful behavior to eternal life, which he has provided to whomsoever he will. Nevertheless, there must be a willingness on man's part to accept the terms and conditions of the author of this change. This change is done through regeneration; it is weaned from the world, through the death and resurrection of Jesus Christ God's son.

The love of Christ that came into our hearts brought on the change, and the world is now under our feet, by having a new change of heart is the new creation and having a new heart, a new nature, all things are passed away and all things are made new 'God has provided a remedy for the reconciliation to bring back mankind to him through the death and resurrection of Jesus Christ his son. We spoke about the sins that so easily beset us and form a hindrance to our prayer getting answered. Now, that we have repented and confess our sins and gained forgiveness we are now ready to make peace with God through reconciliation. We are now ready for a change of lifestyle through God compassion, in a new covenant.

Undergoing in the rite of water baptism, and rise again to new opportunities to walk in humility and Christ righteousness, and God's holiness, these are some of the stages that are relevant to a healthy Christian life, just as a butterfly changes from one extreme to another until they become expert in the art in flying.

There is a remedy of change that is recommended to all who desire a real change, perhaps you are sick and tired of the way you are and have desperately tried everything, yet it does not seem to work, and the condition seems hopeless, let me introduce you to the author of change. He who works in us; recommends a change, it can only be as you surrender your heart to the God who has the power to change and become born again. He says, 'therefore, to be born again is to be borne by the spirit' the change is not wrought by any wisdom or power of our own, but by the power and influence of the blessed spirit of grace.

NECESSITY FOR CHANGES

Some changes must take place at times, but nothing is final. Changes occur in the lives of an individual; can move from good to better, while others change from better to worst. As some children might be slow starters; they slowly develop into who they really should be in later years.

There is a beginning with everything under the sun that is why people should not be too hasty or too rash with one another because of the slowness of their development. There is goodness in every person, no matter how young or how old, though it takes time, yet the author of change has no time limits, he is also the author of time, in his time is right, then all will be revealed. Life in general accounts for all sorts of changes from time to time, people change, time changes, and situation changes, people change from good to an evil person, and so we are in a changing world, that we cannot understand what will be the next change. Sometimes changes are so frequent and unpredictable that we cannot be perfect in our estimation of what next, only because there exists an author of the change; nothing comes or goes as a surprise.

The very important question is; 'what communion can there be between God, who is a Spirit and a soul in its condition?' It is a corruption that is prized in the bone within us, the corrupted nature which is the flesh, takes rise from our first birth, and therefore, the new nature which is the spirit, must take rise from a second birth, thus, corruption and sin are woven into our nature, so we are shaped in iniquity. Therefore, it is not enough to put on a new coat or a new face, but we must put on the new covering on the man, and fortunately, Christ makes it necessary by his own words, 'Marvel not that I say to you, you must be born again.'

Christ had said, he is the great physician of man souls, he knows their cases, and what is necessary for the cure, He said, 'You must be born again' We are not to marvel at it, for when we consider the holiness of God with whom we have to do, and the depravity of our nature; we must not think why so much stress is laid upon, that we *must be born again* 'Christ said so, he is the great physician of souls, he knows man cases and what is necessary for the cure. Therefore, we are not to marvel at it, for considering the holiness of God with whom we have to do, and the depravity of our nature, we should not think it strange that so much stress is laid on the statement, 'You must be born again.

This change is illustrated by two comparisons, first, the regenerating work of the Spirit is compared to water, 'to be born again is to born of the water and the Spirit, that, which is intended here is to show that the Spirit, in sanctifying a soul. Secondly, it is compared to the wind, 'The wind blows where it is listed, and so is every one that is born of the Spirit and the

Spirit dispenses its influences where and when, on whom, and in what measure and degrees, he pleases. He works powerfully and with evident effects, 'thou hear the sound thereof, though its causes are hidden are manifest. The Spirit works mysteriously, and in secret hidden ways, 'Thou cannot tell where it comes from, not whiter it goes, and how it gathers and spends its strength is a riddle to us, so that manner and working of the Spirit are a mystery.'

THE NATURE OF THE CHANGE

The nature of this change and what is wrought, it is by the *'spirit,'* to be born again, is to be born of the spirits, and enter upon a new existence, to have a new mind, a new heart, new views, new principles, new taste, new affections, new disliking, new fears, new joys, new sorrows, a new love for things once hated, new hatred to things once loved, new thoughts of God, and love for self and people and the life to come, and salvation" Wow, this sounds a lot of newness, almost in everything, but read on, those who are regenerated are made spiritual new.

The Christian is now a new man as opposed to the old man that he was before he became a Christian. This concept of newness may be traced to an important choice between two Greek words, both meaning new, one word means new, in the sense of renovation to repair the other in the sense of fresh existence. It is the latter that is used to describe the Christian. He is not the old man renovated or refreshed, no, he is a brand new man with a new family, a new set of values, new motivations, and new possessions. (Act 2:38)

The term *'new creature'* refers to the transformation that occurs within the inner man when a person believes in Christ as Savior.

149

The Christian is now a new man as opposed to the old man that he was before he became a Christian. This concept of newness may be traced to an important choice between two Greek words, both meaning new. The meaning of the word *new*, in the sense of renovation to repair, the other is in the sense of fresh existence. It is the latter that is used to describe the Christian. He is not the old man renovated or refreshed, no, he is a brand new man with a new family, a new set of values, new motivations, and new possessions. The dictates and interests of the rational and immortal soul have retrieved the dominion they ought to have over the flesh. The change is illustrated by two comparisons; to be born again, is to be born of water, and the Spirit, the primary interest is to show that the Spirit is in the sanctifying soul.

To be born again gives new life by the spirit, and all who welcome Jesus as Lord of their lives are reborn spiritually, they receive new life from God. Christ has shown in his word that it is necessary for a change like things, because that which is born of the flesh is flesh, and that which is born of the Spirit is Spirit. We are told what we are, that we are flesh, the soul is still a spiritual substance, but so wedged, so it's justly captivated by the will of the flesh, and that is justly called flesh. Through faith in Christ, the new birth changes us from the inside and rearranging our attitudes, desires and motives, and the Spirit clean and purifies, and the water cools and refreshes. Also as water does to the thirsty hart, and the weary traveler, it was probable that Christ had an eye to the ordinances of baptism which John had used himself. Jesus emphasized, 'that man must be born again by the Spirit which regeneration by the Spirit.'

The Spirit should be signposted as the washing with water, and as a visible sign of spiritual grace. The change is compared to wind, for instance, the wind blows where it is listed, and so is everyone who is born of the Spirit. The wind is life and has no control over the body, it is invisible, yet the wind is strong, you can feel and hear it, but cannot be touched or see it. There are different kinds of wind, for example, strong wind, gales, storms, breeze, tornados, and hurricanes. We might consider how this wind comes about, and why? Are they accidents, do they happen by chance, or, are they come about by God? So does the Spirit in the working of regeneration work, it is arbitrary as a free agent, the same description signifies both the wind and the Spirit.

The Spirit dispenses its influences, where and when and in what measure and degrees, he pleases. The wind is powerfully, and with effective force, the sound of the wind can be heard, though its case although hidden, yet its effect is manifested. The wind works mysteriously and in secret hidden ways. One cannot tell where the sound comes from, how it is gathered, and where it sends its strength, it is a riddle for us, and so is the manner and method of the Spirit working as a mystery. When a person dies to the old life, he is belonging to Christ, a new life will begin.

A person who is an unbeliever's mindset is centered on his or her self-gratification, and those who don't follow Christ have only their determination as to their source of power, by contrast, God is at the center of a Christian's life, God supplies the power for the Christian daily living, the believer will experience that their whole way of looking at the world changes when they come to Christ. A life of change will convince people of Christ power, one of your greatest testimonies is the difference others see in your life and attitudes since you have believed in Christ.

At times you may be afraid to share your faith and changes you have made in Christ, because you might feel uncomfortable, and rejected. Notice, Peter and John's zeal was so strong for the Lord that they could not keep quiet, even when they were threatened about owning Jesus Christ as their Savior and Lord. If your courage to witness for God has been weakened, pray that boldness may increase, and remember Jesus promise, 'whoever acknowledged him before men, and I will also acknowledge him before my father in heaven.' (Matthew.10:8)

CHAPTER TWELVE

FORGIVENESS

God is willing to forgive our sins and cleanse us from all unrighteousness, therefore, there is no sin too great and no sin too small, God can cleanse us completely from anything inconsistent with his moral character. Having receiving forgiveness and cleansing it is reasonable for sinners to forsake their sin and yield themselves completely to God, by taking this leap of faith and even believers who will benefit from this restoration will be restored to full fellowship with God. When God forgives us of sins, he forgets them; we never have to fear that he will remind us of them. Since God forgives so merciful forgiving our sins, we should also forgive others. We may be asked, 'If God has forgiven us of our sins because of Christ's death, why must we confess our sins?

Therefore, we must recognize our tendency to sin and relying on God's power to overcome when we receive Christ forgiveness. We must understand only God has the power to forgive man sin, and he is willing and just to forgive sinners of their sin. The act of pardoning an offender is ceasing resentment towards another because of his offence and giving up all claims to recompense. According to the law God gave to the nation of Israel, for one who had sinned against God, or against his fellowman to have his sins forgiven, he first has to ratify the wrong as the law prescribed and then, in most cases, present it to God.

When Israel was in a covenant relationship with God, they were a holy people, chosen from among all the nations. So often God reminded the people of what he has done for them; he tells them plainly that they should obey his voice in deeds and keep his covenant since they were saved by him, they should also rule by him, he assures them of the honor and kindness he would show them in case they keep his covenant. If the people adhere to God's command, he promises they would be a particular treasure to them giving divine revelation, instituted ordinances, and promises inclusive of eternal life.

He will also send his prophets among them, and pouring out his Spirit upon them. God promise to dignify them above all people. Here, God asserts his sovereignty over, prosperity in the whole visible creation. All true and obedient Christians are promised by God to be adopted into a righteous standing before him, through the new covenant mediated by Christ.

Hence, the principle stated by Paul, nearly all things are cleansed with blood according to the law and unless blood is poured out no forgiveness takes place, since the blood of animal sacrifice could not take away sins of the individual and give a clear conscience. By contrast, the foretelling of a new covenant was made possible that true forgiveness should be based on Jesus's ransom sacrifice, that even while Jesus was on earth he demonstrated through many miracles proving he had the authority to give forgiveness of sins, and healing a paralytic man.

God forgives largely as indicted by Jesus illustrations of the prodigal son, and of the king who forgives a slave a debt of ten thousand talents, whereas that slave was unwilling to forgive a fellow slave a debt but a hundred denarii. Nevertheless, God's forgiveness is not prompted by sentimentality, for he does not leave notorious acts unpunished. God warns Israel that he would not forgive apostasy on their part. Since, all humans have to forgive others for personal offence, regardless of the number of times involved. God's forgiveness is not extended to those who refuse to forgive others. Even in the case of serious wrongdoing among the Christian congregation, prayer must be prayed for God's forgiveness on behalf of others, even an entire congregation.

Moses did so respecting the nation of Israel confessing their national sin and seeking forgiveness, he was favorably heard by God. God's forgiveness should not be resented because Jesus gives a stern warning against forgiveness in general, he said, '*if we refuse* to forgive others, God will also refuse to forgive us, because when we don't forgive others, we are denying our common ground as sinners in need of God's forgiveness. Although God forgiveness of sin is not the direct result of our forgiving others, it is based on our releasing what forgiveness means.

Forgiveness is like a flower that opens up' See the attitude of the prodigal's father when his son whom he thought was lost return home. The father came out and entreated him in, and accosted him mildly, gave him good words, and desires him to come in. He might have justly said, if he will not come in, let him stay outside, even when they are at fault, nevertheless, treats them with compassion, and even in this case assured his son, that the father honored his son's confession, 'father I have sinned, and the received him with opened arms.

Yet the brother of the prodigal son needed to understand the virtue of forgiveness, the father gave him a good reason, he said, 'it was met that we should make merry for the return of his brother, my son, to the family'. Any family would be more transported with joy for the raising of a dead child to life, than for the continued life of and health of many children. The elder brother did not make any reply to what the father has said, which one might suggest that he was well reconciled to his prodigal brother, and his father reminded and said, 'this is your brother'.

How easy it is when you ask God forgiveness, and how difficult it might be to grant forgiveness from yourselves to others, therefore, whenever you asked God for forgiveness, also ask yourself, 'have I forgiven the people who have wronged me?' therefore, you should never hold back forgiveness from others; because God has willingly forgiven all your sins, and take into account and realize how Christ has completely forgiven, this should produce a free and generous attitude of forgiveness towards others.

God has a way of seeking and receiving human sin, it is very important that one acknowledge their sin, and recognized the offence is against God. Thus, every sin must be confessed, it is unqualifiedly and has a deep heartfelt sorrow, of the wrongs done, and a determination to turn from such a course or practice, the guilty one must do what he can to right the wrong or damage done against God, or man. We must be compassionate enough and carefully preserve Christian love and peace with all brethren, and if anyone should breach this, we should labor for reconciliation, until this is done we are utterly unfit for communion with God in holy ordinances. For instance, 'If you have a heart against your brother, make short work of it, do not prolong it anymore, get it sorted, and be willing to forgive, and also forgive the injury.

Love or charity is so much better than all burnt offerings and sacrifice that God is content to stay for the gift, rather than have it offered while we are under guilt and are engaged in a quarrel. Though at times we may be feeling unfit to participate in the rite of communion with God, by a continual fault with a brother, yet they have no excuse for the omission or neglect of duty, and many believers sometimes use this as an excuse not to attend church services when communion is served, or maybe because they are at variance with some neighbor, thus, though your sin will never excuse another, but will rather double the guilt.

Neither must you allow the sun to go down on your wrath, because of going to prayer before going to sleep. Matthew recommends, 'come to term quickly with your accuser while you are on the way travelling with him, lest your accuser's hand you over to the judge, and the judge to the guard and put into prison (Matt 5:25) Jesus was concern regarding even the social life of his disciples that they would not divide and pull in pieces in their minds, he draws an illustration of a disquieting and tormenting thought, which may disturb their joy in God, and break the sleep and hinders the enjoyment of ourselves, our friends and what God has given, it is advice rather, taking the problem to God in prayer to gain his peace.

The Christian believer can confidently recall how God promise to provide for those who are his, in all things needful for life as well as godliness, an example of the life that now is, food and a covering, not dainties, but necessities, so we must cast all your cares on him and take no thought for your life what you will eat or what you will put on. God even promised to look after the creatures who either work or have any care, much more than humans. God who knows how to give what we need, He said, 'he will supply all our needs according to his riches in glory by Christ Jesus our Lord', 'take no thought for your life!

For example, Christian believers who have been forgiven for a lifetime of sin, and yet, to be unforgiving to others, it's unfair, but true forgiveness must begin in the heart of a regenerate man. It is one of the signs of genuine salvation, people who are saved are both forgiven and forgiving, when we don't forgive others, we are settling ourselves outside and above Christ's law of love. Jesus taught his disciples to pray so that forgiveness can become the cornerstone of their relationship with God. God has forgiven all our sins, so we must now forgive those who have done us wrong. To remain unforgiving shows that we had not understood and we deeply need to be forgiven.

The Christian's most powerful resources are communion with God through prayer, the results are often what we thought was impossible. And though some people see prayer as a last when all else fails, prayer should come first, because God's power is infinitely greater than ours, and it makes sense to rely on God through prayer, especially since God encourages doing so, you are encouraged to pray without ceasing, and since we are not aware of when you would be tested and tried by the enemy of our souls.

For example, Job while he was going through his second test, was when he lost his health, and the identification of the disease signified by sore boils was not clear, all over his body was covered with boils and it was very painful. Job recognized that both good and evil comes from God's hands, one by his activity and one by his permissive will God can permit evil things to happen for good ends. Job was at his lowest place in life, yet, he still believes that God could raise him out of his dead condition, he put himself in the posture as a penitent in true repentance; there must not be only conviction of sin, and retribution and godly sorrow, Job thought hardly on himself, he said, 'Wherefore I abhor myself and repent in dust and ashes.' Most Christians undergo testing and sometimes takes comfort by the way Job was also tested, but one cannot compare themselves what Job went through and still, trust remains faithful. Job was so focused during his testing period; he did not blame God or even his friends who tried to comfort him

Peter cowardly and repeatedly denied that he knew Jesus when he was on trial after the cock crowed once, he continued in the temptation, and a second and third time Peter relapsed into the sin then he remembered what Christ said, regarding the crowing of the cock, it was that brought him to repentance, immediately the crowing of the cock'. Peter's conscience arouses, nothing will grieve a penitent more than to remind him of his sins and that he has sinned against the grace of the Lord Jesus, because Jesus is God's Son the Messiah, therefore to reject Christ is futile, Jesus is the only way that God reveals Himself to the world. Some Christians may disagree whether or not people can lose their salvation, but all agree that those who move away from their faith are in serious trouble and need the disciple of Jesus.

A person, who accepts Christ as God's Son, accepts God the Father at the same time, and the two are one and cannot be separated. Many cultists today called themselves Christians, but they deny that Jesus is divine; therefore, we ought to expose their teaching so that this false message does not contaminate some weak believers among us. If anyone acknowledges Jesus as the son of God, God lives in him and him in God; we know that we live in Christ because we acknowledge that Jesus is the

Son of God. When we become Christians, we receive the Holy Spirit, God's presence in our lives is proof that you belong to him. He also gives you us the power to love, that is, the sense of God's love to us, and drawing out our love from us to him.

The ground of all this is the shedding abroad of the love of God in our hearts, and the sense of God's love will make us not ashamed either of our hope in him or our sufferings for him. (1 John 4.15)

Thus, Christianity is both private and public; it is with heart-belief and mouth confession. Our relationship with God and the power he provides result in obedience. Having received the gift of forgiveness and eternal life, we are now challenged to live that life with God's help. We must never pretend to be on God's team, if our living pleases the devil, you will be only fooling yourself. Instead, live a truthful life that shows you are on God's team by doing right from the inside out, and God will always be with you. (1John 2:23)

The believer can now move on in faith and walking in obedience and confidence in Christ who made it possible and granting me his forgiveness. It is reassuring and makes a great difference in my walk with God, it improves confidence and propels me to share this wonderful freedom of being forgiven and set free, free to testify, free to do exploit for God, and do ministry. People are often being robbed of things and possession that means dear to them. If someone has been robbed of money, love, time, peace, business ideas, the guilty person should be brought to justice to restore the loss to the victim and pay an additional interest penalty.

The guilty person must take full responsibility and make restitution for his wrongs and add one fifth to the person he has wronged, and if you have wronged others, you ought to do more than apologies, you should look for ways to set matters right to leave the victim better off than when you have harmed them.

An example of how Solomon turned from God; he did not turn from God at once, or in a brief moment. Solomon spiritual coldness with a mirror of departure from God's laws, over sometimes those little sins grew until it resulted in his downfall, thus, this shows how the first step in turning away from God. It is often the sin that you don't pay much attention to, but the sin you excuse is the greatest trouble. Therefore, you should never let any sin go unchallenged in our lives, is an unchangeable sin spreading like deadly cancer 'does excuse it but confess it to God and ask him for strength to resist temptations.

Families establish homes and watchmen guard cities, but both these activities are futile unless God is with them, yet, family without God can never experience the spiritual bond God brings to the relationship. It is all right to get a right start, but it is important to watch each step upwards that God is still your portion, he who endures to the end will be saved. Therefore, backsliding people have always had a tendency for going backwards turning to evil, turning to Satan, turning back to the world, turning from the love of God. In as much as humans are prone to turn and wonder, yet, Christ knew about their plight and is willing and just to welcome them into his care. This person who has wandered from the truth is a believer who has fallen into sin, one who is no longer living a life consistent with his or her belief.

GOD'S WILLINGNESS TO FORGIVE

Generally, the sinfulness of man breaks fellowship with God, because mankind has a sinful nature, and has a tendency to believe their conduct is involved in many sins, but God is willing to forgive and accept us as we develop a loving fellowship amongst one another. Fellowship is one of the keys to spiritual growth, it occurs when Christian shares their walk with God in an atmosphere of love and respect. Anyone who denies the Son is in the Father, and the father is in him, whoever acknowledges the Son, acknowledges his Father also, to do so John firmly states, 'It is impossible to believe that the son is not in the father, and the father is not in the son.

God is more than willing to pour out his heart and make known his thoughts to us through his son Jesus Christ. To receive God's advice you must be willing to listen, and not allowing pride to stand in your way. However, if the penitent is willing and obedient, God will cause the spirit of wisdom to bubble forth, making his words known to them He invites them to repent and become wise, and turn from their reprove and return to God, turn to your duty, turn and live.

Those that love simplicity may find themselves under moral impotency to change their minds and ways, and no longer live as the heathen in the perverseness and emptiness of their soul and minds. We must be willing to strip ourselves of the former nature, and putting off and disregard our old un-renewed self which characterizes our previous manner of life becomes corrupt through lust and the desire that spring from delusion, because, none of us knows when you will be called on to witness of your faith in Jesus.

Normally there might not be enough time to prepare to respond, this might happen out of the blue someone says something that has challenged your beliefs, or having a casual conversation that turns to matters of principles, and you find yourself put on the spot. That is one reason why you should stay in a state of readiness to defend your faith at any time or for any season.

At the time of conversion, all your sins are forgiven present and future. Yet even after you become Christians, you might sin and still needs to confess, yet this kind of confession is not offered to gain God's acceptance, but to remove the barrier to fellowship that your sins have between you and God. Yet, it is difficult for some people to admit their faults and shortcomings, even to God. It takes humility and honesty to recognize your weaknesses and most of you would rather pretend that you are strong, but you need not fear revealing your sins to God, he knows them anyway.

God will not push you away from his presence no matter what you have done as long as you are willing to tell him all about it and draw to God and he will draw near to you. The availability of God's mercy must not become an excuse for careless living and immorality, forgiveness is the only way to God's power because everything in life comes at a cost.

Forgiveness is tied to obedience, to enable you to keep the words of Jesus, meaning to hear his voice and obey them. Jesus says, those who obey would die, he was talking about spiritual death, and not physical death, but even physical death will be eventually overcome, for those who follow Christ will be raised eternally with him.

Since forgiveness is guaranteed, do you have the freedom to sin as much as you want? The answer is, 'by no means! Such an attitude deciding ahead of time to take advantage of God's forgiveness does not make sin less serious, God Son died for sin shows you the dreadful seriousness of sin that Jesus paid for with his life so you could be forgiven. If this is genuine, it will be followed by a conversion by both all human beings

Conversion requires the commitment of the total personality, intellect, emotion and will. This is how the people respond to the message of the gospel, when they understand the nature of Christ atonement and felt the guilt and conviction, they will love God, and surrender their wills to the offer of salvation. Thus, conversion implies more than a mere attitude or verbal expressions, rather it involves the works that benefit repentance, it's an active, seeking, searching, and enquiring after God.

The apostle Paul in his preaching declared that 'men should repent and turn to God and prove their repentance by their deeds' The apostle Paul sent messengers with letters down to Antioch and having assembled the congregation they delivered the letter, and when the letters were read, it was regarding the gospel, the people rejoiced at the consolation and encouragement it brought them. Paul risks his life for a message that was offensive to the Jews and unbelieving Gentiles, and Jesus receives the same response to his message, to a worldly, materialistic mind. At times it might seem to risk so much to gain so little, but as you follow Christ, you will discover the temporary possession that looks so small comparing to the smallest in eternity.

The preaching of Paul was all practical; he showed the people the importance of repent of their sins to be sorry for them and to enter into a covenant against them. He urged them to change their minds their ways, and turning to God, they must not conceive any antipathy to sin, they must turn to God, but they must come into conformity to God, while they must turn to God in love and affection, and also return to God in duty and obedience, and return from the world and the flesh. Those who profess repentance must practice it, they must live a life of repentance, it is not enough to speak penitent words, but we must do works agreeable to those words that Paul spoke sternly on the subject of repentance.

At every opportunity, God encourages both Jews and Gentiles to repent and turn to him, do good works and live consistent life that is worthy of their repentance, that is necessary for salvation. This act of necessity means seeking God's favor by listening to his voice, as expressed in his word, and showing insight into his trueness through better understanding and appreciation of his ways and will. By observing and doing God's commandments will keep you loving and showing kindness, justice, and constantly hoping in God. It might be a good idea to abandon the use of religious images or the idolization of creatures to direct your hearts unswervingly to God and serve him alone, and not walking in the old ways and not in the ways of the nations, or one's way. (Acts 26:20)

By offering prayers, making a sacrifice, fasting, and observances of sacred festivals are meaningless and of no value with God, unless it is accompanied by good works, justice, the elimination of oppression and violence, this exercise of mercy. God was unhappy with the sacrifice of the people, and was revoking the system of sacrifices he had initiated with Moses; instead, God was calling for sincere faith and devotion. God knew the leaders were making traditional sacrifices and offering at holy celebrations, but they were still unfaithful to God in their hearts. In truth, sacrifices were to be an outward sign of their inward faith in God, but the outward sign became empty because no inward faith exists.

At the time of conversion a person receives a new heart and a new spirit, that person is changed of wrong motive and aim in life, he will produce a new frame of mind, disposition and moral force. For the one who has a life-changing course, the result is a new personality that was created according to God's will in true righteousness and loyalty, must be free from immorality, covetousness, violent speech and conduct.

The penitent must deprive the evil desire that is lurking in their members such as sexual vices, impurity, unholy desires, and all Covetousness. It might be useful to make a conscious decision to remove anything that supports or feeds these desires, and rely on the Holy Spirit power to help us live victoriously. Paul reminds us to consider ourselves as dead and unresponsive to sexual immorality, impurity, evil desires and greed. Just like a diseased limb of a tree, these practices must be cut off before they destroy us, we must make a conscious daily decision to remove anything that supports and feeds these desires, by relying on the Holy Spirit's power. (Col. 3:5-10)

It is easy to stand up for what you believe in church on a Sunday morning or among other Christian friends, nevertheless, we let Jesus down by our attitude when we are with others, we may not say, '*I am a not a Christian*, but by our words, our action, even by our silence, we go along with those who do not acknowledge

Jesus as Lord, because we may not wish to stand out as different and maybe unintentionally, get swept along with the tide.

The corrupted nature of man is called a man, it is the old man, as old Adam, from whom we derived sin, and it was bred in the bone, and was brought into the world with us. It is said to be corrupt, for sin is in the corruption of its faculties, and where it is not mortified, it grows daily more and worst. According to the deceitful lust, and has promise men happiness, but render them more miserable, these must be put off as an old garment; the new man must be put on, for it is not enough to shake off corrupted principles. (Eph. 4:17-24)

A person cannot turn from his sin by any power of their own, to this God answer, 'I will pour out my Spirit' therefore, the person who is converted, is born again; by the Spirit of the Lord. The Spirit will be poured out in the heart of the person as the Spirit was poured at Pentecost thus, genuine repentance has real impact, it generates force, and it moves the person to turn around. There is evidence of great earnestness, and clearing of one's godly fear, longing and fighting, and the absence and concern for rectifying wrongs committed, shows lack of true repentance, for we must all appear before the judgment seat of Christ, so that each one may receive his just reward, according to what he had done, whether good or evil.

FORGIVING ONE ANOTHER

Why we should forgive one another even our enemies? Jesus gave illustration; Peter came to Jesus and asked, "Lord, how many times shall I forgive my brother when he sins against me? 'Up to seven times,' Jesus answered, 'I tell you, not seven times, but, seventy times seven times. These were the guidelines Jesus introduce for dealing with those who sin against one another, and they were meant for Christians, not unbelievers. This is regarding sins that are committed against you and others, and conflict resolution in the context of the church. Jesus words were not meant to be license for a frontal attack on every person who hurts you or slights at us. This was not meant as license to start a destructive gossip campaign or to call for a church trial, they are designed to reconcile those who disagree so that all Christians can live in harmony.

Thus, the religious leaders taught the people their concept of forgiveness, that people should forgive those who wrong them only three times. But Peter was trying to be generous when he asked Jesus if seven times, was the perfect number enough times to forgive someone, but to his surprise, Jesus answered, *'Seventy times seven,'* meaning we should not even be keeping records or keeping track of how many times we forgive someone, but we should always forgive those who are truly repentant no matter how many times. Forgiveness involves both attitude and actions; if you should find it difficult to forgive someone who hurt you, you must respond with kind actions, and appropriate, and telling this person that you would like to heal your relationship between the two of you.

This can be follow up, by sending him or her a gift, lend a helping hand, smile at him or her; many times you will discover that the right actions lead to the right feelings, if we refuse others, we will not receive forgiveness ourselves from God. Forgiveness is an act of pardon, when we receive forgiveness from God our sins are blotted out, and we receive the remission. The truth of confession is admitting our sins; we are agreeing with God that our sin is truly sin and that we are willing to turn from it. This confession is to ensure that we don't conceal our sin from him and consequently from ourselves.

Why forgiveness requires the shedding of blood? The law requires that nearly everything should be cleansed with blood and without the shedding of blood there is no forgiveness of sins. This is no arbitrary decree on the part of bloodthirsty God as some has suggested, thus, there is no greater symbol of life than blood, moreover, there is life in the blood, and blood keeps us alive. Jesus shed his blood for our sins that we would not have to experience spiritual death, eternal separation from God. Jesus is the source of life and not death that is why; Jesus gives us his own life to pay our penalty that we might live. Christ shed his blood and dies on the cross and was buried, after three days Christ rose from the grave and proclaimed victory over sin and death.

A story was told how a servant contracted a debt by wastefulness and willfulness after he was found out, he could be left to lie in the outcome, his lord commanded him and his wife and children to be sold, and all that he had, for payments are made to pay his debt. Whatever sin deserves, this is its wages. Notice even by selling everything it could not amount to the total worth of the debt owing. Thus, the servant fell at his Lord's feet and worshipped him, he begged submissively and very importunate, he pleaded, '*have patience on me and I will pay all.* (Hebrews 10:22)

In this instant, sinners are commonly careless about the pardon of their sins, till they come under arrest of some awaking word, the stout heart will fail, when God set the sins in order before them. Although he begs his master time to pay the debt, time, patience and forbearance are a great favor, yet it is folly to think that, these alone will save us, therefore, retrieves are not pardons, he promise payment, have patience awhile and I will pay, he promised, although he knew he had nothing to pay with, this is the state of sinners, how close their pride stands out, they are convinced, but not humbled.

The God of infinite mercy is very ready, out of pure compassion, to forgive the sins of those that humble themselves before him. If God should deal with us in strict justice as we would be condemned as insolent debtors. Therefore justice demands satisfaction. Adam and Eve probably had no idea of the vast consequences that would result from their brief and singular act of disobedience.

Examples can be traced of the carelessness of most people who follow unlawful pleasure and believe it is easy to give them up whenever they please, but, ah, sin that repeated will become customary, and customs will become an ingenious habit, and habit, in the end, assumes the form of necessity; and the man becomes bound with his cords and be led captive by the devil at his will.

Sharing one's faith and fellowship can be an effective way to win others to faith, also communicating love in the church and the assembly; will be strengthened as best practice. Sometimes fellowship requires confessing one to another as we strive to develop a unity of spirit and mind. Some work to hinder fellowship of the brethren and practice sin that is hated by God, even though there are facts of the basic truth that all people are sinners by nature and by practice, but love will prevail over evil.

It may seem as if there were no end to the consequences of sin, but blessed be the Lord and Savior of our Lord Jesus Christ who came with a remedy of salvation to justify the wrath of God on the human race. Before Christ coming Gentiles and Jews kept themselves apart from one another. Jews considered the Gentiles were beyond God's salvation and therefore without hope. The Gentiles resented the Jewish claims, thus, Christ revealed the total sinners of both Jews and Gentiles and, and there he offered his salvation to both.

Only Christ breaks down the wall of partitions and reconciles all believers to God, and unites us in one body. Christ alone destroys the barrier that people build between themselves, because these walls have been removed, we can have real unity with people who are not like us. Our hostility against each other often has been put to death by the Holy Spirit; therefore, we are no longer foreigners or aliens to God. We are all built into a holy temple with God our chief cornerstone.

CHAPTER THIRTEEN

CONVERSION

Conversion has various aspects, for example, the conversion of a building, a car, place, and other sorts of conversion. Normally conversion of a build might be in a state of dilapidation and needs to be pulled down and rebuild. The foundation of that building must be examined to see if the foundation is firm to endure the knocks of rebuilding.

Conversion is consisting of repentance and faith in Christ, therefore, human response to the offer of salvation that God provides for mankind. When a person becomes a Christian; the dilapidated state of old life needs renewal; this is where regeneration takes place. Thus, regeneration is when God comes down to the site of the worst disaster in the universe, we as sinners and completely removes the deadly toxic elements from the core of our being. It is called regeneration, meaning God's provision for us to be born again through the new birth, to give us his life.

Conversion implies more than a mere attitude or verbal expressions, rather, it involves the works that befit repentance. It is an active, seeking, inquiring for God with all one's heart and soul. It is of necessity, means seeking God's favor by listening to his voice as expressed in his word, and showing insight into his trueness through better understanding and appreciation for his ways and will. Why do we need regeneration? It is because a disaster has stricken each of us and has rendered us uninhabitable by God, and human's nature from birth is uninhabitable to God. We were born with a heart that was emitting a deadly radiant far worse than the gamma rays of that exploded reactor; we are producers of the element most hated by God in the universe which is called conversion, people offer prayers, sacrificing, fasting and observance of sacred festivals accompanied by good works, yet, it is of no value to God. By abandoning the use of religious images of the idolizing creatures are meaningless and of no value with God unless accompanied by good work, justice, the illumination of oppression and violence and exercise of mercy.

The expressions of a man that is newly converted or who is recently converted can means a newly planted or newly grown. Such a man must not be assigned ministerial duties in a congregation lest he becomes puffed up with pride and fall into judgment and becomes Devilish in behavior. Thus, true Christians are those who believe inwardly and outwardly that Jesus death has allowed God to offer forgiveness and eternal life as a gift. They have accepted the gift through faith and are seeking to live a life of obedience and gratitude for what God has done for them. Thus, conversion marks a halt in a person' wrong course, and the rejection of that wrong way and the determination to take a right course, if genuine it will follow by conversion.

Conversion means simply to turn back, turn around, or return, or, if it is used in a spiritual sense it can mean, and refers either a turning away from God, or turning back to a sinful course, or turning to God from previously wrong way (1Kings 8:3) The converted sinners on earth are a matter of joy and rejoicing in heaven. The greatest sinner may be brought to repentance, while there is life there is hope, and the worst is not to have despaired of God's will, he delights to show them mercy. God rejoices in all his works in particular in the works of his grace. He rejoices not only in the conversion of nations but even over one sinner that repents through one. There is no joy over one sinner that repents lesser than the ninety and nine just persons. God rejoices to do good to the penitent, and the good angels will be glad that mercy is shown to them. The redemption of mankind was a matter of joy in the presence of the angels, for they say, *'Glory to God in the highest.'*

A NEW HEART SPIRIT

All converted human needs a new heart that Christ may live in them. A person cannot continue living with an old heart, old, old things pass away and all will become anew. The expression of a newly converted person, or recently, is referred to as a new plant, such or newly grown. Such a person should not be assigned to ministerial duties in a congregation, lest he becomes puffed up with pride and falls into the judgment passes on the Devil. God promise to give a new heart to those who believe in him, in society people admires assertiveness, independence, and defiance of authority. A change of motive and aim in life produces a new frame of mind, disposition and moral force. For the person whose life course has changed, the result is a new personality that was created according to God's will in true righteousness and loyalty, free from immorality, covetousness, violent speech and conduct. From such ones God causes his spirit to bubble forth, and making his words known to them. Thus, genuine repentance has a real impact; it generates force and can move the person to turn around.

Hence, Jesus says to the church in Laodicea, *'be zealous and repent'* there will be evidence of great earnestness that clears away Godly fear and longing to right the wrongs. In a new relationship with God, these qualities can become stubbornness, self-importance, and refusal to listen or change, but rather if they allow unchecked stubbornness can become a way of life and hostility towards God, and sometimes to other people.

The prophet Jeremiah was called and used by God to speak to the people on his behalf. He was not afraid to openly give unpopular criticism, he bravely, spoke about the king, the officials, the priest and prophets. The prophet spoke to the people and challenges them regarding their social and moral behavior. The people could either obey, or silence him, but they chose to silence him, even though they did not think they needed Jeremiah to correct them, because their false prophet did already tell them what they wanted to hear. It is important to carefully listen to what people might be telling you regarding your faith in God, sometimes they come in different forms trying to test if you truly believe or are just a follower. (Jer. 18:18)

NEW SPIRIT

The spirit in man has must be changed in every aspect since man was born in sin and happen in iniquity, and although Jesus died to set men free there is still a tendency in man to sin and needs a change of spirit. God promises to give a new heart to those who believe and obey follow him. God promise he will put a new spirit in the believer, though God is a God who loves, he is also a God of perfect justice. His perfect love causes him to be merciful to those who recognize their sin and turn back to him, and God cannot wink at those who willfully sin. Wicked people die from both physical and spiritual death, and God takes no joy in their deaths he would prefer they turn to him and have eternal life. Likewise, we should never rejoice in the misfortunes of non-believers, instead, we should do all in our power to bring them back to faith, and making statements, *'I told you so'*.

People should not spend time looking for loopholes in God's law, instead, look for and find God's standards and obey them. If men renounced their old direction and turn to God he will abundantly pardon. You can begin by faith, and trusting in God's power to change the heart, and help you to live for him.

RETURNING

Not everyone finds it easy to make a right turn, either to the right or to the left, more so those who run away from God and are warned to return to him on his terms. People have always felt comfortable doing their own thing until they find themselves in deep waters, then will decide to cry to God for help. For instance, the people of Israel mourned and sorrow gripped the nation for 20 years when the ark was put away like an unwanted box in the attic, and it seems as if the Lord had abandoned his people. (1 Samuel 7:3)

Samuel was now a grown man who aroused the people to action by saying if there were truly sorry they should do something about it. It is so easy for us to complain about our problems, even to God, while we refuse to change and do what he requires, sometimes we refuse to take the advice God has already given us. Have you ever felt as if God has abandoned you at a time when problems seem to overtake you? It is best to check if there is anything God had already told you to do; you may not receive new guidance from God until you acted on his previous instructions.

Samuel urged the Israelites to get rid of their foreign gods, idols that are useless gods of wood and stone that are just as dangerous. Therefore whatever holds the first place in your heart will control us will act as our god. For example money, success, material goods, pride, or anything else can be an idol; and takes the place of God in your life. The Lord alone is worthy of our service and worship, therefore, we must not allow anything to rival him, if anything stands in our way and God we must ask God to dethrone it and make the true and living God our priority.

PRODUCTIVE LIFE

The life of a person can only achieve productively by the remission from sin; thus remission means to forgive based on Christ's death. Therefore, people who lived before Jesus under the old covenant could only approach God through a priest, or an animal sacrifice. Now all people can come directly to God through faith because Jesus death made us acceptable in God's eyes. After all this bad news about our sinfulness and God's condemnation, Paul gave the wonderfully news, he said, 'there is a way to be declared not guilty' only, by trusting Jesus Christ to put away our sins, making us right with God, and to empower us to live, the way he taught us.

Therefore, God's solution is available to all regardless of what background, or our past behavior. Here, the questions have ended the discussions stopped with the report that God had given the Holy Spirit to the Gentiles, this was a turning point to the early church, they had to accept those whom God had chosen, even the Gentiles. But the joy over the conversion of Gentiles was not unanimous, this continues to be a struggle for some Jewish Christians throughout the first century. The Old

Covenant was a shadow of the new, and point towards the day when Jesus himself would be the final and ultimate sacrifice for sin. Rather, an unblemished Lamb slain on the altar, the perfect Lamb of God was slain on the cross, a sinless sacrifice so that our sins could be forgiven once for all, and all those who believe in Christ receive forgiveness.

REMISSION OF SIN

Repentance is changing of mind for the better, and hearty amending your ways with abhorrence of your past sins' After repentance the repented sinner must now seek baptism is immersing in water, except in the case of Jesus, he was divinely provided symbol associated with repentance both on the part of those among the Jewish nation which had failed to keep God's covenant while it was in force, and on the part of the people of the nations who turned around to render sacred service to God.

The beginning of the New Testament was the gospel of John the Baptist, his baptism and the saving of the great day. In John' way of living there was the beginning of a gospel spirit, for it bespoke great self-denial, mortification of the flesh, a holy contempt of the world, and nonconformity to it. The more we get loose of the body, and live above the world, the better we are prepared for Jesus Christ.

After John was put in prison, Jesus went into Galilee, proclaiming the good news of God, 'The time has come, he said, 'The kingdom of God is near. 'Repent and believe the good news' In John's preaching and baptizing there was the beginning of the gospel doctrine and ordinances. John preached the remission of sins, which is the great privilege, and preaches repentance; he preached the great preeminence of Christ. To guide people there must be a renovation of their heart and reformation of their lives. (Mark1:22)   We have gone through some of the requirements necessary to bridge sin's gap and brought mankind back to God.

Please turn your attention to the second introduction of God's recovery plan for man's existence.

CHAPTER FOURTEEN

PART TWO

SPIRITUAL UNION

Spiritual union is the Holy Trinity designates one eternal God in unity, yet, existing in three eternal persons. The member of the Trinity is equal in nature, distinct in person, and subordinate in duties. For example, the Son is eternally begotten by the Father, so Jesus is submissive to do the work of the Father, yet he is equal in nature to him. The father is the source of authority, the Son is the channel, and the Holy Spirit is the agent whereby authority is exercised. Therefore, all members of the Trinity as God, and a distinct person, and, each member of the Trinity should be so recognized in worship, by Christian congregations.

When a person becomes a Christian you receive evidence from the Holy Spirit to live in Christ because you acknowledge that Jesus is the Son of God and acknowledged the Holy Spirit, and God's presence is in our life as proof that you belong to him. The Holy Spirit also gives you the power to love with one another and love even the unlovable, that is the sense of God's love for you, and also drawing your love for him. The ground of all this is by the shedding of the love of God in our hearts and the sense of God's love will cause us not to be ashamed either in our hope in him, or our suffering for him.

God has poured his love in the believer through the Holy Spirit, whom he has given, and all three members of the Trinity are involved in salvation. The father loved the world so much that he sent his Son to bridge the gap between us. The father and the Son send the Holy Spirit to fill our lives with love and enable us to live by his power, and with all this loving care we can never do less than serving him. John gave a true account about Jesus, he stated that he talked with him, touched him, and he knew Jesus was more than a mere spirit. In the very first sentence of John's letter, he established that Jesus had been alive before the world began, and also that he lived among men and women, in other words, he was both divine and human. Therefore, Jesus divine-human nature is the pivotal issue of Christianity' and anyone can claim to speak for God, and the world is full of these, especially the false teachers.

As you consistently training your conscience to be employed both to search and judge ourselves, but not only in one particular way, but seeking the right way to follow. During the times of affliction, it is reasonable to consider our ways what is amiss and to repent, and amend for the future, by so doing we all need to turn again to the Lord. Since it has never been well with us since we forsook him, but as we turn again to him, our hearts must go along with our prayers we must lift our hearts with our hands, and pour out our souls in humility, because praying is lifting our souls to God in heaven forever. (Lam 3:40-42)

PROMPTED BY HOLY SPIRIT

The Holy Spirit is the third person in the Holy Trinity. Since Jesus departed from his earthly ministry, the responsibility was put on the Holy Spirit to be with Jesus followers here on earth. The work of the Holy Spirit's working among believers is vast, it is deep to discern the depth of men's thinking, wide as the ocean, and he covers all human needs. Why God sent the Holy Spirit? The Trinity is a description of the unique relationship of God the Father, the Son and the Holy Spirit. If Jesus had stayed on earth, his physical presence would have limited the spread of the gospel, because physically he could be in only one place at a time. After Christ was taken up to heaven, he would be spiritually present everywhere through the Holy Spirit. The Holy Spirit was sent that God would be with and within his followers after Christ return to heaven.

The Holy Spirit has many functions, some of his functions Holy Spirit are to give comfort, guidance, and teaching Christian believers to know the truth, and reminding them of Jesus's words, giving them the right words to say, and filled them with power. At Pentecost the Holy Spirit was made available to all who believed in Jesus, we receive the Holy Spirit and are baptized by him when we receive Jesus Christ. 1 Corn 12:3

The Spirit marks the beginning of the Christian experience; therefore we cannot belong to Christ without his Spirit, and we cannot be in the body of Christ except by baptism by the Spirit. The spirit is the power of our new lives, and he begins a long life of change as we become more like Christ. When we receive Christ by faith, we begin an immediate personal relationship with God, and there is a particular assurance given they should now shortly receive the Holy Ghost.

At Pentecost the apostles were given a command to wait; this was to raise their expectations. They must wait till the time appointed, which is not yet, and not many days, hence. Those who have this promise must be patient and wait. They must wait in the place appointed; in Jerusalem was where Christ was put to shame, therefore, this hour he will have this honor done to Jerusalem to teach us to forgive our enemies and persecutors.

The apostle was now put on a public character and Jerusalem was the fittest place for the lights to shine, the blessings 'they should receive, 'You shall receive the Holy Ghost' The disciples were already being breathed upon with the Holy Ghost, and they had found the benefits of it, but now they shall have larger measures on his gifts, grace, and comforts. You shall be cleansed and purified by the Holy Spirit, as the priest was baptized and cleansed with water when they were consecrated to the sacred functions. (John 20:22)

First, the gift of the Holy Ghost was given by promise of the father; the spirit of God is not given as the spirit of men is given us, by the word of God, that the gift might be more valued able, and be surer, it is by grace and might receive by faith. As Christ, so, is the Spirit is received by faith. (Act 1:4-6)

Secondly, it was the promise of the Father, of Christ's father, our father, he will give the Spirit, as the fairer of mercies; it is the promise of the father. **Thirdly,** this promise of the father they had heard from Christ many times, confirms the promise we have heard from Jesus. The Spirit unites the Christian community in Christ, the Holy Spirit can be experienced by all, and he works through all. The message concerning faith, if we declare Jesus is Lord and believes with our heart that God raised him from the dead. (Romans 10:9)

The apostle Paul informs us no one who is speaking by the Spirit of God says, *Jesus is cursed'* and no one can say, *Jesus is Lord*, except by the Spirit, he says, anyone can claim to speak to God, and the world is full of them, for instance, false teachers.

Paul gave us a test to help us discern whether or not a message is really from God if anyone does not confess Christ as Lord, do not believe them, and anyone acting under the influence, nor by the power of the Spirit of God, who disowned and blasphemed Christ. For the Spirit of God could never so far contradict itself as to declare Christ accursed, and therefore, no man can be called to Christ Lord without believing and dependence upon him, unless their faith is wrought by the Holy Ghost.

JESUS INCARNATION

Scripture spoke regarding Jesus incarnation; it was the act of pre-existent of God voluntarily assuming a human body and human nature, without ceasing to be God. Jesus became a human being, the man called Jesus. He did not give up his deity to become human but set aside his right to his glory and power. In a submission to the father's will, Christ limited his power and knowledge, Jesus of Nazareth was subjected to place, time, and many other human limitations.

What made his humanity unique was his freedom from sin in his full humanity; Jesus showed us everything about God's character that can be conveyed in human terms. The carnation is explained further in Romans 8:9 you are not controlled by the sinful nature, but by the Spirit, if the Spirit of God lives in you, and if anyone does not have the Spirit of Christ, he does not belong to Christ.

You may wonder if you are a Christian, here is your answer; a Christian is anyone who has the Spirit of God living in him or her. If you have sincerely trusted Christ for your salvation and acknowledged him as Lord, then the Holy Spirit has come into your life.

The apostle explained the mystery of godliness, the secret of how we become godly, Jesus appeared in a body. As a man, Jesus lived a perfect life and so he is a perfect example of how to live, as God Jesus gives us the power to do what is right. Jesus was a man, his incarnation is the basis of us being right with God, and was vindicated by the Spirit. Jesus resurrection power showed that the Holy Spirit's power was in him. He was seen by angels, and was taken up to glory, Jesus is divine, therefore we cannot please God on our own, and we must depend on Christ. (1Tim 3:16)

John says how to recognize the Spirit of God; every spirit that acknowledges that Jesus Christ came in the flesh is from God, the mutual relationship living in Christ as he lives in us shows itself in Christians who keep these three essential commands. Those who believe in Christ will love the brothers and sisters and live morally upright lives. The spirit presence is not only spiritual and mystical, but is also practical, and our conduct will verify his presence. (1 John 4:2)

The Lordship of Christ is at the name of Jesus, every knee shall bow in heaven and on earth and under the earth, and every tongue confesses that Jesus Christ is Lord to the glory of God the father. God the Father hath exalted Jesus his whole person the human nature as well as the divine. His exaltation here is made to consist in honor and power; he had a name above every name, and every knee must bow to God. The whole creation must be in subjection to God and things in heaven, and things in earth, and things under the earth, the inhabitation of heaven and earth, the living and the dead. The kingdom of Christ reaches to heaven and earth and all the creatures in each, and all the dead as well as the living, to the glory of God the father. (Phil.2:11)

CHAPTER FIFTEEN

JUSTIFICATION BY FAITH

The acts of Justification are God's of declaring us *'not guilty* for our sins, the moment we believe we are put into a state of being justified. We are justified by Christ blood, and our justification is ascribed to the blood of Christ, and without blood, there can be no remission of sin. In all the propitiatory sacrifices, the sprinkling of the blood was the essence of the sacrifice. The great privilege that flows to us from the death of Christ is justification from sin, and therefore, we were acquitted from that guilt which alone could have ruined us, as we have accepted the favor of God which alone could set us free. Christ is who have purchased our justification for us, and applied it to us by his intercession.

Christ currency is eternal life, a new life with God that begins on earth and continues with God, 'Have you made your choice?' Have you ever felt worried whether you are a Christian or not, even though you believe that Jesus Christ is Lord? Be reminded someone who is a Christian has the Spirit of God living in him or her. If you have sincerely trusted God for your salvation and acknowledged him as Lord, then the Holy Spirit will come into your life, and you will become Christian. If you are waiting on some sign and feelings, you will know the Holy Spirit has come; you must believe he has come because Jesus promises he would send you the Holy Spirit.

The Holy Spirit working within will reveal the reality that Christ is God's son and eternal life comes through him. If God justifies and reconciled us when we were still enemies, how much more will he save us when we are justified and reconcile? Therefore, being justified by faith, we have peace with God through our Lord Jesus Christ. Since it was man's sin that breeds the quarrel between us and God, therefore, justification takes away the guilt immediately by removing the obstacles, and the peace is made, by faith, so we lay hold of God's arm and receive strength to receive his peace, like Abraham who was justified by faith, and it was accounted to him for righteousness.

For instance, justification can be described as when a judge in a court of law declares the defendant *'not guilty'* all the charges are then removed from his record. Legally, it is as if the person had never been accused. When God forgives our sins, all our records are wiped clean, from God's perspective, it is as though we had never sinned. Justification is the fruit of the death of Christ, and thus, Christians are justified by the blood of Jesus, our sin is pardoned and the enemy is slain, an end is made of iniquity, and everlasting righteousness is brought in.

From the example of Abraham, his faith was fastened on the promises of God and on believing, he accepted God as righteous man, therefore, those of faith are the children of Abraham and so are we, God would justify the heathen worthy in the way of faith, therefore, in the seed of Abraham is in Christ, and not the Jews only, but also the Gentiles. We are blessed as Abraham was; it was through faith in the promises of God that he was blessed and it is only in the same way that others obtain this privilege, otherwise, we can't be justified but by faith, because the law condemns us.

PEACE WITH GOD

There is more in God's peace than only a cessation of enmity, now there is friendship and loving-kindness, as we acknowledge that God is neither the worst enemy nor the best friend. Christ has called his disciples friends, and a man would not do any more to make him happy than to have God as his friend, this is made perfect Christ as our great peacemaker between God and man. We have access by faith into God's grace in wherein we stand.

This is a further privilege afforded us, not only peace but also grace, having peace with God, which may differ from peaceful feelings such as calmness and tranquility. Peace with God means that we have been reconciled with him, and there is no more hostility between us, neither there is any sin blocking our relationship with God. The happy estate of the saints is a state of grace, we have access into his grace, and we could not have gotten into it by ourselves, but we were led into it as a blind man, or lame, or weak people are led. Paul says, as believers were are standing in the place of the highest privilege, this grace in which we now stand where God has declared us not guilty, and he has drawn us close to ourselves, instead of being enemies, we have become his friend.

Paul's experience of conversion how he was made nigh, it was Christ who introduces him and led him by the hand into this grace. By whom we have access by faith, by Christ who is the author, and by faith as the means of this access, and have a happy standing in this state, we must not lie down, as if we have already attained, but stand as if we are pressing forward. We stand firmly and safely as soldiers stand that keeps their ground. Grace is God's gift of salvation in Christ, receiving it brings peace. In a world of noise, confusion, and relentless pressures, people long for peace. Many have given up the search, thinking it is impossible to find it, but true peace of heart and mind is available to the Christians through faith in Jesus Christ. God's peace is different from world peace, true peace is not found in passive, thinking in the absence of conflict or good feelings, and it comes from knowing that God is in control. Our citizenship in Gods kingdom is sure, our destiny is set and we can have victory over sin, let Gods peace guard your heart against anxiety.

Imagine not be anxious about anything, it would seem impossible; we have worried at work, in our homes at school, neighbor, Paul advice to turn over all our worries into prayers. Sometimes we may believe our peace should come to us with no effort, but David says, we are to seek and peruse peace. A person who wants peace cannot be argumentative and contentious, because the peaceful relationship comes from our efforts at peacemaking, working hard at living with others each day.

PEACE WITH OTHERS

Peace is the opposite of unrest and uneasiness, a broken relationship can hinder our relationship of peace with God. Believers are to seek lasting peace with one another and peace with God. It is most comforting to be with peace within ourselves, and then we will be able to maintain peace among, family, church, community and even among our enemies. If we have a problem or grievance with a friend, we should resolve the problem as soon as possible; otherwise, that space can be blocked with corroded with malice, forgiveness, hatred, resentment and the rest of the works of the flesh. We are hypocrites if we claim to love God while we hate others. Our attitudes towards others reflect our relationship with God.

If anyone says I love God and do not love his brother whom he has seen, he cannot love God whom he has not seen. It is easy to say we love God when that love does not cost us anything more than weekly attendance at religious services, but the real test of our love for God is how we treat the people right in front of us, our family members and fellow believers. Therefore, we cannot love God and neglecting to love those who are created in his image. Even though the psalmist reported that when he was for peace his enemies were for war because peacemaking is not always popular. Some people prefer to fight for what they believe, rather, thinking that peacemaking is in the hope of winning, but someone must be the loser.

The glory of peacemaking may actually produce two winners; and peacemaking is God's way so we should prayerfully attempt to be peacemakers, and times of peace are not just for resting, it allows us to prepare for times of trouble, and restlessness, therefore, we must use our times well. David was a man of prayer, he prays not only for his peace and prosperity but peace for his brothers and friends in Jerusalem. This was an intercessory prayer on behalf of others. David was praying for peace which is more than the mere absence of conflict, but it suggests completeness, health, justice, prosperity, and protection. Real peace comes from faith in God because he alone embodies all the characteristics of peace. Finding peace of mind and peace in others, you must first find peace with God, and then in yourself. (Psalms 122:6-9)

By making peace with God and with others acts as a building block that even in the face of turmoil, creates a sense of stability and dependability. There are times when the sea is calm and seemly undisturbed, such as at sunset on a calm summer's evening, yet there are other times when the sea rages, driven by high winds, with huge waves. Even when the sea is raging on the surface, research findings indicate there is no noticeable effect of a few hundred feet down. Christians must possess the deep, abiding, inner peace and stability that the Holy Spirit gives in his abiding presence. Those who have this kind of inner peace will be able to edify others as they interact with them.

CHAPTER SIXTEEN

WATER BAPTISM

The word *baptism* derives from a verb meaning to immerse, or to identify with, Spiritual baptism happens when the new believer is united with Christ and his people and is identified with his death, burial, and resurrection. Water baptism should be practice after conversion; hence it is sometimes called the first step to faith. Christians should seek water baptism after conversion. Baptism through emersion indicates burying old sins and old habits from our former life before conversion, but perhaps Christ example is the compelling one, thus, water baptism is the act of immersing the new believer in water as a testimony that he or she has experienced the reality of conversion. Baptism symbolizes submission to Christ and a willingness to live God's way, and identification with God's covenant people.

There are four different aspects of baptism together with related questions, *John's baptism,* *water baptism* of Jesus and his followers, *baptism into Christ death,* and *baptism with fire.*

Baptism is an outward sign of commitment to be accomplished by an inward change of attitude leading to the change of life, by the work of the Holy Spirit, and all who were baptized are obliged to commit to Christ their rule, so, we are by baptism bound to obey. Except in the case of Jesus who was a divine symbol associated with repentance both on the part of those among force the Jewish nation, which had failed to keep God's covenant while it was in force and secondly, on the part of the people of the nation who turned back to render sacrifice to

God. *Secondly*, baptism must be administrated in the name of the Father, the Son, and the Holy Ghost. This was an authority from heaven, and not of man, for Christ ministers act by authority from the three persons in the Godhead.

Calling upon the name of the Father, Son, and Holy Ghost, and actions must be sanctified by prayer and particular the waters of baptism, this was intended the summary of the first principles of the Christian religion. Our assent is to the scriptures revelation concerning God the Father, Son, and Holy Ghost.

Christ gave instruction to his disciples for executing the commission by the sacred rite baptism, 'Go into all nations, preach the gospel to all nations work miracles among them, and persuade them, to come with themselves and bring their children with into the church of Christ' It is in the name of the Father, believing him to be the father of our Lord Jesus Christ, and our father, our Creator, Preserver, and Benefactor. The disciples were expected to be baptized believers because baptism unites believers with Jesus Christ, in his, or her death to sin, and resurrection to new life.

Another explanation put it, it is into the name of the Son, the Lord Jesus Christ, the Son of God, in baptism we assent, as Peter said, 'Thou are the Christ Son of the living God, and consent as Thomas did, My Lord, and My God. We accept Christ to be our Prophet, Priest and King and give ourselves to be taught and ruled by him.

Seeking water baptism has a long history since the days of Jesus and John the Baptist. Some desire the rite of baptism by sprinkling water on the head, but in reality, baptism is emersion in water. Water Baptism is a foundation to be rightly recognized and daily remembered, but should not be repeated.

Baptism is for those who believe in Jesus and requires an understanding of God's word, and make an intelligent decision to present oneself to do the reveal will of God. It was evident when at Pentecost, when Peter was confronted regarding baptism, Peter gave a clear and concise answer, he echoed, 'Repent change your views and purpose to accept the will of God in your inner selves. Instead, of rejecting the warning, 'Repent and be baptized every one of you, in the name of Jesus Christ for the forgiveness and be released from your sins, and you shall receive the gift of the Holy Spirit.

Some rebelled after hearing the message and chose to stay in their comfort zone of unrepentant condition that will eventually lead to death. Instead of accepting Christ as Savior would create newness in Christ Jesus and this will occur within the inner man. Thirdly, before and after baptism the believer must be taught and encouraged to observe, in the teaching the bible, to observe all things, whatsoever the gospel have commanded.

The believer must have a desire to be obedient learners to grow and develop spiritually. The believer might have a question, but as they follow on they will be enlightened by the Holy Spirit guidance for the rest of their Christian journey. Our consent to covenant relationship to God the Father, Son, and Holy Ghost, the sacrament that is an oath, it is an oath of abjuration, by which we renounce the world and the flesh, as rivals with God for the throne in our hearts. An oath of allegiance, by which we resign and give up ourselves to God, to be his, body, soul, and spirit, to be governed by his will, and made happy in his favor, we then will become his men.

John's the Baptist made disciples, his ministry was successful, never mind the opposition he had to encounter. It was Christ prerogative to make disciples, to form and fashioned them according to his will. The Christian is made and not born as such, John baptized those whom he made disciples not himself, but by the ministry of his disciples. John baptized the people who came to him to be baptized, as a sign that they had asked God to forgive their sins and has decided to live as he wanted them to live., and John owned himself to be the minster of the outward sign, he directed the people to the one who was greater than himself, and John reminded the people, he said, '*I baptized with water.*'

Therefore, after baptism, the guilt of sin is buried, although guilty feelings can come from many directions, sometimes guilt is brought on by the complexities of life, but the Spiritual mandate rings true that, 'There is now, no condemnation to them who are in Christ Jesus, who walk not after the flesh, but after the Spirit' This was to demonstrate an unspeakable privilege to those who are in Christ that there is, therefore, no condemnation, He does not say there are no accusations against, for this was thrown out, and he does not say there is nothing in them that deserves condemnation, for this they see it and own it, but it shall not be their ruin, neither did he say there is no cross, no affliction to them, for this there maybe, but no condemnation.

If we should think of our old sinful life as dead and buried, then we should have a powerful motive to resist sin, we can consciously choose to treat the desire and the temptations of the old nature as if they were dead. Then we can continue to enjoy our wonderful new life with Jesus. The repentant must therefore seek to be baptized in water. The process of baptism is immersion including submersion in water, in the bible to immerse in water was the same as being baptized. Jesus was baptized immersing into his death; therefore, believers were buried with him through our baptism. When a person is immersed in water by baptism that person is temporarily buried under out of sight, and then lifted out. Baptism identifies us with Christ and with the community of believers; it is a condition of discipline and a sign of faith.

This benefit arises from them being in Christ, and by their union with him through faith. Thus, this privilege came by justification, which the law could not do, it could neither justify nor sanctify. Therefore, the law could not make anything perfect, because it was weak, and yet, the weakness of the law was not through any defect in the law, but through the flesh, the corruption of human nature. There was an argument between the disciples of John and the Jews regarding baptism, the matter in dispute was about purifying about religious washing.

We may suppose that John's disciples were much taught by John their leader was regarding the right path. No doubt with much assurance applauded the purifying that was in among them. It was not expected that the Jews in this dispute could deny the excellent nature and design of John's baptism. (Romans 8:1)The complaints what John's disciples made to their master concerning Christ and his baptizing, they said, *Rabbi*, he that was with you, he baptized, and all men come to him, they suggest that Christ was setting up a baptism of his own, it was a piece of presumption as if John first set up this rite of baptizing if it were a patent for the invention.

They thought it was a piece of ingratitude to John, they complain as if Jesus owns all his reputation to the honorable character John gave of him, but Christ did not need John's testimony; John was just bearing witness of Christ. The problem was, 'All men came to him' John's answer was no disturbance to him; he checked the complaint and took the occasion to confirm the testimonies he had formerly borne was of Christ the Superior.

John reminds his disciples not to envy those that have a larger share of gifts than we have, or move on in a larger sphere that would have promoted him, except he received it from above, from God Spirit whom he gives without measure. Therefore, we should never grudge or feel inferior to others in the gift of usefulness, John echoed, let me remind you again, and again that I'm not the Christ, yet, I am sent before him.

The apostle Paul declared that Christ did not send him to baptize, he wasn't minimizing the importance of baptism but he was commanded by Jesus himself and practice by the early church. Paul was emphasizing that no one person should do everything, his gift was preaching the gospel, and that was what he did. However, Christian ministers should be a team effort, no preacher or teacher is a compatible link between God and people, and no individual can do all that Paul did, and must be contented with the contribution God has given us and carry it out wholeheartedly.

In the church in Paul's day, water immersion was the usual form of baptism. That is, the new Christian was completely 'buried' in water. The people understood this form of baptism to symbolize the death and resurrection of new life with Christ. If you want to follow Christ, you must repent and be baptized.

Therefore, baptism in New Testament theology is a loyalty oath, a public avowal of who is on the Lord's side in the cosmic war between good and evil. Andrew one of Jesus disciples found his Brother Simon and says to him, we have found the Messiah, which, is being interpreted, the Christ, and brought him to Jesus. His finding implies he was seeking him, when Jesus saw him he knew who he was, and says to him, and; 'You are Simon the son of Jonah' Jesus saw not only who Simon was, but whom he would become.

This is a testimony of a new convert who wishes to share his glorious discovery with others, especially with another member of his family. Andrew's testimony was positive, he speaks excellently, we have found, Andrew did not confess and say, 'I think I've found a good thing" or hope this is it" he said, rather, "I have found the Christ" How heartwarming it is to see new converts crying out, *"I have found him,'* and he brought him to Jesus, the fountain-head, this was an instance of true love to his brother. We ought to have a particular concern and application to seek the spiritual welfare of those that are related to us, it was an effect of his conversion with Christ and Andrew knew there was enough in Christ for all. (John 1:41-42)

JESUS BAPTISM BY JOHN THE BAPTIST

Christ stood among the common people and was one of them who was baptized by John; God himself is often near to us than we are aware of. The principles of the commission of baptism to the disciple all nations, was to carry out this instruction first they must admit themselves to a sacrifice of baptism, Jesus command to his disciples, 'Go into all the world, preach the gospel to them work miracles among them, persuade to bring their children with them into the church of Christ, then admit them into the church by washing them with water.'

Jesus the Messiah and presented himself to John for baptism, after a few questions from John Jesus, John eventually accepted the honor to baptized Jesus. After Jesus was baptized, then he was anointed by God's Holy Spirit. Jesus thereby became the King – Designated, the one recognized by God court as having the legal right to the Davidic throne. John the Baptist cried out in the wilderness, 'I indeed baptize you with water, but there is one coming after me, he shall baptize you with the Holy Ghost not many days hence.

The book of Matthew informs us that John was explaining how Jesus baptism would be greater than his, while, one day while John was baptizing in the Jordan River, suddenly Jesus came to him and asked to be baptized. John felt unqualified; rather he wanted Jesus to baptize him, we may want to ask, why did Jesus need to be baptized?
Good question!

Jesus baptism was not for the repentance for sin, because Jesus never sinned, but, it was to fulfill all righteousness, and to accomplish God's mission. Jesus saw his baptism as advancing God's work, therefore, Jesus was baptized because he was confessing sin on behalf of the nation, as Nehemiah, Ezra, Moses and Daniel had done, he was showing support of what John was doing. Jesus was inaugurating, in his public ministry, he was identifying with the penitent people of God and not with the critical Pharisees who were only watching, in truth, Jesus as a perfect man didn't need baptism for sin, yet, and he accepted baptism to obedient service to the father.

CHAPTER SEVENTEEN

RESTITUTION

God has included restitution as a unique concept as part of the law for Israel, in cases of wrongs done against God and people. These were not a collection of picky laws but they were case studies of God's principles in action. These cases had several objectives; such as to protect and organize the nations, to focus their attention on God. Since the laws did not cover every possible situation, yet, it gives practical examples to help to decide what God wants from his people. First, the penitent must confess his sin to God, and confess it to his neighbor, and so, take shame to himself. It can be very humiliating when someone reminds us of our past offence, how different, how God responds.

When confession and wrongdoing against others are made, satisfaction must be made for the offence done against God whose law was broken, as well as the loss sustained by neighbors. Therefore, restitution, in this case, is not sufficient without faith and repentance. When someone was robbed, the guilty person was required to restore the loss to the victim and pay an additional interest as a penalty. For instance when the Lord said to Moses, say to the Israelites, 'when a man or woman has wronged another in any way, and so become unfaithful to the Lord he has sinned, he must make full restitution for his wrong and add one-fifth and give it to the person he has wronged.

When we have wronged others, we ought to do more than apologies; we should look for ways to settle the matters, and take heed not condemning men, for example, the story of Zaccheus, whose name indicates that he was Jewish, also a thief tax collector and a rich one. In Jesus day Publicans and Sadducees were the two main sects that people held in high esteem, and tax collectors were known for being corrupted. Thus, Zaccheus as a publican was not very ethical in his business practice, and perhaps Jesus reputation with him owing him as a friend was a touching moment, and publicans reached him. When Jesus came to the place he looked up and saw Zaccheus sitting in a tree looking hopelessly for the help of his sick conscience, Jesus looks up and saw him and said' 'Zaccheus make hast and come down for today I must abide at your house.'

This was a remarkable example of Jesus excursing supernatural knowledge, implying as part of God's plan for Jesus, and for Zaccheus that this appointment should take place. It had an overwhelming joy that stem from Jesus willingness to dine with him, because having table fellowship with someone normally was a sign of a certain amount of mutual acceptance, and this is why the Pharisees would not eat with publicans.

God allows room for repentance, and so we must also demonstrate the proof as Zaccheus gave, he was now a penitent, and by his good work, and gave evidence of the sincerity of his faith and repentance. As a new man in Christ he bravely stood up, which denote him saying deliberately and with solemnity, like a vow, he addresses himself to Christ and not to the people, he makes it appears that there was a change in his heart and that he had repented. 'If any man is in Christ, he is a new creature, old things have passed away, and now all things have become new'.

Before Zaccheus conversion he was ready to resolve his will to do well towards God, and do well to others, he pledged, 'Behold Lord, the half of my goods I will give to the poor although I was uncharitable to the poor, now I will relief them the money and the duty I have neglected'.

Thus, Zaccheus confession reveals a penitent's heart, it does not suggest any doubts that he is guilty of wrongdoing, but illegally gaining money had to be returned plus one fifth, a fourfold return was legislated where lives stock were concerned. Christ approved and accepted Zaccheues's conversion. It was not surprising for the people to take offence; and murmured that Christ had gone to be a guest at a sinner's house as if they were not sinful men as he was. Yet, the people did not understand that it was Christ mission to seek and to save, though the man was a sinner, God makes room for repentance, and so we should, and though he was a sinner they should not blame Christ for going to him.

This is the result of a man who was scorned and criticized before by others, he becomes a new creature; all old things have passed away, all things become new.

The term '*new* creature' refers to the transformation that occurs within the inner man when a person believes in Christ as Savior. When a person receives salvation, they are now a new man as opposed to the old man that he was before he became a Christian. This concept of newness may be traced to an important choice between two Greek words, both meaning *new*, one word means *new*, in the sense of renovation to repair the other in the sense of fresh existence. It is the latter that is used to describe the Christian, rather he is not the old man renovated or refreshed, no, he is a brand new man with a new family, a new set of values, new motivations, and new possessions. However, the old man is still present in the new life and will from time to time express himself in corrupting deeds such as lying. For the new man to be visible he must put on as one put on a new suit of clothes. In other words, the new nature must be cultivated or nurtured by spiritual decisiveness to grow in Christ.

The great change must be shared with the unchanged every day, live it out, be an example among believers, work friends, and even enemies. We should take all precautions not to revert by putting on the old suite of the former life; rather, we must continue to grow in the new life. Christ came into the world to seek and save sinners, and he took all possible means to affect that salvation, Christ mission, he seeks for those who have not sought him, and those who do not ask for him. (Luke 19:8) Christian should help urge back-sliders to return to God by taking the initiative, praying for the person, and acting in love.

Consider the turning of someone as Peter denying his Master, and it comes as part of Christ sufferings. Peter fell miserable, but by God's grace, he got up. The immediate sin of Peter, when he sat in the palace among the servants of the High Priest, the bad company is the route of many sins, and sitting or standing on the devil's ground, you can scarcely or easily come out of his territory without grief or guilt or both.

The temptation came to Peter when he was challenged as a retainer to Jesus of Galilee, by the first maid, and then by another, and then the rest of the servants, charging him. 'You were also with Jesus, and again this fellow was with Jesus of Nazareth, and again 'you are one of them for your speech betrays you.' The sin itself, when Peter was charge as one of Christ disciples and he denied it, he was ashamed and afraid to own himself, and pretend that he did not understand the charge, that he did not remember it was a speech of lying which we are all prone to do. The worse part of Peter's sin is when he said, '*I know not the man*, and that was the way of his downfall.

This is written that we do not sin after the similitude of Peter's transgression, that we never, either directly or indirectly, dent Christ the Lord, dissembling our knowledge of him, and being ashamed of him and his words. This sin was aggravating knowing who Peter was, an apostle one of the first three. Christ had given Peter of his danger, and how solemnly he had promised to adhere to Christ in this night of trial, he had said again and again, '*I will never deny you.*'

Most Christians undergo testing and sometimes takes comfort by the way Job was also tested, but one cannot compare themselves what Job went through and still, trust remains faithful.

PARDON OF SIN

The prophet Isaiah wrote regarding God's pardon, God declares, 'I the Lord who blotted out your transgressions for my own sake, and I will remember your sin no more' This declaration of God's readiness to pardon sin comes in very strategically; the charge rang very high, he said, 'thou hast wearied me with your iniquity' One might think that it should follow, 'I am he who would destroy you, and will burden myself no longer' but God says, I, even I is he who will forgive you. It is the great God would teach us forgiving injuries, it is the best way to keep ourselves from being wearied with them. The sin of every believer present pardon, it expressed God will blot them out their sin, as a cloud is blocked by the beam of the sin. When God forgive, he forgets for his own mercies sake, and especially for his own Son sake. (Psalms 32:1-5)

Sometimes the temptation often aroused to remind others of their past offences. When God forgives us he forget them, we never have to fear that he will remind us of them later, because God's forgiveness is total. We must also forgive others of theirs. God wants to forgive sinners, it has always been part of God's loving nature, he announces the same to Moses, he renewed it to David, and he dramatically showed it to the world through Jesus Christ.

Many scriptures' have shown several aspects of God's forgiveness, he forgives transgressions, covers sin and does not count our sins against us, and we can have this joyous of forgiveness through faith in Jesus Christ. The believer should never be condoned or attempt to excuse their sin, there are only two things that should be done about sin. *'Confess it and forsake it.* Thus, confessing means to acknowledge or to say the same thing, as the truth regarding my sinful attitude, all the thought, actions that displease God.

The believer is instructed to speak the same thing as God about his or her sin, and when the believer confesses his sin he has the assurance that God is faithful, he can be counted on to keep his word, and it will all be d is just in dealing with our sins because he paid his price for them. For the non-believer, the same is require in confessing sins to God and be ready to turn and forsake sins when God says so.

RENEWING THE MIND

The focus according to Romans 12 regarding the individual who lived within the Christian community; they are advised to walk in God's purposes towards their Christian brothers and sisters, towards suspicious outsiders, and towards their government. Christians are admonished through the word 'not to conformed to this world, but be transformed by the renewing of the mind, that you may prove what is that good, and acceptable, and perfect, will of God.

What is the great effect of this renewal? That you may prove what is that good, and acceptable, and perfect will of God, the will of God has three excellent properties of law, it is good in itself, it is good for us, and it is acceptable and pleasing to God' and the only way to attain this favor is to conform to God's will as the rule. It is perfect, to which nothing can be added. The process to renew the mind, is renewing of the whole man, for out of it are the issues of life.

There are some enemies to renewing of the mind; one is conformity to the world, we are warned not to conform to the world' but be transformed, by the renewing of the mind that you may prove what is the acceptable and perfect will of God. The disciples and followers of the Lord Jesus were constantly reminded not to conformed according to the pattern of this world, or conform to the men, or follow the multitude to do evil, and if sinners entice us, we must not consent to them, but instead, finding a way of witnessing to them.

Although it might seem as if some Christian has the world system inside his or her heads; we are constantly bombarded by its images, words, and values, that often echoing in our minds, to avoid such bombardment the individual mind Christians must seek renewing in habitual, thought patterns and behavior that will reflect on the contrasting values of Christ's kingdom. It will cause you to make a continuous quest to discover the will of God. In each successive life challenge, the good and pleasing will of God must be understood that God can save and keep you from falling into sin.

A person who is sick in mind must seek help through God's word for a solution to fix what is causing the illness. There are so many matters that affect our minds, and it might be disappointing that the mind cannot be touched by human's hands; it can only respond to the word from God who makes human minds in the first place. Thus, conversion and sanctifications are the renewing of the mind, it makes a change not out of the substance but the qualities of the soul, for instance, a man is not what he was before his mind was renewed now all things are passed away, behold all things becomes anew.

It concerns Christians to prove what the perfect will of God, acceptable, is and know experimentally and approve excellent things. The spiritual renewal comes through the Holy Spirit work according to John 6:63, the Spirit gives life, the flesh counts for nothing. Without the work of the Holy Spirit, you cannot even see your need for a new life, and all spiritual renewal begins and ends with God.

He reveals the truth to us; he lives within us, and then enables us to respond to that truth. Christ makes perpetual intercession before God for us, his continuous presence in heaven with the father assures us that our sins have been paid for and forgiven. To reflect such favor our daily application of God's word must have a purifying effect on our minds and hearts, as the Scriptures points out sin and motivates us to confess, and renew our relationship, and bring back our fellowship with Christ, and be guided back in the right path.

CHAPTER EIGHTEEN

RESTORATION

Restoration will renewed fellowship; is needful and necessary of all humans, because we were born as sinners our natural inclination is to please ourselves rather than God, and many people followed that inclination, for example, David when he looked on another man's wife with lustful eyes and leads to the sin of adultery. Like David we must ask God to cleanse our heart and spirit for new thoughts and desires because right conduct can comes only from a clean heart and spirit, you must ask God to create a pure heart and a right spirit in you.

David experienced a broken fellowship between him and God, he cried out to ask God to restore his fellowship, he asked, 'Restore the joy of thy salvation and uphold me with your generous Spirit' Restoration is a renewal of something to its former state, such as things that have been worn and dull can be beautifully restored as new using the right products, old clothes can be restored as new by those who have an interest and value in the garment. If restoration is available to things and people, how much more is the restoration of the human relationship between God and man, family, community, body of Christ we all need restoration. (Psalms 51:12)

The relationship between God and man was broken through Adam's disobedience, and God wants to restore man in fellowship with him through his son Jesus Chris. God was willing to restore mankind to his former state in relationship with him. Before man disobeyed and commit sin, the man had a close relationship with his creator in the Garden of Eden. For instance, when God restored a right relationship with the Israelites, he does so by demonstrating his great love for them, by treating them tenderly. Peter spoke of the times of restoration of all things of which God spoke through the mouth of his holy prophets of old times until which time the heaven must hold within itself, the Christ appointed' Jesus. Both the rich and the poor needs restoration; In the days of the Old Testament whenever a census took place, everyone, both rich and poor were required to pay a ransom. God does not discriminate between people. We all need God's mercy and forgiveness, because of our sinful nature.

There is no way that a rich person can buy God, and no way can the poor avoid paying God. God demands that all of us come humbly before him to be forgiven into his family. In Jesus ministry, he restored a man with a withered hand that caused uproar among the rulers of the law, as Jesus saw the man with a need Jesus was touched with compassion to do something. Unfortunately, the onlooker accused Jesus of healing the man on the Sabbath day, they said he did something unlawful because of the day, Jesus was angry of their uncaring attitude, and being angry it is not wrong, it demands on what makes angry, and what we do with our anger.

Jesus expresses his anger by correcting a problem by healing the man's hand that was a factor that hinders him from doing work. Jesus demonstrated his restoration power by speaking healing to a man with the shriveled hand, 'Stand up in front of everyone' Then Jesus asked the religious leaders, 'which is lawful and right to do on the Sabbath day, to do evil, or to do well? 'Since these religious leaders have always found fault in Jesus work, they remain silent, and when Jesus looked around the man's hand was completely restored. They did not understand that God can excel beyond our understanding. For example, in a forest that is burned down and can grow back, broken bones are healed, and even those who are in grief can be restored to laughter. In so much as our tears can be seeds that will grow into a harvest of joy because God can bring good out of tragedy.

If you are feeling burden by sorrow and grief, resentment, bereavement, you can be assured that none of these will consumed you. It might mean evil, but God has meant it for good, and you will know that not one sparrow will fall to the ground without God consent.

Some time ago, I was feeling low in spirit even so still having a burning desire for more of God and less of me, on that note, I did not ask or consulted anyone, knowing what was to be done to address my situation without making matters worse, I immediately ask God through the medium of prayer for his help. During those times there was a hungering and thirsting developing within me, I wanted to be closer to God, my soul longs for God, nothing else seems to satisfy that pangs of hungry and thirsting. I thought maybe I should do a deeper search through the scriptures; there might be a verse that would speak life into my situation, and with an alarming determination to get it right.

It works' it was tears and prayers, and more tears that finally brought me to that place I was longing for. And endeavoring to set a plan and stick to that plan, brings exceptional results, I cried, Lord, my need is great, I need more of you, and less of me, without you I'm lost, Lord if you can do anything, please help me.

This prayer was mingled with faith and brought me a much closer desire for God, you must pray, amid struggles, even when it seems as if you are eased off from the problem, don't be fooled, at times you must turn up the prayer flame and pray without ceasing, and believe and accept you are the righteousness of God through Christ, 'I thought me?, yes, me, as times goes on, faith begins to bud and starting grow again, through more prayer and fasting, my faith seems as if it was stretch to a limit like an elastic band, nevertheless, I was determined to be enlightened and restored to the sweet fellowship with God, my father.

When you believe with all your heart that God is always right, in all he does, and say is the right approach to live, you will experience the assurance that comes from the light of God's countenance. God understood when we are experiencing trials, loneliness, and tempted to question matters that don't seem to make sense, but wait, consider, these are light affliction, it is not meant to take your life away, only to learn submission to God. It can be like pressing with the expectation of pressing the seed to bring out the oil. After a while, you will feel restored, you will know when this happens, and you will experience a calm and sweet feeling that comes in as if to drive out all fears, anxieties. This beautiful experience has enabled me to begin again as it were *a new beginning* to *take* my lawful position in his care, and fellowship was finally restored, and thanks be to God my misery are now behind me, because of God's grace that covers me like a blanket. It is only through God's mercies that locate me from where I was, I am restored and made righteous, God has the power and ability to restore his people from the pause of the enemy and any difficult situations, he has restored my soul, to find joy again.

SPIRITUAL RESTORATION

It is a fact that a child of God knows no true or solid joy, except the joy of God's salvation, joy in God, his divine favor and in the hope of eternal life. 'The joy of the Lord is my strength', and I will dwell in the house of the Lord forever, and feast at the table spread for me, surely goodness shall follow me. Our Christian grace must be exercised in joy; we must not sink into a sad disconsolation frame of mind which would make us faint under our trails. Though many philosophies may instruct men to be calm under their troubles, and Christianity teaches men to be joyful because our trials will brighten our graces until we receive our crown.

We are always encouraged through the prayers of David's prayers, he prayed for the countenance of God's will towards him, and the progress of the good work in him, he asked, 'Cast me not away from thy presence' as one who God abhorrent and cannot endure looking upon. David plea, 'take not thy Holy Spirit from me'.

We would be all undone if God should take his Holy Spirit from us. King Saul was an example of this instance, how exceedingly miserable he was when the Spirit of the Lord departed from him. David knew this, so he begs, and he earnestly pleads, 'Lord whatever you take from me, nor my children, my crown, not my life, yet take not thy Holy Spirit from me. David is always making significant prayers to God that can be our example through dark times.

We cannot help but read and acknowledge David's prayer, he asked God not to cast him away from his presence, but to renew a right, preserving, and steadfast spirit within him, restore the joy of his salvation, and uphold him with his Holy Spirit. David must have felt miserable without God's relationship; he had a longing to be in close fellowship with God so he cried out in desperation for God's forgiveness, David prayed for the restoration of divine comforts and the perpetual communication of divine grace, he prays, 'Restore unto me the joy of thy salvation.'

The prophet Jeremiah is another example of faithfulness to carry out God's messages to the people. An example, when the Lord spoke to Jeremiah on behalf of the people, saying, 'All those who devour them, they shall be devoured, every one of their adversaries will all go into captivity, those who plunder them, they shall be plundered, and all who prey on them' God says, 'I will restore health to you, and heal you of your wounds because they call you an outcast, saying 'this is Zion and no one seeks her' when they look on the people that formally dwell in Zion, but they were now in captivity, thy called them outcast, these are those who belong to Zion, but no man seeks after them' For all this God will work deliverance and salvation for them in due time.

Although the people were in fear in an off land, yet they shall be preserved, God said, 'though he made a full end of the nation where he had scattered them, yet he will not make a full end of thee, 'yet I will restore health unto thee. Because people had medical conditions, and no one cares about them, God promises to restore health, and heal their wounds. The medical disease was caused by sin, however, God's medicine cures every disease, even the disease of sin, if people were willing to allow and accept him to cure them. (Jeremiah 30:17)

FINDING RESTORATION IN THE CHURCH

The church is composing of people with various backgrounds and characters, a variety of these people has multicultural gifts and abilities. The church is the people and believers are the church and are not the building, but rather it is made up of the chosen called out of the world, though believers are in the world but, not more of the world system and behaviors. The church of God was purchased by the blood of Jesus when he died on Calvary.

The Church is compared as a tent that is soon taken down and shifted, and when God pleases it will soon be fixed somewhere else. Also, the church can be compared to a human body which has many members of the same body that makes one body. All members are baptized into the same body and made the church of the same spirit. Christians become members of the body by baptism, they are baptized into one body and communion, at the other ordinances, we sustained by drinking into one Spirit. It is by the baptism of the Holy Spirit of Christ that makes us true members of Christ body.

All who has the Spirit of Christ are the members of Christ, whether Jew or Gentiles, bond or free. Each member has its particular form, place and use. The meanest makes a part of the body so every member of the body mystical cannot have the same office. The meanest member of the body is as such a member as the noblest, his entire member are dear to him, so it is in the body of Christ. There are varieties in the body that contributes to the beauty of it, so it is for the beauty and good appearance of the church that there should be a diversity of gifts and the disposal of members and their situation are as God pleases.

As members of Christ body, we should do the duties of our place, and not quarrelling with others because we are not in theirs. All beavers of the body are necessary and useful to each other. Some members might feel to be more feeble are also necessary, and every member serves some good purpose or another, nor is there a member of the body of Christ, but ought to be useful to his fellow members and in some cases is needful to them. There might be differences between individuals to divide people as the case in Corinth, because of the multiculturalism exist among Christian of different races, classes, and beliefs it stirs division, but despite the differences all believers having one thing in common, 'Faith in Christ.'

All believers are formed into the body of Christ and as a group of individuals unite in purposes and love for one another in service to the Lord. If at any time an individual stumbles, the rest of the group is there to pick him or her up and help him on his feet to walk with God again. If an individual has sinned, he or she should seek restoration through the church; meanwhile, the rest of the body must continue witnessing God's truth. Believers of the church should edify, comfort or exhort themselves and to one another, by communicating our knowledge and experience one to another, and join in prayer and praise with one another. (Eph. 4:15)

Ministers of the gospel have a crucial input in all this, most time they distance themselves from the big problem until it gets bigger before they take action. Ministers are described by the work of their office; therefore the people must know them, as they labor with diligence because they are called laborers together in God's kingdom. Ministers are to rule their people, not with rigor, but with love. They must rule as spiritual guides, by setting a good example to the flock, and they must also admonish and instruct the people, to do well, and rejoice in the Lord and the power of his might.

Minister should implement various training and uplifting project that stretches believers ability to study to show themselves approved like a workman that should not be ashamed and seeking to learn the art of winning souls for Christ kingdom. Christians must always remember and keep the great commission fresh and alive in minds and hearts, this should give an excellent desire to go tell with lamps of the gospel shining brightly so that others might see and find their way to the house of God. Therefore, the church should be a place of recovery in a position for wounded people, who from time to time will be injured especially, believers.

It is not unusual for believers to feel discouraged, disappointed, rejected, dejected, hurt, and lonely and a tendency to depart from the church. In such cases, the rest of the believers have a duty of care to reach out and encourage those who need to restore their fellowship with God and with one another. It is of vital importance that individuals receive relevant training on how to restore each other in times regarding misunderstanding, and other contributing factors, that may attach and try to destroy faith. It could make matters worse by blaming, and judging, instead of excreting patience, understanding, sometimes we make more mistakes to walk away from the causality. Let us ask God for his compassion to restore, to love with bowels of hope to the individual so that they will gain confidence in accepting Christian counseling.

The church must be in a position to accept casualties binding broken bones, broken relationships, broken promises and any other factors that may need healing and deliverance until they recovered. Some might be seriously injured from persecution, fear, discouragements, while others may feeling the strain from weariness and need an encouraging word from someone who understands what it is to feel that way. The worse thing that can happen in these cases is for a person who has never experience what it is to be feeling weary and drained, sharing their experience to persons who had never experience a headache, but finding the time to be high and lifted to criticized those who are going through hell and high waters.

The church should welcome those seeking refuge and rescued them from sin's cold; also, anyone needs treatment from all-natural sickness and diseases. The church needs to find the right plaster for the right sore, by selecting a person without any offence, to minister healing and assurance to the ailing persons. *What is your church doing in the community?*

Members of the body of Christ should be encouraged to reach out to the lost, the aged, to people everywhere, and lonely. It might seem impossible to reach so far, but reaching one and encourage that one to reach to others, would soon be developed as a pyramid going upwards, outwards until the house of the Lord is filled with new converts all year round. Believers who belong to the church should grow and become strong members who encourage others to study to show themselves approved, and become soul winners for Christ kingdom. Does your church provide restoration for members who might fall into temptation? 'If not, why not try Jesus example by going after his lost sheep, and bring them back to the fold.

WHEN DOES THE CHURCH BEGIN?

The church was a mystery for example hidden, not revealed. In the Old Testament it was first prophesied in the spoken words to Peter, 'On this rock, I build my church. In this prophecy the word 'rock which also happens to be Peter's name, Jesus said, 'You are Peter, *Petros,* and on this rock, I will build my church. (Matt. 16:18)

Many suggestions are offered for various reasons, though the simplest view is to understand the New Testament church as beginning on the Day of Pentecost in response to Peter's Pentecostal sermon. On that remarkable day, three thousand souls were added to the church. The group was called the first time the, *church,* those who listened to the preaching accepted the message were baptized and added to the church. These new Christians were united with the other believers; they were thought by the apostle and were included in the prayer meetings and fellowship. New believers ought to be in small groups where they can learn God's word pray, and mature in the faith. (Acts 2:41)

The great commission should exist widely in many churches all over the world, minister must encourage the believer to go tell, and go bring the lost for Christ. Yet, some church leaders will avoid this command and would prefer to recommend yet more activity on the church program to keep members occupying the seat and within the four walls. Some minister has failed miserably in caring for lost believers who might lose the desire to share fellowship, instead of going after such person they would prefer welcoming by passing members who are just popping in. To recovery others the church must be a praying church equipping believers with the tools of prayer, love one another, praising only the one and only God, living a consecrated set apart lifestyle, always remembering who you are, and who calls you out of darkness into his marvelous light.

THE PURPOSE OF THE CHURCH

The ultimate purpose of the church is to bring honor and glory to its head, Jesus Christ. It is done by fulfilling the two purposes related to God's program to the world. The purpose of the church as it relates to the world is evangelism. The program is spelt out in the Great Commission, which has never been rescinded. The program is to make disciples of all nations. The way is to be done in two-fold, 'baptizing them in the name of the Father, and the Son and the Holy Ghost, and by teaching them to observe all things that I have commanded you' Baptism is not an optional afterthought; it is a vital part of evangelism, and making disciples. (Matt. 28:19-20)

Another purpose of the church, as it relates to the world, is edification, according to Paul to the Ephesians, the saints need to be edified and build-up for two goals.

1. For the equipping of the saints for the work of ministry, the believer who composes the church's membership needs to be built up so that they would realize all that God has provided for Christian living and that they may come to maturity.
2. They also need to be equipped to perform that work in the body of Christ. In a real sense, each member of the church is to be a Christian worker so that the work that God wants to perform through the local church can be accomplished. (Ephesians 4:12)

God has given the church an enormous responsibility to make disciples in every nation, this involves, teaching, preaching, healing, nurturing, giving, administering, building and many other. If we had to fulfill this commission as individuals, we might as well give up without trying, because it would be impossible, but God calls us as members of his body. Some of us can do one task, some can do another, and together we can obey God more fully than any of us can alone. It is a human tendency to overestimate what we can do by ourselves and to underestimate what we can do as a group. As the body of Christ, we can accomplish more together than we could dream possible working by ourselves.

CHAPTER NINETEEN

RIGHTEOUSNESS OF CHRIST

The significance of Christ righteousness has shown one of the most awesome requirements God made upon the men and women that they are righteous, that is conforming to his ethical and moral standards. Righteousness is not an overnight achievement; it takes time to get it right, since only God who is always right, is righteous in all he does. The human heart, mind, and thinking process would need renewing, to become right with God. In so many ways humans might attempt to do all that lies in their power to achieve a righteous standard that pleases God, but alas all man's effort has proven futile.

Paul demonstrates considered and thought of making the distinction between goodness and righteousness when speaking of Christ's sacrificial death, he says, 'Very rarely will anyone die for a righteous man, though for a good man someone might dare to die, by God demonstrate his love for us in this. While we were still sinners Christ dies' A man can be termed righteous, if he fulfills his proper obligations, is just, impartial, honest and not guilty of doing wrong, or immorality, and knows that integrity of conduct and unrighteousness.

On the other hand, Paul statement implies certain superiority in the good man, to be good the individual could not be unrighteous or unjust, yet other qualities may distinguish him from the man that is primarily known for his righteousness. A man that is termed righteous is someone benevolent and beneficent, he is not merely concern with doing what justice requires, but goes beyond this, and is motivation by wholesome consideration for others. (Romans 5:7-8).

Paul gave another example of the man who is termed as righteous as a man who wins the respect of others, he may not appeal to their heart as strongly as to impel anyone to die for him. However, the man is outstanding for his goodness, which is warm, helpful, considerate, and merciful. It is no wonder Paul was upset with himself he said, when he wants to do good evil presents itself, for, in my inner being, I delight in God's law, but I see another law at work in the member of my body, waging war against the law of my mind and making me a prisoner of the law of sin at work within my members, he asked what a wretched man I am, who will rescue me from this body of death, he concluded, thanks be to God, through Jesus Christ.

The apostle Paul change his word and declare, nothing can separate him from the love of God which he found in Christ Jesus' 'Neither life nor death, principles, or power' can separate him from the love of God which is in Christ Jesus our Lord. Separation from the world involves more than keeping our distance from sinners, it means staying close to God, it involves more than avoiding entertainment that leads to sin, it extends how much we spend our time and money. However there is no way to separate ourselves from all sinful influences, nevertheless, we are to resist the sin around us, without either giving up or giving in to sin.

The apostle Paul described his findings, he said, the work of the most honorable Holy Spirit is designed to help us become right with God. Paul refers to the facts; 'there is no one righteous; meaning no one is innocent; every person is valuable in God's eyes because he created us in his image and he loves us' notwithstanding, there is no one righteous, that is, no one can earn right standing with God through valuable, we have all fallen sinners, yet God through Jesus Christ has redeemed us and offers to forgive us if we return to him in faith. You might even be expecting to think comfortably, 'I'm not too bad, or, I'm pretty good, but the bible says, 'there is no one good' 'can you think of the last person who has accused you of wrongdoings? How does it make you feel?

What was your reaction? And because of the law, we know that we are helpless sinners and that is why we must come to Jesus Christ for mercy? Bearing in mind that we do not earn salvation by keeping the law, but we do please God when our lives confirm what he reveals in us. The righteous demands of God that are coupled with the inability of man might present an insoluble; however, God himself has graciously solved the problem.

Justification of believers, in the righteousness of God, revealed' will show you the way of salvation and the way of justification. The gospel makes known God's righteousness, there is such righteousness that is revealed in the gospel. It is called the righteousness of God, it is God's appointing. It is so-called to cut off all pretensions to the righteousness of Christ. It is said to be from faith to faith, from the first faith, by which we are put into a justified state, to after, by which we live, from faith engrafting us into Christ deriving virtue from as our root, both implied in the next words, *The just shall live by faith.'*

Thus, David gave some insight, he asked, 'Lord who shall dwell in temporarily in your tabernacle, or who shall dwell permanently on your holy hill' There is a clear distinction between those who worship God and those who refuse to worship him. David worshipped God under his leadership Israel obeyed God and prospered. After several years later Israel forgets about God, and it became difficult for the people to distinguish between God's followers and those who worshipped idols.

The prophet Isaiah called the people to repentance who went astray, he made the imagery of straying sheep even more general, referring to all people, since the whole human race, both Jews and Gentiles alike have turned away from God. The nature of Christ's righteousness, and how it is brought in, is by his obedience. The disobedience of the first Adam has ruined us and the obedience of the second Adam has saved us.

It was by Christ obedience that he wrought righteousness for us, it satisfied God's justice, the fruit of it, and that there is a gift upon all men in their salvation which is called common salvation. Jesus invitation to whoever will come and drink the waters of life, as the gift is unto justification, whereas, it is not only just that frees from death, but that entitles to life, men shall be made righteous, shall be constituted by letters patent. The answer is, 'He who walks and lives uprightly and blamelessly, who works righteousness and justice and speak and thinks the truth in his heart'.

He is consciously honest and just in all his dealings, faithful and fair with whom he has to do, he works righteousness, he does all the good he can to his neighbors, but very careful to hurt no one, in particular, and is tender to his neighbor's reputation, he makes the best of everybody and the worst of nobody, his charity will cover a multitude of sins, and he is one that always prefers a good conscience before any secular interest.

There is a faith that is justifying us; living by faith, there is a faith preserving us, and there is a faith maintaining us. Faith is all in all, both in the beginning and progress of Christian life. It is increasing, continuing, preserving faith, that show that this is no novel upstart doctrine, he quotes that famous scripture, 'the just shall live by faith, but if any man draws back, my soul hall has no please in him. The writer encourages his readers never to abandon their faith in times of persecution, but to show by their endurance that their faith is real, faith means trusting in what Christ has done for in the past, but is also resting him for what he will do in the present and the future. (Hebrews 10:38)

The righteousness which salvation produces is by faith, from first to last. As the apostle Paul used the term, *faith*, means total acceptance and absolute trust. It means being utterly sure what Jesus said is true and accepting time and eternity on that assurance. In full-fledged faith when a person hears the Christian message, agrees that it is true, and then, cast himself, or herself upon it in a life of total submission. Since God is holy, therefore, he cannot allow sinners into his presence, or in his sanctuary or his holy hill.

Interchangeable words are describing the focal point of Israelite worship, the dwelling place of God. There, God calls for his people to be morally upright, and in these psalms, he gives us ten standards to determine how we are doing. Since we are living among evil people whose standards and morals are eroding, our standard for living should not come from our evil society, but God. Since all persons are sinners, they could not be saved apart from the supernatural invention of God.

Your sin was poured into Christ at his crucifixion, and his righteousness was poured into us at our conversion, this is what

Christian means, by Christ atonement for sin. In the world, a bargain works only when two people exchange goods relatively of equal value, but God offers to trade his righteousness for our sin that is something of immeasurable worth for something completely worthless, how grateful we should be for this kindness. On the other hand, when we believe in Christ, he treated us as though we were as righteous as Christ.

BENEFITS OF CHRIST RIGHTEOUSNESS

God sent Christ who never sinned, to die for our sins, and thus to satisfy his wrath towards us, we can simply be assured and say, God at the cross treated Christ as though he committed our sins, even though he was righteous, so there is need for human righteousness. Humanity has largely turned away from the goodness of God, and preferring passion and lusts over his will since the righteousness through religion has been derailed by ethnic identity and ethnic conflict, but in truth, religion is supposed to produce a family, but instead, it has produced division, trusting in Christ will make an exchange of our sin for righteousness.

The bible called this type of righteousness *imputed* righteousness' This simply means that God puts to our spiritual account the very worth of Christ, much as though he were a banker adding an inexhaustible deposit to our bank account and sadly many people who refuse to believe that such abundant blessings can be theirs as a gift, nevertheless, the Bible urges all men to trust in Jesus Christ as Savior and thus to be reckoned as the righteousness of God. God loves the righteous and cares for them, and God will provide for them in all seasons, they shall dwell in the secret place of his abiding place, he will guide with his eyes, his rod and staff shall comfort them, though they walk through the shadows of death they shall fear no evil.

They promise long life and fruitful days of joy and prosperity. The Joy of the Lord is their strength, they shall run and not be weary, and they shall run and not faint and eternal life is the promise at the end of their days, for instance, David wrote, 'I use to be a young man, and now I have grown old, and yet I've never seen the righteous left entirely, nor his offspring begging bread' When God justifies the believer he treats them as if they had never been sinners at all; he treats you as a child to be loved.

God does not treat his children as his enemies, but like his friends, he says, 'You are my friends if you do whatever I command you not as lawbreakers to be punished, but as men and women to be loved. As Solomon declared, 'God will not cause the soul of the righteous to be hungry, but the craving of the wicked he will push away' Thus, God is the judge over the inhabitable earth in righteousness by Jesus Christ, and he will create, 'new heavens and a new earth in which righteousness will dwell, yet because a person is righteous, it does not mean being perfect, and it is would be impossible for human beings; instead righteous people are those who love the Lord and seeking to follow him, like the path of a Christian, and they are given the power of the Holy Spirit to help to live a Godly righteous life.

The prophet Jeremiah testified against the folly of the impenitence as senseless who would not be made wise by all the methods that God took to bring them to themselves. The people refuse to take actions in the fairness of their soul, with the same common prudence which they acted in other things,

yet God in his mercies invited them to come and reason with him, he asked, *Shall men fall and not rise?'* If men happen to fall into the dirt in the ground, will they get up as fast as they can? The prophet, asks, 'why when men fall into sin, they make no hurry and hasten to get up again through repentance?' 'Why do they not reform when they missed their way and return? 'Therefore, sin is backsliding, it is going back from the right way, and not only into a wrong, but rather, but a path that leads to destruction.
(Jeremiah. 8:4-6)

As part of the Christian mission on earth it is to demonstrate God's righteousness and to be a light for the Gentiles and to all nations. Christians have the opportunity to share in his mission, since God called us to be servants of his son, demonstrating God's righteousness and brings his light, what a rare privilege it is to help the Messiah, but we must seek his righteousness. Before we can demonstrate it to others, we must endeavor to shine our Christian lights among others in our homes, communities, shine positive action so that others may see where they going, we must also keep our light burning, to benefit ourselves.

Eventually, the possession of the earth is promised to the righteous, by God the creator, and the wicked to be cleared out of the earth as a ransom for the righteous, and also the possession of the wicked will go to the righteous as the proverb states, 'The wealth of the sinner is something that is treasured up for the righteous, and the ill-gotten treasures have no lasting value, but righteousness delivers us from death, and Lord does not allow the righteous to go hungry, but he thwarts the craving of the wicked.

The person who is preserved in righteousness is assured of God's goodwill and the approval of right hearted men, and for time to come in due season for a blessing, but the very name of the wicked will rot. Respect and wisdom will count whom God declare righteously, and to follow their counsel and reprove, which will bring good to those accepting it. For example, David received reprove from God through righteous men, as God's servants and prophets, and he said, should the righteous one strike me, it would be a loving-kindness, and should he reproves me, it will be an oil upon my head which my head would not want to refuse' Those who are desirous in the effectiveness of enjoying the flow of God's mercy must seek him, and showing a right heart condition by abandoning wrong ways and harmful thoughts, and seek and inquire of the Lord while he may be found, claiming Him by necessity and by doing right, calling on him while he is near, the wicked forsaking his way and the unrighteous man his thoughts, and let him return to the Lord and he will show love, pity, and mercy to him and will abundantly pardon.

Therefore, it is only reasonable to show proper fear of God and appreciation for his righteous precepts, and if they deviate from the righteous course they have been following, they must not try to cover up sin, but confess it and manifest genuine contrition and heartfelt sadness. Another absolute and essential is they must be merciful, as Jesus said, 'Happy are the merciful, for they will be shown mercy as followers of Christ they are sanctified, and set apart for sacred use. Thus, such ones are cleansed and made holy through believing and obeying the word of God, and having an understanding of the word of God, that God's words are not simply a collection of words, but it is a vehicle to communicate ideas, it is living, life-changing, and dynamic as it works in us. It can be compared to the incisions of a surgeon's knife, so God's word reveals who you are and what you are not.

If we should allow God's word to penetrate the core of our moral and spiritual life, it will discern what is in us, both good, and evil, therefore, the demand of God's word requires decisions, we must not only listen to God's word but we must let it shape our lives because he or she have already accepted forgiveness through Christ sacrificial death, thus the Christian life is equality earthly and spiritual. We should draw a sharp line in the demarcation between the two. Our spiritual acts of worship are to live according to God's expectations daily.

THE BREASTPLATE OF RIGHTEOUSNESS

In the Old Testament God gave instructions regarding the designing and making of the breastplate. The breastplate was worn by the high priest as garments of protection. The most considerable ornament of the high priest was the breastplate; it was made from a rich piece of cloth, curiously wrought with gold and purple. This precious and significant garment was made in fashion like the ephod which had wreathen chains of gold, both fasten at the top so that the breastplate might not be loosed from the ephod. The ephod was a garment for service, and the breastplate was the garment of judgment and not an emblem of honor, but these two must not be by no means be separated. In the breastplate, the tribe of Israel was recommended to God's people in the twelve precious stones. Christ wears the breastplate of judgment and the holy crown; for the church high priest is her prophet and king. All believers are clothed with the robe of righteousness and girt with the girdle of truth. Therefore, righteousness must be our breastplate. It secures the vital part of the upper body and shelters the heart, which is a very vital organ of the human body.

The righteousness of Christ is implanted in you it is to fortify the heart against the attacks which Satan makes against you, and may wonder what does this mean because the bible tells you more than all else, and safeguard your heart, for out of it are the issues of life, and your helmet should be the hope of your salvation for its object; even when you are tempted by the devil you would not become despair, the God of your salvation will keep you rejoicing in him. Ephesians chapter six urges the believer to put on the whole amour of God to be able to stand the slaughter of the enemy.

Your Christian should be well-armed with each piece of amour and having no amour of your own. The amour of God was to be worn in all times, to withstand the wicked darts of the enemy. Therefore; the whole amour of God must be put on and worn and all pieces of the amour must be put on to be effective in battle. The Christian amour is designed to cover all parts of the body from the crown of the head to the sole of the feet. The resolution must be as the gravest of your legs, and is having your feet shod with the preparing of the *gospel of peace*; *shoes'* in military times walking on graves of brass were formerly part of the military amour to defend the feet against gall-straps and sharp sticks which was laid to obstruct the marching of the army.

The *word of God* is called the sword of the spirit because he renders it officious and powerful. *Prayer* must be buckled on all the other graces, and you must pray always. We must pray in the Spirit, we must *watch*, thereto, and endeavoring to keep our hearts in a prayerful frame, and perseverance, and supplication,

232

not for ourselves only, but for all saints. Our heart, our feelings of love and desire dedicates to a great extent to how we live because we always find time to do what we enjoy. That is why Solomon urged us to guard our hearts above all else, making sure we concentrate on those desires that will keep us on the right path.

Your heart should be inflamed with love, true and fervent love to God, and the things of God, it will keep you watchful and sober, and to keep your heart occupied with the word of God, as a storehouse keep those things for future use. The heart of man needs much discipline and training. The Christians are urged to stand firm wearing the belt of truth buckled around our waist, with the breastplate of righteousness in place and making sure your desire pushes us in the right direction. Therefore, it is advisable to put boundaries on your desires, and not going after everything you see, but looking straight ahead and keeping your eyes fixed on your goal, never be sidetracked will cause detour and leads to sin. Christian is advised to wear the breastplate of righteousness since the heart of fallen man is treacherous and desperate, and following God's righteousness is essential as a protection against its turning back.

The Christian has to endure battles against rulers and authorities, the power of evil forces and fallen angels headed by Satan, who is a vicious fighter, to withstand their attacks; you must depend on God's strength and use every piece of amour of the weapon provided, for protection. Thus your whole body needs to be armed against the power of this dark world; thus you must prepare to fight in the power of the church whose power comes from the Holy Spirit.

The Christian can be assured of the course by sticking close to the Scriptures that the apostle Paul wrote, 'The word of God is beneficial for teaching, for reproving, for setting things straight, for disciplining in righteousness, that the man of God may fully competent, completed equipped for every good works'. Thus Christian's believers should accept gratefully the discipline that they have received from righteous men who made such use of God's word, therefore, righteousness exalts a nation but sin is a reproach to any person.

CHAPTER TWENTY

THE NEW COVENANT

A covenant is an agreement between parties; a covenant was designed for mutual protection, such as securing peace, and covenant of friendship;

The new covenant is the culmination of God's covenant-making with Israel and may be view as a document of God prophetic program and the policies of admiration. As an administrative document, it renders obsolete and succeeds the old Sinitic covenant that serves as the manual of procuring for carrying out the moral, civil and ceremonial regulations relative to national Israel in the pre-Christian era. Some features of the old are carried over to the new covenant. There is in the new covenant stress of importance of the unchanging principles of God's law, however, these will be written in the hearts of God's people, and they shall become part of the inner ward code for a living, and will conform in all respect in the moral law of the scriptures.

As a document of prophetic promises like the Abraham, and Davidic covenants, the new covenant is unconditional, it corresponds to the Royal grant treaties of the ancient near east land. The purpose of the old covenant was good and served well, in the old covenant people could only approach God through the priest and the sacrifices system that was provided. Jesus death on the cross ushered in the new covenant or agreement between God and man, and now with the new covenant, all people can approach God and communicate with him in confidence.

The people of Israel first agreed to their Exodus journey from Egypt. It was designed to point to the day when Jesus Christ would come, thus the new covenant completes, rather than replaces the old covenant, fulfilling everything the old covenant looked towards.

The covenant of grace in Christ is a treasury of merit and grace, and hence we receive pardon and a new nature and made us free from the law of sin and death, both from the power of sin. We are under another covenant, under the law of the Spirit, the law that gives the Spirit, spiritual life to qualify us for eternal. The foundation of this freedom is laid in Christ's undertaking for us, of whom he speaks, according to God's covenant made between him and all flesh after the flood. God promised he would never again bring a flood of water over all the earth.

There is no possibility of God changing his mind concerning the covenant or regretting it. It is similarity, with God's covenant with Abraham, as God step in with an oath, as a legal guarantee demonstrates more abundant to the heirs of the promise the unchangeableness of his counsel. God's promises and his oath being two unchangeable things, in which God cannot lie, and for instance, many of the promises God made to Abraham seemed impossible to be realized, but Abraham trusted God.

The promises to believers in God's word might seem too incredible, but we can trust God to keep all his promises. God sworn covenant with his Son for priesthood like that of Melchizedek, it was like a wise something over which God would feel no regret. Ever since Adam eats the forbidden fruit, humans have been fond of the forbidden path. Without the law, sin was dead, as a snake in the winter, which the sunbeams of the law quicken and irritate. We may all confess that sin is a deceiver and sin puts a cheat upon mankind, as a fatal cheat, and the worst thing that sin does is the perverting of the law.

CONTRAST OF NEW AND OLD

The apostle Paul illustration regarding the old covenant that was made with the fathers of the Jewish nation at Mount Sinai said this covenant was not found faultless, it was perfect in its kind, and fitted to answer, but very imperfect in comparison of the gospel. It was not sure or steadfast, it will decay and grow old and vanished away, and it was antiquated of no more use in gospel than candles are when the sun has risen.

Comparing the New Testament dispensation it has a better covenant, it is without fault and is well ordered in all things, it requires nothing but what it promises grace to perform; it is put into good and safe hands. The new covenant is established upon better promises, it promises covenant contains in it promises of progress and perseverance in grace and holiness by the power of God. It is a new covenant, and it will also be that way, in which all who take hold of it shall be always found preserved by the power of God.

The articles of the covenant are sealed between God and his people by baptism and the lord supper. God once wrote his laws on them, now he has written his law in them, there shall be a table and transcript of the law of God. These articles will take them near and very honorable relation to himself, and he will be their God, and they shall be to him a people, to love, honor, observe, and obey him in all things. This they will do and God will enable them to do so, because God himself who first found the relation, and then fills it up with grace, suitable and sufficient. God's article with the nation was about the pardon of their sins, the freeness of his pardon that does not result of merit in man, but from mercies in God. The fullness of this pardon is extended to all kinds of sin. It is so fixed that God will remember their sins no more, he will not recall his pardon, and therefore we have all reason to rejoice that the former dispensation is antiquated and has vanished away.

God's word in the form of a Beautiful covenant promise came to Abraham. Covenant people are the true children of Abraham, they are not just his biological descendants, but they are all those who trust in God and in what Jesus Christ has done for them. However, in stating a promise or making a covenant, God may set out requirements, conditions to be met by those whom the promise or covenant is made. They would become God's special property, and a kingdom of priests and a holy nation, if they strictly obeyed his voice and keep his commandments. From the beginning, God has held to his side of the covenant, but Israel failed to violate that covenant time and time again.

God finally annulled the covenant he did it with complete justice. For example, the responsibility for the non-fulfillment of the promise rests entirely with the offending Israelites. A new and old covenant, the old was the covenant of the law between God and Israel, and the new and better was the covenant of grace. This covenant is new in extent and goes beyond Israel and Judah to include all Gentile nations. It is new and applicable because it is written in our hearts and our minds. It offers a new way to forgiveness, not through animal sacrifice, but faith.

The people who had entered into a covenant with God and Moses were commanded to hear, learn and follow God's statutes. The Christians also have entered a covenant with God through Jesus Christ and should be responsive to what God

238

expect. Moses threefold command to the Israelites is excellent advice for all God followers, for example, *hearing* is absorbing and accepting information about God, learning and understanding its meaning and implication. Following is putting into action all we have learned and understood all these three-part are essential to a growing relationship with God.

Christ offered to forgive our sin and brought us back to God through his sacrificial death. Under God's new covenant, God's laws are inside us, it is no longer an eternal set of rules and principles. The Holy Spirit reminds us of Christ words, activates our consciences, influencing our motives and desires. (Jeremiah 31:31) For if there had been nothing wrong with the first covenant, no place would have been sought for another, but God found fault with the people and said, 'the time is coming declares the Lord when I shall make a new covenant with the house of Israel and with the house of Judah.' It will not be like the covenant I made with their fathers, when I took them out of the land of Egypt, because they did not remain faithful. (Heb. 8:7-9)

The membership in God's family is based on eternal, not external, qualities. Notwithstanding all whose hearts are right with God are real Jews, that is part of God's family. Church attendance or being baptized, confirmed, or accepted for membership is not enough, just as submitting to circumcision was not enough for the Jews. God desires our heartfelt devotion and obedience. All believers in every age and every nation share Abraham's blessings, this is a comfortable promise to us, a great heritage for us and a solid foundation for living.

COVENANT OF FRIENDSHIP

There are many types of the covenant that people make between themselves; here is one between David and Jonathan. When these two friends met, they immediately became close friends; their friendship was closer than brothers from the same parents. Their friendship was is one of the deepest and closest recorded in the bible. Their friendship was based on the commitment to God, and not just on each other. These two friends did not allow anything to come between them, not even career or family problems. David and Jonathan drew closer together even when their friendship was tested, yet, they remained a friend to the end.

Jonathan was heir to the crown entered into a covenant with David; God ordered this so that David's way might be clearer when his rival was his friend. Jonathan conceived an extraordinary kindness and affection for David. The soul of Jonathan was immediately knitted with David. Jonathan and David became one in spirit, David, loved Jonathan to prove this close friendship between them. Jonathan took off the robe he was wearing and gave it to David, along with his tunic, instead of staff and a sling, a sword and a bow, and instead of the shepherd strip a girdle, either a belt or a sash, the same he wore himself. For example, David was often seen in Jonathan' clothing that all make notice that he was Jonathan' friend, and at a later date when Jonathan realized that David would become the king of Israel, but, that did not weaken his love for David and Jonathan would rather losing the throne of Israel rather than losing his friend. Jesus called those who obey him his friends, he said, 'You are his friends if you do whatever he commands. (John 15:14)

FRIEND WITH AN OBEDIENT SPIRIT

Christ loved his disciple for he took them into a covenant of love with him. The followers of Christ are friends of Christ, those who do the duty of his servants are admitted and advance to the dignity of his friends, and this honor has all Christ servants. Christ takes believers to be his friends, though they often show themselves unfriendly. He is a friend that loves at all times. He will not call them servants, though Christ called them his friends they call themselves his servants.

What kind of friend are you? A friend loves at all times, and there is a vast difference between knowing someone well and being a true friend. The greatest evidence of genuine is loyalty, loving at all times, being available to help in times of distress and personal struggles, sadly some people are fair-weather friends, they stick around when the friendship helps them and leaves when they are not getting anything out of the relationship.

Who is your friend? 'He who walks with the wise grows wise, but a compassion of fools suffer harm' There is an old saying, 'A rotten apple spoils the barn, it is often applied to friendships, and with good reason. Our friends and associates affect us sometimes profoundly, we need to be aware of whom we chose as our dearest friends, you should be spending time with those you would like to be because you and your friend will surely grow to resemble each other. (Pro. 13:20)

A good friend will be willing to make the sacrifice for their friend, whether, in time, making provision, standing in duties were allowed and mortal man is not expected to make the sacrifice for their friend as Jesus did by dying. His sacrifice was once for all and was good enough. The proof and sacrifice of

Christ love, he loved his disciple, for he laid down his life for them, 'Greater love hath no man than this, to lay down his life for his friends, and this is the love wherein Christ has loved us. Christ ask us to see the extent of the love of the children of men, the highest proof of it is laying down one's life for a friend, to save his life, it is love in the highest degree which is stronger than death. Others may thus lay down their life for their friends, but Christ lay down his life for us who were enemies.

CHAPTER TWENTY-ONE

THE LORD'S SUPPER

The author of the Lord's Supper was Jesus Christ. The time of the institution was the very night when Jesus was betrayed, just as he was entering in his sufferings, our Savior took bread, and when he had given thanks, he broke, and said, 'Take eat this is my body, broken for you, this do in remembrance of me, and like manner Jesus took the cup, when he has supped, saying, 'This is the cup in the New Testament in my blood' this do, as often as you drink it, in remembrance of me'.

The material for this sacrament was the visible signs, the bread and the cup, what was eaten is called bread, although at the same time is said to be the body of the Lord. The bread and the cup are both made use of because it is a holy feast, the cup was sacred for what was in it, without once specifying what the liquor was. The things signifying by these outward signs were Christ body and blood, his body broken, his blood was shed. Similarly, Christians participate in Christ's once for all sacrifice when they eat the bread and drink the wine symbolizing his body. Therefore, Thus, eating at Christ table means communing with Christ and identifying with his death.

The apostle explains the sacredness of the institution regarding the Lord's Supper. He tells us how he came by the knowledge he had received from the Lord. He explains, The institution was supposed to be done in remembrance of Christ to keep fresh in our minds his dying for us, as well as to remember the absent friend, even as Christ interceding for us. Our savior took sacrament actions at the institution; he delivers his body and blood, with all the benefits procured by his death, to his disciples. Jesus continues to do the same every time the ordinance was administrated true believers. It illustrates that Christian believers are taking Christ as their Lord and life, and yielded themselves up to him. The sacraments were barely in remembrance of Christ death, but to commemorate his glorious condescension and grace to our redemption. We are to be examples before the world by this service that we are of Christ disciples who trust in him alone for salvation and acceptance with God. Sharing in the Lord Supper should be frequent, just as how our bodily meals are eaten often; it is fit that the spiritual diet should be taken often too, to be perpetual, and observed until the Lord return.

The Lord's Supper is not temporary, but standing and perpetual ordnance. It was celebrated in the early church, and it includes a feast or fellowship meal, followed by the celebration of Communion. In the church at Corinth, the fellowship meal had become a ritual, that is, when some eat and drank excessively while others went hungry, there were little sharing and caring. These actions did not demonstrate the love and unity that should characterize the church, nor was it preparation for communion. The apostle Paul condemned the church for these actions and reminds the church of the real purpose of the Lord's Supper.

Records show that the early Church remembered Jesus celebrated the Lord's Supper on the night of the Passover meal, according to the gospel of (Luke 22-13-20) the breaking of Christ's body as a sacrifice for us is here commemorated by the breaking of bread, this is my body which was given for you 'this bread that was given to us as food for our souls. The bread that was broken and given to us to satisfy the guilt of our sins, and to satisfy the desires of our souls, and this we do for the memorial of what Christ did for us and joining ourselves to him in joining ourselves in an everlasting covenant. The shedding of Christ blood by which the atonement was made, and as represented by the wine in the cup. It commemorates the purchase of the covenant by the blood of Christ.

In all the commemoration of the shedding of Christ blood, we must be concerned with it as a shed for us, who loved me, and gave himself for me. Some Christians posed different possibilities for what Christ meant when he said, 'Take *eat, this is my body'* Some believe that the wine and bread become Christ's physical blood and body, others believe that the bread and wine remain unchanged, but Christ is spiritually present with the bread and wine, and symbolized Christ body and blood.

There are three meanings of commemorating the Lord's Supper. The Passover commemorated Israel's escape from Egypt when the blood of a lamb was painted on their door frames as an emblem to saved their first-born sons from death. The event foreshadows Jesus work on the cross, as the spot Lamb of God; his blood would be spilt to save his people from the penalty of death brought by sin. Just as the Passover celebrated deliverance from slavery in Egypt, so the Lord's Supper celebrated deliverance from sin.

The bread and wine become Christ's body and blood, and secondly, the bread and wine become unchanged, yet Christ is spiritually present by faith in and through them. Thirdly, the bread and wine which remain unchanged are lasting memorials of Christ's sacrifice. No matter which view they favor, all Christians agree that the Lord's Supper commemorates Christ death on the cross for our sins and points to the coming of his kingdom in glory. When we partake we show our deep gratitude for Christ work on our behalf, and our faith is strengthened.

The idea of unity and fellowship with God through eating a sacrifice was strong in Judaism and Christianity as well as in paganism, in the Old Testament days, when a Jew offered a sacrifice; he eats a part of that sacrifice as a way of ensuring his unity with God, against whom he had sinned. It is expected that the Lord's Supper is participated by the believer who is born again, by eating the bread and drinking the cup.

This would take our minds back to remembering Christ's death, and renewing, and remembering, our commitment to our service to him. Jesus to his disciples 'Do this, in remembrance of me' How do you remember Christ, in the Lord's Supper?

Some Christian believed those who share communion in an unworthy manner, might sin, however, Christians can commit the sin of course, but they must immediately ask God forgiveness and then continue serving him. God has freed believers from their slavery to Satan. Unfortunately, the world does not have the Christian's freedom to obey God, unless they come to Christ in faith, there is no idle ground, a person either belong to God, and obey him, or they live under Satan's control. There is a danger of receiving the Lord's Supper unworthily and using the purposes of feasting and factions to be guilty of the body and blood of Christ.

They eat and drink judgment to themselves, and they provoke God and are likely to bring down punishment on themselves. Rather, a fearful believer should not be discouraged from attending these holy ordinances by the sound of these words. The Holy Spirit never deters serious Christians from their duty, although the devil has often taken advantage of it, and robbed good Christians of their choicest comfort. In the case of such ones who have strayed, repentance from all known sin should lead that person to the restoration of the right relationship with God, such as pagans the non-Israelites nations during the time of God's covenant was in force with Israel, and also those persons of whatever race or nationality who are outside the Christian congregation. As Gentiles living in the corruption of their natures, they were reproached by the formal Jews because they were not circumcised.

They were in a Christ-less condition, it must be a sad and deplorable condition to be without Christ, and they did not belong to a church. Paul the apostle reminded the church at Ephesians, he urged believers, 'Be reminded that at one time you were Gentiles, heathen in the flesh, you were called the un-circumcised by those who called themselves circumcised, in itself a mere mark in the flesh by human hands' Those who are newly converted needs frequent reminder reflecting on the sinful and miserable state they were once in by nature. They were in a Christ-less condition without any saving relation to Christ, it must be a sad and deplorable thing for a soul to be without Christ, being without Christ they are aliens from the commonwealth of Israel; they did not belong to Christ church, there was a happy change made in their state, 'But now, through Christ Jesus, you who were sometimes far away from Christ, and from God himself, and all good, 'But now in Christ Jesus, you are made nigh' they were brought home to God, and if any man is in Christ you are a new creation, all things are passed away, behold all things have become new' It is a fact that repentance is a primary and essential step forward.

Both Jews and Gentiles were found guilty of spiritual pride. The Jews believe that their faith and traditions elevated them above everyone else. The Gentiles trusted in their achievements, power or position. Spiritual pride will blind the individual to our faults and will magnify the faults of others. We ought to be careful not to become proud of our salvation, but rather humble and thank God for what he has done. God has granted both Jews and Gentiles, the grace of repentance unto life it is God's gift, it is not only his free grace but his mighty grace that works in us. Wherever God designed to give grace, he gives repentance also, to men everywhere. God has exalted his Son Jesus not only to give repentance to Israel, and the remission of sin, but to the Gentiles also.

WASHING THE SAINTS FEET

In the generally warm climate of the ancient Middle East where people customary wore open sandals, walking on dried soil, and travelling on foot along dusty roads, the Oriental gesture of washing the feet was a welcome and hospitable act that often proceeds the eating of a meal. Foot washing was not only a host's hospitality towards his guest but the feet were also customary washed before returning to bed, and Levites priests wash their feet and hands before going into the tabernacle or before officiating at the altar. Jesus Christ washed his disciple's feet on the last night of his earthy life. He did so to teach them a lesson and set the pattern, rather than to establish a ceremony. That evening there was a discussion among the apostle as to who was the greatest. Jesus was washing his disciple's feet as a lesson in humility and willingness to serve one another most humbly. Jesus laid aside his outer garments, girded Himself with a towel, put water in a basin and washed their feet. Thus Christ showed humility each one should be the servant of the others and should show love in practical ways, doing things for the comfort of others.

Christ asked, 'know you what I have done? Before explaining, he asks them if they could construe it, 'Know you what I have done?' Christ reason for putting this question to his disciples was not only to make them sensible of their ignorance but to raise their expectations of instruction. Christians ought to wash one another's feet from the pollution of sin, although we cannot satisfy one another's sin, we must help to purify one another from sin in tears. Christ closes this part of the discussion and said, 'If you know these things, happy are you if you do them'

The disciples were all Christ immediate followers and in particular the twelve, whom Christ have in them especially. These Christ were counted to be his own in the world, they were his boson friends. Christ allowed them to be free with him and share their infirmities. Christ could have owned others of more quality, but he stuck with his poor fishermen, though he reproved yet, he never ceases to care for them, as man's wife and children are his own, so Christ has a cordial love for his own in the world, and nothing can separate believers from the love of Christ, he loves his own unto perfection.

Christ manifested his love for his disciples by washing their feet. Thus he showed them his love, for them it was condescending and would put honor on them as great and surprising for a lord to serve his servants. The disciples had just betrayed the weakness of their love to him, in grudging the ointment that was poured on his head. (Matt. 21:8) Christ chose his time to show his example, he knew he should soon depart out of this world to return to his father, as Christ himself depart, so will all Christ-followers will depart from this world. Christ washes his disciple's feet to let the world know how low he could stoop to his own. The action itself was very mean and servile, which servants of the lowest rank were employed in.

If Christ had washed their hands or faces, it would have been condescending, but for Christ to stoop to such a piece drudgery as this may well excite our admiration.

CHAPTER TWENTY-TWO

GOD'S AMAZING COMPASSION

Compassion refers to suffering from another with mercy, and God is described as overabundant. The psalmist spoke graciously, for your great mercy towards me, and you have delivered my soul from the depth of hell 'but thou O Lord, you are a full God of compassion, and gracious, long-suffering and abundant in mercy and truth. Human is bad and very wicked and vile, no mercy is to be expected from God, but thou are a God full of compassion, and gracious. Men are barbarous, but God is gracious, men are false, but God faithful, and in him, mercy rejoices against judgment.

NEW EVERY MORNING

The prophet confessed bad as things might have been it owning to the mercy of God, by his grace makes it return to our hearts, he said he recall it to mind, therefore I have hope and I'm kept from despair. We are afflicted by the rod of his wrath, but it is by the Lord's mercy that we are not consumed.

Thus, the church of God is like Moses bush, burning but not consumed, it is persecuted of men, but not forsaken of God, and therefore, though it is cast down, it is not destroyed. It is refined in the fire as silver, but not consumed as dross. These streams followed up to the up the fountain, it is the Lord's mercies. God is an inexhaustible fountain of mercy, the father of mercies, if we were dealt with according to our sins, we should have been consumed long ago, but we have been dealt with according to God's mercies.

There are certain circumstances when God repent, but not when it comes to divine decrees, to every promise God has ever made, He says, *'I am the Lord, 'I change not'* However, when a lost person believes in the Lord Jesus Christ and surrenders his or her life to him, God's attitude changed immediately, therefore, everyone faces mercy or judgment, when one becomes a believer and accepts Christ as savior, God changes his attitude from Judgment to forgiveness.

This change of God's heart consisting of nature; meant that if he called people to repentance, then he would respond to their repentance by shifting the judgment he had against them. The people were dependent on God's mercy that made it possible in the atoning by the faith of his rightful wrath, thus by faith in God, they placed themselves under the covenant of his holiness and love.

Those failing and rejecting to believe in Christ teachings will face everlasting destruction, are those following a course like many scribes and Pharisees, who willfully and knowingly fought the manifestation of God's spirit through Christ would receive no resurrection, thereby to flee from the judgment of Gahanna. (Mark 3:22)

Another example of God's compassion has displayed the thief on the cross who showed a measure of faith in Jesus, impaled alongside was given the promise of being in Paradise. While some have endeavored to read into this promise the idea that the thief was thereby guaranteed life everlasting, while the evidence of the scriptures already considered does not allow this.

This man was about to die, he turned to Christ for forgiveness, and Christ accepted him. This has shown that our deeds cannot save us, yet, our faith in Christ does. It is never too late to turn to God with all our heart, soul and mind, even in the misery of the thief on the cross Jesus had mercy on this criminal who decided to believe in him. Rather, our lives will be much more useful and fulfilling if we turn to God early, but even those who repent at the very last moment will be with God in paradise, it's never too late to call and accept God's forgiveness.

Example of the thief who admitted the wrongness of his criminal activity in contrast with Jesus innocence, yet there is nothing to show that the thief had come to hate badness and love righteousness. In his dying state, he was in no position to turn around and produce the works that benefit repentance. He had not been baptized; therefore it appears as he is allowed to take this course upon Jesus resurrection from the dead.

It would have the view that the dying criminal had more faith than the rest of Jesus followers put together, for although the disciples continue to love Jesus, yet, their hopes for the kingdom were shattered, and most of them had gone into hiding. As one of the followers said two days later, 'we had hoped that he was the one who was going to redeem Israel' By contrast the criminal looked at the man who was dying next to him and said, 'Jesus remember me when you come into your kingdom' and by all appearances, the kingdom was finished.' (Luke 23:39-43)

How, was the faith of this man who alone saw beyond the present shame to the coming glory? John in the revelation said, 'I saw the dead, great and small, standing before the throne, and books were opened, another book was opened which is the book of life' These books also contained the recorded deeds of everyone, good or evil, and everyone's life will be revealed and evaluated. Although no one is saved by deeds, however, deeds are seen as clear evidence of a person's actual relationship with God.

The dead will be judged according to what they had done as recorders in the books; at the judgment, the books will be opened. The records represent God's judgment, and in them are recorded the deeds of everyone deeds whether good or evil. Therefore, a sinner is not saved by deeds, but deeds are seen as clear evidence of a person's actual relationship with God. It is by grace we are saved through faith, and not of ourselves, it is the gift of God'.

The grace that saved sinners is free undeserved goodness and favor of God, he saves them not by the works of the law, but through faith in Christ Jesus, thus faith and salvation are the gifts of God. God had ordered all this so that the whole thing should be by grace. It was grace that brought salvation's plan, and the love that brought it down to man, and the might gulf that God did span, at Calvary. Jesus will examine how we have handled gifts, opportunities and responsibilities, because, God gracious gift of salvation does not free us from the requirements of faithful obedience and service, therefore, each of us must serve Christ in the best way we know, and live each day, the books of our life records are kept and will one day be opened, as each person will stand before God to hear their fate. (Rev 20:12)

RESURRECTION TO OPPORTUNITY

The glorious resurrection of our Lord and savior Jesus Christ allowed every human to receive salvation by faith. There is no excuse of crying condemnation or setting and dying the way we are, without hope, certainty not, there is hope and opportunity to start all over again if at first, you don't succeed.

Resurrection to opportunities is rising, getting up, and not only getting up, but looking around for opportunities, that may be the missed, or miss-used, ones that were ignored, believing that it had worth nothing, you must be willing to trust God's son who raised him from the dead. There is an opportunity of resurrection from sin to repentance and be converted to Christ, it is offered to all living humans by the death and resurrection of Christ from the dead. Christ took the occasion to represent the sad character and condition of the generation in which we lived, a generation that would not be reformed, thus person and things might appear under false colors, characters and conditions are here changeable, things are really what they are eternal.

Jesus did not want his disciples to miss the opportunity to reach others who may have missed their opportunity to hear the gospel, so he directed the disciple on what to do when they entered a strange city. If they were not welcome by the people, they were to shake off the dust off their feet and leave. Jesus disciples received such instructions because the Gentiles' city was known for the pious Jews, when they visit the city and were about to leave they shook the dust from their feet to show their authority over Gentiles practices. If the disciples shook off the dust off their feet from a Jewish town, it would show their separation from Jews who rejected their Messiah and also to show the people that they were making a wrong choice by rejecting Jesus the Messiah.

Sadly, this opportunity to reject Christ might not present itself again; maybe an opportunity will only come but they should listen to the teaching of Jesus through his disciples. The doom was passed on those who willfully refused to hear the gospel and despise God, they are lightly esteemed. It shall be more tolerable, in the Day of Judgment, for the land of Sodom, as wicked place as it was. The people who refuse to adhere to the gospel that was meant for them, they shall be made to hear the sentence that would ruin them, and therefore, we must not ignore the prompting of the Spirit otherwise. It is not for certain we might be given another chance to repent, therefore today is the day of salvation; it is the day of the Lord. Nevertheless, upon true repentance through Christ, even the greatest sin shall be pardon, and the greatest ruin prevented. People from all places, including the Jewish cities, will be resurrected. They will have the opportunity to manifest humility in repentance and turn around in conversion to God through Christ.

When Jonah got out of the belly of the fish by God's mercy, he grudgingly went to Nineveh, and preach God's message and saw the city repented. By contrast, when Jesus came to his people they refuse to repent also, here, Jesus was clearly saying, what his resurrection will be, three days after his death, he Jesus will come back to life, just as Jonah was given a new chance at life after three days in the fish belly. The change was not in God's but the people because the people of Nineveh took action to repent, the men of Nineveh will stand up at the judgment with this generation and condemn it; for they repented at the preaching, and behold, someone more than Jonah is here, a prophet sent to the Assyrian the city of Nineveh. Jonah tried desperately to get out of the command that God had assigned to him because Assyria was such a cruel and warlike nation. Jonah tried to run from this assignment and ended up three days in the belly of a huge fish.

BLESSINGS OF GOD

A blessing is pronounced on those who endure their exercise and trials, blessing was one way of asking for God's divine favor to rest upon others. It is not the man who suffers only is blessed, but he who endures affliction and does not make him miserable, a blessing may raise to such, and therefore, suffering and temptations endure blessedness, when he is tried he shall receive a crown of life. The trail of Christians shall be a crowned one, and the crown he shall wear shall be a crown of life, thus, The Lord said to Moses, 'Tell Aaron and his sons, 'This is the way you are to bless the Israelites, Say to them, The Lord bless you and keep you, the Lord make his face to shine upon you and be gracious to you, the Lord turn his face towards you, and give you peace.'

The ancient blessing in these verses helps us to understand what a blessing was supposed to do, here are five parts conveying that God would, bless and keep them, favor and protect, make his face shine upon them, be pleased, be gracious, merciful and compassionate, turn his face towards them, give his approval, give peace, the blessing that you are offered will not only help the other person receiving it, but, it will also demonstrate, love, encourage others, and provide a model of caring to others. The blessings from God cannot be stopped, retrieved or *cancelled* by men, therefore, whom God chose to bless, no man can put a curse.

God has promises believers, that in the last day he will pour out of His Spirit on all flesh, both old and men shall experience this mighty outpouring of God's spirit. The outpouring of the Holy Spirit was predicted by Joel, it occurred on Pentecost. While in the past God's spirit seemed available to kings, prophets and judges, Joel envisioned a time when the spirit would be available to every believer. God's spirit is now available to anyone who calls on the Lord, they shall be saved. (Joel 2:8)

We often read in the Old Testament of the Spirit of the Lord coming by drops, as it were upon the judges and prophets whom God raised for extraordinary services, but now the Spirit of the Lord shall be poured out plentifully in a full stream as was promised in Isaiah. The fixed time was afterwards, after the fulfilling of the forgoing promises, this shall be fulfilled. The spirit shall be poured out upon all flesh, not upon on Jews only, but also the Gentiles, for with Christ, he has no distinction between Jews and Greeks, and God will reveal himself by dreams and visions both to the young men and old, they shall prophesy, they shall receive discoveries of divine things, this will not to be for their own only, but the benefit of the church.

In those days the believers shall interpret scriptures and speak of things in the distant, and future, these wonders would give a hint or a picture of a coming event. The outpouring of the Spirit predicted by Joel occurred on Pentecost. While in the past God's Spirit seems available to kings, prophets and judges, but Joel envisioned a time when the Spirit would be available to every believer. God's Spirit is available now to everyone who calls on the Lord. (Joel 2:28)

Some blessings are conditional, God promises great blessings to his people, but many of these blessings required our active participation, for instance, God will deliver us from fear, save us out of troubles, guard and deliver, show his goodness, supply our needs, listen when we talk to him, and redeem us, but we must do our part. We can appropriate the blessing when we seek him, cry out to him, turn away from evil, as you humble yourself and serve him obediently.

God's blessing comes from reverencing him, maybe you have never thought of persecution as a blessing, as something worth rejoicing about. Peter and John were physically beaten for their faith. These men knew how Jesus had suffered and they praised God that he had allowed them to be persecuted like their lord. If you are mocked and ridiculed and persecuted for your faith, it is not that you have something wrong, but because God has counted you worthy of suffering and disgracefully for his name. Believers are blessed by staying together as a family of God; it includes all who believed in him in the past, all who believe in him in the present, and all who believe in him in the future.

In Christ believers form part of the family of God because we all belong to the same father, he is the source of all creation, the rightful owner of everything, but God promises his love and power to his family, the church.

If we receive God's blessings, we must stay in contact with other believers in the body of Christ, those who isolate themselves from God's family and try to go alone, are cut them off from God's power. Believers are blessed in the heavenly realms with every spiritual blessing, which means that in Christ we have all the benefits of knowing God. We are heirs of salvation, being adopted as his children, received forgiveness, blessed with insight, having the gifts of the Spirit, with power to do God's will, and having the hope of living forever with Christ. We can enjoy these blessings now because these blessings are eternal and not temporal, the blessing that comes from Christ Christ's Spiritual realm is not the earthly realm of the gods of this world.

Because Abraham was blessed by God, therefore, all believers from every age and every nation share Abraham's blessings. This is a comforting promise to us, it's a great heritage for us, and a sound foundation for every believer, because the believer is forgiven; he or she is blessed because God does not count against his sins. The person who God discipline are blessed and receives God's law, and his word, believers are blessed because they walk not in the counsel of the ungodly and not seated in the seat of the scornful, nor stands in the way of sinners, but delight himself in the law of the Lord, and his law he meditates day and night. He is like the tree planted by the streams of water which yields its fruits in season and whose leaf does not wither, and whatever does will prosper. (Psalms 1:1)

CHAPTER TWENTY-THREE

CONSECRATION

Consecration means separation, to set apart for sacred purposes, to purify, dedicated to God service; consecration plays a vital role in Christian development. It is a daily process for the mind and body, to present oneself to the service of the Lord. The Christian believer must take on the responsibility to consecrated themselves and set apart. It involves more than avoiding entertainment that leads to sin, it extends to how we spend our time, money, There is no way to separate ourselves from all sinful influences, nevertheless, we are to resist the sin around us without giving up, or giving in. It means staying close to God.

Consecration is more than going to church, keeping the Ten Commandments, tithing, sharing your faith, repeating the sinner's prayer, raising your hands in worship, all of those are good and enjoyable acts, but cannot fill the role of being consecrated. In the days when a priest was used by God on behalf of the people, the priest was required to separate themselves from sin and evil, this was done by washing themselves and their clothing in a special ceremony.

The utensils that were used in the temple worship were considered consecrated, set apart exclusive for God's use. However, consecration means dethroning yourself and enthroning Jesus as Lord of your life, and losing all self-interest and surrender all to Jesus. We will soon understand and recognize that all that you have is a gift from God, and all must

261

be consecrated for his service, therefore, consecration is an ever-depending love for Jesus. God commission Moses who was God's reprehensive in the solemnity to produce his order of consecration to the congregation, this is what the Lord commanded to be done and deliver the priesthood which he received from the Lord.

The ceremony should be performed according to divine rites. Aarons and his sons were washed with water; this was to signify that they ought now to purify themselves, from all the sinful disposition and inclination, and ever after to keep themselves pure. They were clothed with the holy garment, Aaron with his, typified the decency of Christian, who is a spiritual priest. 'Take the Levites from among the other Israelites and make them ceremonially clean, meaning purifying them, do this, 'Sprinkle the water of cleansing upon them, then instruct to shave their whole bodies, and wash their clothes, and so purify themselves. (Numbers 8:5-8)

Whilst people are not required for carrying out the ceremony today, yet we must seek to purify ourselves by reading God's word and prepare ourselves to participate in worship. The Christians are consecrated by Christ; Jesus prayed to his father, he wanted his disciples to be unified among them, based on the unity with him and the father. Therefore, Christians must be separated from the world system; although they are still living in the world but should not be of the worldly system. Believers were urged by the apostle Paul not to form a binding relationship with non-believers because this might weaken their Christian commitment, integrity, or their standards.
(2 Corinthians 6:14-8)

The believer has a sacred anointing refers to the pouring out of special olive oil. This olive oil was used to consecrate kings and special servants for service. Oil was used by the church as part of the emblem of healing when someone was sick, coupled with the prayer of faith by the elders of the church. Members in the church are not alone, they all make up the body of Christ, and they should be able to count on each other for support and prayer, especially in times of sickness. Elders of the church should be on call to respond to any illness of a member while the church stays alert for the needs of all members in the body of Christ.

The believer has an anointing by the holy one since the Holy Spirit has been given by the Father and the Son, and when a person becomes a Christian, he or she receives the Holy Spirit. One of the many ways in which the Holy Spirit helps the believer and the church is by communicating truth, as Jesus is the Truth, so the Holy Spirit guides believers to him, those who are opposed to Christ is opposed to the truth also, and the Holy Spirit will not be working in such person's life.

Before Jesus left earth to return to his father in heaven, Jesus told his disciples how he had much more to say to them more than they can now bear, but when the spirit of truth, comes, he will guide them into all truth, he said 'The Holy Spirit would inform them what is yet to come and the nature of their mission and the opposition they would face, and the final outcome of their efforts'. The Spirit will guide them as a skillful pilot guides the ship into the port it is bound for, to be led into the truth is more than barely to know it, but it is to be intimately and experimentally acquainted with it. It denotes a gradual discovery of truth shining more and more. During times of uncertainty, it is comforting to rediscover a light in the word of

God that points to a better way or a more positive path that leads to the shore.
(John 16:13)

The apostle urges believers not to form binding relationships with non-believers because this might weaken the Christian commitment, integrity, or standards, and become a mismatch, instead of earlier, Paul reminded believers to remain with their non-believing spouse he explains that he did not mean of isolating oneself from non-believer, rather, he wants believers to be active in their witness for Christ to non-believers, and not lock themselves in personal or business relationships that could cause them to compromise the faith; rather believers should do everything in their power to avoid situations that could force them to divide their loyalties.

For people who might feel guilty and condemned, John offers reassurance, even though they know they have sinned and Satan the accuser is demanding the death penalty. Those who feel this way, should not give up hope, the best defense lawyer in the universe is pleading your case. Jesus Christ our advocate, your defender is the Judge Son. He has already suffered your penalty in your place, you cannot be tried for a crime for which you have already being acquitted; he has already won our case.
(1 John 2:1-7)

PURITY-PURIFICATION

Purity is a state of being or process to becoming free from an inferior element of ritualistic uncleanliness. The primary Hebrew root word for pure (Tahar) is often referred to pure or flawless as gold is purified. A basis Old Testament meaning without flaws, purified, perfectly clean (Lam 4:7) To be ritually pure means to be free from flaws and uncleanliness which would bar people from contact with holy, and objects or places especially from coming contact with the holy presence of God in worship. God is the ideal of purity, and those who are to come in contact with God's presence also must be pure, this indicates that God's eyes are too pure to look upon evil. (Habakkuk 1:13)

Most New Testament used words 'purity' relates to the cleanness of some type in Old Testament, meaning are often reflected the word of the Lord is pure, words as silver tried in a furnace of earth, purified seven times. Some Hebrew and Greek words describe that which is clean and pure or the acts of purification that is, restoring to a condition without blemish, spotless and free from anything that soils, for instance, adulterous or corrupt. All together these words in their different forms occur more than two hundred times in the scriptures and describe not only the state of physical cleanliness but more often, moral or spiritual cleanness. The physical cleanness and personal habit made the nation of Israel a comparatively healthy people, but their nomadic wanderings in the wilderness for forty years has polluted their minds and body.

Thus, God's law governs their camps life, including the diagnosis and treatment of disease which they were unquestionably responsible for, and very importantly, the importance of clean water was emphasized under this arrangement. Christian *cleansing*; Christians are not under the law and its cleansing requirements, even though such law and its customs were still in force when Jesus was on earth. When it was almost time for the Jewish Passover, many went up from the country to Jerusalem for their ceremonial cleansing before the Passover, they went looking for Jesus (Jn.11:55) The law had but a shadow of good things to come; these were expected, but not yet discovered, therefore, the law was not the very image of the good things to come, but was only a shadow. As it were, the law was a rough draught of the great design of divine grace, and therefore, not to be much doted on.

For instance, the legal sacrifice, that the priest offered year by year, could never make the comers perfect, but under the gospel, the atonement is perfect as well as the sinner is once pardoned, and only needs renewing his repentance and faith. The believers in Christ are circumcised with the circumcision made without hands, not by the power of any creature, by the power of the blessed Spirit of God. For instance, during that period the Jews thought they were complete in the ceremonial law, but the Christians are complete in Christ. Thus, we have communion with Christian and the world undertaking of Christ operation.

Purification comes through sacrifice is also mentioned in the New Testament that is applied to the death of Christ, it is a purification that does not need repeating and this is a higher level than Old Testament. The sacrifice of Christ brings purification and Christ as a part of the work of the high priest as his blood cleanses from sin. (1John 1:2)

The apostle Paul had concerns about purification matters, he said, 'nearly all things were cleansed with the blood according to the Law of Moses, he sprinkled both the book, the people, the tenth and the vessels with blood, and unless blood is poured out there is no forgiveness.' Therefore the physical requirements of the things in the heavens needed to be cleansed by these means, 'For if the blood of goats and bulls, and the ashes of a heifer sprinkled on those who have been defiled sanctifies to the extent of cleanness of the flesh.'

Paul asked how much more will the blood of the Christ, through an everlasting spirit offered himself without blemish to God; he urged them, 'cleanse your conscience from dead works that you we may render service to the living God. Therefore, Christians should maintain a high standard of physical and moral cleanness to guide them against all defilement of flesh, by placing the greatest emphasis on spiritual cleanness.

Given what Jesus said, 'It is not what enters into the man that defiles a person, it is what comes forth from him defiles him, and who benefits from the cleansing blood of Christ will maintain with a clean heart and clean conscience before God. Likewise, those having a desire to remain clean and pure in the heart needs to obey the counsel that said, 'Depart, go out from there, touch nothing unclean, keep yourselves clean,' because you who are carrying the utensils of God. (Isaiah 52:11)

Ethical Purity is also listed in New Testament; the person who is in the right relationship with God should live a life of purity. Therefore, to the pure all things are pure, but to those who are corrupted and do not believe, nothing is pure. Paul made believers aware whatever you chose to fill the mind with will affect the way you think and act, he urged, instead turn your thought to God and his word, and you will discover more and more goodness' Even in this evil world it is unusual for some people to see positive all around them, while others see nothing but evil, what a difference it makes when your soul become filters through which you perceive goodness or evil.

The pure are those who have Christ in control of their lives; rather, we should learn to see goodness and purity even in this evil world. Instead, corrupt and unbelieving people find evil in everything because their minds and hearts color even the good they see and hear. Whatever you chose to fill your minds with will affect the way you think and act, and turning your thoughts to God. The apostle Paul urged believers to program the minds with thoughts that are true, noble, right, pure, admirable, and excellent and praiseworthy. It is a good principle to replace daydreams, television programs, books, conversations, films with wholesome material that will inspire your minds.

It seems impossible to function in an impure environment, and sometimes it seems as if you are drowning in a sea of impurity, everywhere you look there are temptations to lead impure lives, you might ask, how do you stay pure in a filthy environment, seems impossible and you cannot do this on your own, but you can seek counsel and strength that is more dynamic than the tempting influences around you. There is some tendency especially among younger people in society that are often bombarded with technology, and spend little time reading God's word and obeying what it says, to avoid being overcome with temptation, both young and older believers should be careful of ignoring reading and taking heed to the word of God regularly.

The spiritual benefit is hidden in God's word and act as is a deterrent to sin; this alone should inspire you to memories scriptures, and put God's word to work since it gives a vital guide to everything you do.

CHAPTER TWENTY-FOUR

RECONCILIATION

Reconciliation means to bring back into harmony, or cause to be friendly again; In Greek, the words related to reconciliation are derived from the verb -al-las-so) which, means to change. The word (hi-la-smos) signifies 'a means of appeasing an atonement.' God made Christ who had no sin for us so that in him we might become the righteousness of God. For instance, men who exchange the glory of immortal God images made to look like mortal man and birds and animals replies.

This attitude causes us to lose sight of our own identity as those who are higher than the animals, made in the image of God. Many have been reconciled to God through the sacrifice of Christ Jesus, such reconciliation was necessary because of alienation that existed, for instance, a separation, a lack of harmony, and friendly relations, even more than a state of enmity. How this comes about? This enmity was through the first man Adam's sin and the reluctant sinfulness and imperfection that were inherited by all his descendants. Here is a question. 'How can we declare guilty for something that Adam did thousands of years ago?

Many may feel we should not judge us because it was Adam who had sin, but each of us confirms our solidity by our sin each day because we are made of the same stuff and we are prone to rebel, and we are a judge for the sins we have committed because we are sinners and needs God's mercy. Therefore, the apostle says the minding of the flesh brings enmity with God, for it is not under subjection to the law of God, nor, can it be, due to its inherited imperfect, sinful nature, so those who are in harmony with the flesh cannot please God.

Paul the apostle divides people into two groups, those who leave themselves to be controlled by their sinful nature, and the others are those who follow after the Holy Spirit leadings. Those in the first, category, Jesus had offered a way out, when we said, yes, to him, and we may still want to continue following him because his way brings life and peace. Every day we must consciously choose to center our lives on God, we can use the bible, the word of God to discover God's guidelines and then follow them, and you will discover that the enmity exists because God's perfect standards do not allow for his approval or condoning wrongdoings.

Examples of God's Son Jesus hoe he reflects his Father's perfect qualities; as it is written, 'You love righteousness, and you hated evil.' Even though God is love and he loved the world of mankind, so much that he gave his only begotten son, yet, the fact remains that mankind as a whole has been in a state of enmity towards God. God's love towards the world of mankind was love towards his enemies also. Therefore, if we love God we must also love our enemies, and that has always caused one to feel restful loving our enemies whom we can see. Loving God whom we cannot see, but God's love is guided by principles rather than fondness or friendship, and it is only through the ransom sacrifice of Christ, that it can be possible. As a result Jesus made that full reconciliation with God possible. Jesus is the way and no one comes to the Father except through him, thus, Christ death serves as a proprietary sacrifice for our sins. Indeed, the basics meaning can be change from enmity to friendship, for example, a woman's and her husband making up again after they had separated, it demands love from each of other, to the glue that love, again. It is always a fresh feeling when separating and cutting out the middle man, or that thing, that wrong attitude, negative thinking that stands between us and God. The middle man has been identified and removed, so that God's love penetrates as a sunshine, refreshes our lives to bloom again, ready for an abundant of harvest. However, Jesus instructed that man should first make his peace with his brother before presenting an offering at the altar.

The experience in such cases, while in my daily devotion in and entreating the Lord regarding my attitude with others, as I started to reach out in a deep self-examination, suddenly someone came into my thoughts, and I could not proceed any further, my conscience was at war to fix what came to mind. I rose and went to the phone and made a call to the person whom my conscience was pressing to make contact with. As I got to the phone it seems as if this person was also summoned to receive a call of the same nature, we spoke briefly and buried the *little* thing that was blocking my offering from being accepted.

We did not argue or indulged in any other matters except the only little fox that was hidden and eating our relationship. By acknowledging the work of the Holy Spirit for the s tremendous work he wrought, so smoothly and brought peace and clarity. The bible reminds if anyone brought their gift to the altar and remember that there exists a discord among others, either must leave their gift at the altar and go and make peace, then return and offer the gift. Our conviction will make it easy, for reconciliation with one another, when the heart is broken with a bitter woeful cup it's time to go to God alone. The heart must be free from the least minute dust before it develops into a pool of mud, begin to clean it while it's easy to do so. An example can be shown with Paul and Philemon, the runaway slave.

When God found the runaway he would often send him back to the very place and people from which he ran away, notice, the difference with true forgiveness, it means that we should treat the one we've been forgiven as we would want to be treated, 'Is there anyone you may say, 'you have forgiven? They still need your kindness?'

The sacrifice of Jesus Christ was not a means of appeasing in the sense of smoothing hurtful feelings on God part and mollifying him, for the death of his beloved son, certainly, it would produce no such demands of God's perfectness. Rather, sacrifices were never meant to appeased or satisfied the demands of God's perfect justice. God provided the just and righteous basis for pardoning sin so that he might be righteous when declaring man, the hereditarily sinful man that has faith in Jesus, and supplying the means for expiating or making complete satisfaction for man's sins and unlawful acts.

Christ sacrifice made it propitious, favorable for man's seeking and receiving a restoration to right relations with the Sovereign God. Thus, through Christ death, God made it possible to reconcile again to him all other things by making peace through the blood Jesus shed on the tortured state. Thereby persons who were alienated and enemies due to having their minds on wicked works could now be reconciled through that One's fleshy body through his death. To present them holy and unblemished and open to no accusation before God, some will question the truth if Christ is fully human and he is not fully divine, by the apostle refute the idea of the Greek that Christ has always been God, and always will be God.

When we accept Christ as a savior, we have all of God in human form, we should not dismiss any aspects of Christ either his humanity or his divinity, and He is God! Here, is some truth that is revealed when you recognized God's greatness. You should never be tempted to question and analyze God and try to reduce him to your terms, and you are less likely to try and manipulate him and his will or explain to him his ways. Sometimes while listening to people having aggressively conversation to God in prayer and telling God which way they want things to be and he should do about their request.

They were ignorantly forgetting major aspects about God, first, he is always right, his ways are past finding out, and maybe because we cannot see God face to face, we lose great respect and adoration for him. Nevertheless, I would suggest to you to seek to know who God is, and then find yourself through reading his word, perhaps you will change your attitude when approaching God's mercies, and find their place in humility in prayer. I thought who these people are, and whom they believe they are talking to, God is God and he is always right.

Therefore, we can only give thanks for his kindness and thank him that we are not consumed in our presumptuousness. What can we say of men who served God in times before Christ's death, such as Abel, who had witness borne to him that he was righteous when God bore witness respecting his gift?

In fact that some men may have a more grossly degree of sin than others, even in open rebellions, but sin is sin, whether the degree or extent and God through his son Jesus Christ provided the only sacrifice for man's sin. All this exalts the importance of Christ's position in God's arrangement and demonstrates that, apart from Christ Jesus, men have no righteousness that could qualify them for a right standing before God. Therefore, condemnation has been destroyed because believers have been empowered not to walk contrary to their sinful nature. Because we are now reconciled, the image of God has been restored, and we can now live up to our true self and potential by walking according to the spirit, now, a new law is at work, and not the Old Testament commandments, but the law of the Spirit in the life of Christ Jesus, his sets has us free from the law of sin and death.

GOD RECONCILING A WORLD TO HIMSELF

The apostle explains how God reconcile the world to himself through Christ, and not reckoning to them their trespasses. This should not be misread that all persons are automatically reconciled to God by mean of the sacrifice of Jesus. The apostle went on to describe the ambassadorial work of entreating men to become reconciled to God. The means were provided for all those of the world of mankind who were willing to respond could gain reconciliation. Hence, Jesus came to give his soul a ransom in e exchange for many, and he who exercises faith in the Son of God has everlasting life, he who disobeys the Son will not see life, but the wrath of God remains upon him. Jesus was a ransom that was the price paid for a slave from bondage. Jesus often told his disciples that he must die, but he told them why it is to redeem all people from the bondage of sin and death. The disciples thought that as long as Jesus was alive he could save them, but Jesus revealed that only his death would save them and the world. Jesus says those who believe in him will have eternal life, and to receive eternal life is to join in God's life which by nature is eternal, and this eternal life begins at the moment of your spiritual birth. By the offence and disobedience of one man, many were made sinners, and judgment came upon all men to condemnation.

The sin of man has reached the highest height to pull downward, the depth of sin is so deep it is enough to drown the human race and cause a person never to be found by human searching. The sin of ma travels wide and is capable of consuming the whole world, and sin will be active in human's life as long as a person chose to remain in sin.

Thus, that judgment comes upon all of Adam's disobedience were made sinners, and all the race of mankind lies under a sentence, like an attained upon a family. Mankind can be free from the bondage of Satan abusing, and as a cruel taskmaster, he pays an unreasonable wage at the end of life to those who serve him faithfully, in like manner by the righteousness and obedience one were made righteous, and so the gift came upon all who believe and accept it.

ATTAINING RECONCILIATION

Since God is the offended party whose lawman has violated, thus, it is the man who must now become reconciled to God, and not God to man. Man does not meet God on equal terms, nor is God's standing to what is right subject to change, emendation or modification. God's condition for reconciliation is, therefore, not nonnegotiable, not subject to questions or compromise. God invites us, 'Come now let us reason together' or come now you people 'let us settle matters straight, let us settle the issue.' God still longs to restore people today, so he invites us to come as we are, and repent of the sins we have committed. The Lord is a God of mercy, compassion, and justice. God wants us to enjoy an unbroken relationship with him.

The fault which produced the disharmony lies entirely with man and not with God, yet, this does not prevent God from taking the merciful initiative in opening the way for reconciliation, and he did so through his son. Paul the apostle writes, 'For indeed, while we were yet weak, Christ died for ungodly men at the appointed time, for hardly will anyone die for a righteous man, for the good man, perhaps, someone even dares to die' 'But God recommends his love, in that while we were yet sinners Christ died' much more since we have been declared righteous now by his blood we shall be saved through him from the wrath to come' God additionally displays his mercy and love by sending out an ambassador to sinful mankind. In times ancient ambassadors were sent out primarily in times of hostility, and not peace, but when nations wars against each other.

The ambassador's mission is frequently being used to see if war could be averted or to arrange terms for peace where a state of war prevailed. God sends his Christian ambassadors to men enabling them to learn his terms for reconciliation and to avail themselves of such terms and conditions. As the apostle writes, 'we are, therefore, ambassadors substituting for Christ,' as though God was making entreaty through us, and as substitutes for Christ we beg those whom we come into contact with, *'become reconciled to God'*.

Such entreaty does not signify any weakening neither of God's position nor his opposition to wrongdoing, surely not, but is instead a merciful urging to the offenders to seek peace and escape the inevitable consequences of God's righteous anger towards all who persist in going contrary to his holy will. Therefore, destruction will be the certain end of such, even Christians must be careful not to reject the undeserved kindness of God and miss its purpose by failing to seek continually God's favor and good. It will during the acceptable time and the day of salvation. We must recognize the need for reconciliation and accepting God's provision for reconciliation namely, *'the sacrifice of his son Jesus'*.

The individual must repent of his sinful course and be a convert, or turnaround from following the way the sinful world. This can be possible by appealing to Christ's on his basis of Christ's ransom, whereas, the forgiveness of sins and reconciliation can be obtained bringing 'seasons of refreshing from the God. Since the death of Christ on the cross, mankind is no longer enemies under the wrath of God; they have in fact, passed over from death to life.

Therefore, the individual must retain God goodwill by calling upon him in trueness and continuing and not being shifted away from the hope of the good news, for there is no respect of persons with God; and this might presents a strong case for realizing God's goodness to individuals, even when faced with their sins. For God's forbearance and long-suffering does not erase his wrath and judgment on sinners, for God will give to each person according to what he has done. The wrath of God exists for those who are self-seeking and continually rejecting, even though there can be a delay in executing judgment for sin, although sin deserves his wrath, without His restrain there would be no opportunity for repentance and salvation. However, God has equal concern for each person who submits to his will regardless of ethnicity, gender, or age, he shows no favoritism in offering forgiveness, and a person sin cannot be too many or so hideous that God's mercy will not offer when they seek his forgiveness. In contrast, those who accepted Christ as Savior and Lord and living a life of righteousness bring divine rewards, therefore, God's forbearance must never be interpreted as cheap grace.

The term is used to describe the concept of choosing to sin and then repenting afterwards, or to continue in this manner will indicate a person state of his heart, it will show that they are not concerned with regularly following the Lord's holiness, but they want to live in worlds, serving God, yet pursuing self.

CHAPTER TWENTY-FIVE

THE HOLINESS OF GOD

God is always right and is holy, perfect. Holiness is described as the state or character of being holy, the English word, holy and holiness are translated from Hebrew words having the possible root meaning, 'to be bright,' or fresh, untarnished or clean, in a physical sense, although it is used in the Bible mainly in a spiritual or moral sense. Accordingly, holiness means cleanness, purity, sacredness, and also, the original Hebrews conveys the thought of separateness, exclusiveness, or sanctification to God, who is holy, a state of being set aside to the service of God.

Holiness is morally perfect, pure and set apart from all sin; Holiness also means being devoted to God, set aside for his special use and set apart from sin, and its influence. We are to be set apart from the world and be blending in with the crowd, yet not being different just for the sake of being different. We also need to discover God's holiness. Christ Jesus is in a special sense, God's Holy One. His holiness came from the father when God created him as his only begotten Son, and he maintains his holiness as the closest one to his father in the heavens. When his life was transferred to the womb of the Virgin Mary, he was born as a holy human son of God. Jesus was born without the sin that entered the world through Adam.

The key to God's eternal reign is his holiness. God's glory is seen not only in his strength but in perfect moral character as well, therefore we must never use unholy means to reach a holy goal because, God say, 'be holy because 'I the Lord is holy is holy'. (Luke 1:35)

He is such a high priest who was fitted for us, who is holy, harmless, undefiled, separated from sinners, and has become higher than the heavens' in our case, as sinners we needed a high priest to make satisfaction and intercession for us. No priest could be suitable or sufficient for our reconciliation to God, but one who was perfectly righteousness.

The Lord Jesus was exactly such a high priest as we wanted, for he has a personal holiness, he holy, no sin dwells in him. He is harmless; he has never done the least wrong to God or man. He is undefiled, though he took on himself the guilt of man. However, he never involved himself in the fact and faults of them. He is separated from sinners, though he took on true man nature, yet the miraculous way in which it was conceived set him upon a separate footing from all the rest of mankind. He is made higher than the heavens, for he is exalted at the right hand of God to perfect the design of his priesthood. (Hebrews 7:26)

Jesus was 'declared righteousness on his merit. 'And having been set free from sin, you because servants of righteousness' Although some were guilty as servants of sin, nevertheless, on obeying the law of Christ will be evidence of our relation to Christ's family. Those who are now the servant of God would do well to remember the time when they were servants of sin, to keep them humble, and quicken them in the service of God. A status of holiness, 'what makes us different?' It is God's qualities in our lives. Our focus and priorities must be his; it's all about him, and not us. All this must be in contrast to our old ways. There should be no excuse that we can't help doing the old ways we use to live. We should never be like spoiled children, but grateful children who love to show respect to our heavenly father. (Romans 6:18)

Believers are set free from sin and have become slaves of righteousness. We have been made perfect, yet we are been made holy, through Christ death and resurrection. Christ has made his believer once for all perfect in God's sight. At the same time he is making them holy, progressively cleansed and set apart for his special use in their daily pilgrimage here. We ought not to be ashamed, or surprise that we still need to grow; God is not finished with us, we must be encouraged that this growth process by deliberately, we must, therefore, applying scriptures to all areas of our lives, and allowing the word of God to dwell richly in our hearts while accepting the disciplining and guidance that is found in the word of God.

It is very important on keeping these principles and doing them, and then God will remember our sins no more. When God forgives, there is no need to confess past sins any more, we should be confident that when we confess and renounce our sins, they are forgiven. The prophet Isaiah had a lofty view of God; 'it gives us a sense of God's greatness, mystery, and power. Isaiah's example of recognizing his sinfulness before God and encourages the importance of confessing our sin. The picture of God's forgiveness reminds us that we too are forgiven, being born as a human was not the first time God made Jesus so small, and even so we could have access to him. First, he shrunk himself when he revealed the Torah at Mount Sinai. God shrunk himself into tiny Hebrews words, to man's finite language, so that we might get to him that way. Jesus shrinks himself to a baby, to fit manager infiniteness. (Girl meets God: 'on the path to spiritual life.)

Thus, Isaiah wrote regarding the holiness of God; our greatest failing is not realizing who God is, and what his character is like, firstly, we must understand that God is not human, he is God, and so there is an infinite gap between man and God. The gap is unbridgeable from man's side, and if the gap was to be bridged, it must be from God's side, for he is holy. To be holy means to be set apart. God is set apart from the power, practices, and presences of sin. God is set apart to absolute righteousness and goodness, not only does God require holiness in our heart, but also purity in our bodies. The body is called the vessel of the soul which dwells within, and it must be kept pure from defiling lust, and what can be more undesirable than a rational soul to be enslaved by bodily affections and brutal appetite?

The sin of uncleanness is a sin especially adultery, which is a great sin, although, all sins are an offence to God, yet, there is no sin in God, and God can have nothing to do with sin. If we are to approach God we must do so on his terms. We cannot afford to take this opportunity lightly. Somehow, we must be made holy, just as how God is holy, therefore, any holiness that comes short of God's holiness will not able to stand in the presence of God. Thus, because of the holiness of God, we must have a new life in which our sins have been forgiven and done away with so that we actually can be as separated from sin as God is. Those who desire to receive membership in the kingdom of God are not easy to gain. It is not like approaching an open city with little or nothing to make an entrance, it is difficult. Rather, the Sovereign God had placed barriers to shut out anyone who was not worthy.

Those who would enter must traverse a narrow road, find the narrow gate, keep on asking, keep on seeking, keep on knocking, and the way would be opened. They might figuratively have to lose an eye or a hand to gain entrance. The kingdom would be no plutocracy in which one would buy the kingdom's favor; therefore it would be a difficult thing for a rich man to enter. It would be no worldly aristocracy; in a prominent position among men would not count, and those apparently *'first'* and having an impressive religious background and record would be last, and the last would be first to receive the favored privileges connected with that kingdom.

The qualification of those gaining entrance in the kingdom of God would be those putting material interest secondary and seeking first the kingdom of God's righteousness. For example, when God anointed King, Jesus Christ, they would love righteousness and hate wickedness. They would be spiritually minded, merciful, pure-hearted, peaceable persons, though the object of reproach and persecution by men would become prospective members of the kingdom. Jesus invited those to take up the 'yoke' upon themselves meant 'submission. This is the good news of the gospel that Christ died for our sins, having taken them upon himself, and has set us apart from them. Now, our possession before God will not be changed, because of what God has done, we now can enter bodily into the presence of God. Bear in mind that we do not earn salvation by keeping the law, but we do please God when our lives confirm what he reveals in us. (Is 6:3)

We all need to discover God's holiness, because our daily frustration, societal pressures, and our shortcomings sometimes reduce and limit our view of God. We need the bible view of God as high and lifted to empower us to deal with our problems and concerns. The God of Israel and the God of the Christian church is holy. He sets the standard for morality, unlike the Roman god he is not war-like, adulterous, or spiteful, and he is

God of mercy and justice who cares personality for each of his followers. Our holy God expects us to imitate him by following his high moral standards. We should be just like him both in mercy and just, and sacrifice ourselves for others.

Therefore, we don't need to cover up our sins before God because we can talk openly and honestly with him, and he knows all the terrible information about us, God still loves and wants to forgive us, so it is not healthy to cover up our sins, tell God about every area of our heart, and believe he will forgive and set us free. When we confess our faults one with another, we are helping others to do the same. Although it might seem difficult to begin, but not long from there, we can ask the Holy Spirit to help us to be transparent with each other. Let us, therefore, follow after the things which make for peace, and things wherewith one may edify another. (Romans 14:19)

Although we cannot become holy on our own merits, that is one of the reasons why; God gives us the Holy Spirit to help us obey him and gives us the power to overcome the grip of sin. The key to God eternal reign is holiness. God's glory is seen not only in his strength but in his perfect moral character, as well that God will never do anything that is not morally perfect. This is sure evidence that we can trust God, yet, it places a demand on us also. We must have a desire to be holy to God and morally clean, it must be our only suitable response. As Moses was ordered to deliver the summary of the law to all the congregation of the children of Israel, shows how God cares for his people.

Many precepts have been given and been had received before, but it was necessary to be repeated, that the people might be reminded of the severity of breaking the law. Israel must be holy because God is holy. 'Therefore, we must never use a holy means to reach a holy goal, because God says, 'be holy because I the Lord your holy God is holy.' (Leviticus 19:1.2)

Some sins seem bigger than others because their obvious consequences might be much more serious. Since creation God has made it clear that any sin separate people from him, and that those who sin deserve to die. Because all have sinned, murder, for example, seems to us to be worse than hatred, and adultery seems worse than lust. But this does not mean because we do lesser sins we deserve eternal life.

There is no way a person can have eternal life, only God can redeem a soul because the ransom for a life is costly. The book of Proverbs gives guidelines of the things that God hates, it is best to avoid these things to keep in harmony with God. Christians can help each other and pray on behalf of others while not affecting God's application of justice, since Christ's ransom alone serve to bring remission of sins, we can connect with God in petitioning his giving help and strength to the one who has sinned and is seeking aid. (Proverbs 6:16-19)

If only man could realize that salvation is a gracious gift from God, and how God chose us out of his love exclusively for himself. Jesus died to pay the penalty for our sin and the Holy Spirit cleansed us from sin when we believe. Eternal life is a wonderful gift for those who trust in Christ. I'm indeed satisfied as I set my heart to re-read and meditate in the word of God and in alignment with my finger to write as if I was going to war.

Therefore, we should not minimize little 'sins or overrate 'big sins, all sins separate us from God, but they all can be forgiven. Since Jehovah God is the originator of all righteous principles and laws and is the basis of all holiness, any person or thing that is holy becomes so because of relationship with God and his worship. One cannot have an understanding of wisdom unless he or she has spiritual knowledge of the Most Holy One. God taught his people to worship; he places much emphasis on worshipping in spirit and truth. Sacrifices were God's Old Testament tradition for people to ask forgiveness for their sins.

The high way referred to as the way of holiness, is the way from the desert of suffering to Zion that is the pilgrim's way. It is only by following God you can walk in this way, only the redeemed will travel on God's high way, they will be protected from the wicked and any harmful animals. God is preparing a way for his people to travel to his home and he will walk with them and God never stop at simple pointing, he is always beside us as we go all the way. (Isaiah 35:8)

The foundation of true holiness and true Christian worship is the doctrine of the Gospel, what you are to believe, so when Christ doctrine is neglected, forsaken, or corrupted, true holiness and worship will also be neglected, forsaken, and corrupt. Although man has chosen to live in sin, yet, God's hands are still outstretched calling sinners to repentance, his words remain 'Come unto me all who have labored and are heavy laden, and I will give you rest. You must encourage yourselves and also encourage one another, a good discipline to keep track of this, create a daily list of the good things you do, but your deeds will speak volumes about your character

Over the centuries, many believers overcame by an awareness of their sins, they found in the word of God regarding a penitential confession as a ray of hope in the psalms of David. The book of psalms shared with us the depth of sorrow and repentance, as well as the height of joy of being forgiven.

Believers can truly rejoice in the knowledge that God would respond to confession and repentance with complete forgiveness, and as believers living on the other side of the cross of Christ, you can rejoice more because you understand that your sins are forgiven. Thus believers must seek to discern the will of God and also commit to doing his will that is revealed in his word, thus, God is God, and is always right.

GOD IS ALWAYS RIGHT
PHYLLIS JEMMOTT

The main reason for deliberating and writing this book is to express my concerns for everyone who choose to read the contents of this book. The next step would be to take the opportunity of reviewing and evaluating your own status in Christ and taking the necessary steps to put things right. There is nothing out of the character in taking actions to evaluate one's desire over many years of journeying on this particular road.

I discovered that doing a regular checkup using the word of God as a master tool is effective for the Christian status. It gives a clear and concise reading and guidelines that must be followed and obeyed. God has provided his word as a road map to assist those who believe in his son Jesus Christ, that we might be lost.

ACKNOWLEDGMENT

With much thanks and heartfelt gratitude to the following;

Almighty God
Mr. Marcel Marshall
Rev. R. Anderson
Mr. & Mrs. Natta Bailey

Thanks to all the above for their constant support, much appreciated.

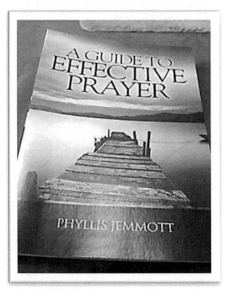